THE POLITICS OF TERRORISM:
TERROR AS A STATE AND REVOLUTIONARY STRATEGY

THE JOHNS HOPKINS
FOREIGN POLICY INSTITUTE

The Johns Hopkins Foreign Policy Institute (FPI) was founded in 1980 and serves as the research center for the School of Advanced International Studies (SAIS) in Washington, D.C. The FPI is a meeting place for SAIS faculty members and students as well as for government analysts, policymakers, diplomats, journalists, business leaders, and other specialists in international affairs. In addition to conducting research on policy-related international issues, the FPI sponsors conferences, seminars, and roundtables.

Current research activities at the FPI span the complete spectrum of American foreign policy and international affairs. In the project on "U.S.-Soviet Relations: An Agenda for the Future" FPI fellows and outside experts evaluate the recent evolution of U.S.-Soviet relations and develop original ideas for increased superpower cooperation in new and established areas. Through the project on foreign policy consensus the FPI seeks to advance the national dialogue on central issues of U.S. foreign policy: specific recommendations are prepared by selected experts and endorsed by a bipartisan commission for wide distribution in the policy community.

Other current FPI programs examine the impact of the landmark Goldwater-Nichols defense reorganization act; the relation of arms control to force structure and military-political doctrine; the politics of international terrorism; the role of the media in foreign policy; American and Soviet national security policymaking; and other leading international issues. These programs are usually directed by FPI fellows.

FPI publications include the *SAIS Review*, a semiannual journal of foreign affairs, which is edited by SAIS students; the FPI Papers in International Affairs, a monograph series designed to make public the best and most cogent scholarly work on foreign policy and defense issues; the FPI Policy Briefs, a series of analyses of immediate or emerging foreign-policy issues; the FPI Case Studies, a series designed to teach analytical negotiating skills; and the FPI Policy Consensus Reports, which present recommendations on a series of critical foreign policy issues.

For additional information regarding FPI activities, write to: FPI Publications Program, School of Advanced International Studies, The Johns Hopkins University, 1619 Massachusetts Avenue, N.W., Washington, D.C. 20036-2297.

THE POLITICS OF TERRORISM:
TERROR AS A STATE AND REVOLUTIONARY STRATEGY

Barry Rubin, Editor

FPI Foreign Policy Institute
School of Advanced International Studies
The Johns Hopkins University
Washington, D.C.

Library of Congress Cataloging-in-Publication Data

Terror as a state and revolutionary strategy / Barry Rubin, editor.
p. cm.—(FPI papers in international affairs. The politics of
terrorism)
Includes bibliographical references.
1. Terrorism. 2. Terrorism– –Government policy. I. Rubin,
Barry M. II. Series: FPI papers in international affairs. Politics
of terrorism.
HV6431.T4564   1988   88–29434 CIP
303.6'25– –dc19
ISBN 0–941700–45–3 (alk. paper).
ISBN 0–941700–44–5 (pbk. : alk. paper)

Distributed by University Press of America,® Inc.,
4720 Boston Way, Lanham, Md. 20706/(301) 459-3366
3 Henrietta Street, London, WC2E 8LU England

CONTENTS

FOREWORD

Mostly indiscriminate and often state supported, terrorism has emerged over the years as perhaps the most complex and least predictable threat to the security of the United States, its allies, and other nations as well. No longer a weapon used only by marginal, isolated groups, terrorism relies on networks of communication that transcend international boundaries linking these groups with one another. Money is readily available, and weapons flow freely, with new dangers raised by possible terrorist access to ever more sophisticated devices. On occasion, national governments sponsor the activities of terrorist groups, at home and abroad, which suit their immediate interests.

Terrorism is, or may be, used to achieve unusually diverse goals: to win new recruits for revolutionary movements that aim at the takeover of a state or the creation of a new state; to destabilize nation-states by forcing a dislocation of their economy, the disruption of political structures, and a breakdown of citizen morale; to strengthen the hands of factions in domestic political rivalries; to weaken opposition to the government; as a proxy for the interests of foreign countries or movements; to blackmail third countries into changing their policies; and to spread a terror that may eventually be conducive to some, many, or all of the above objectives. In sum, in an age when terrorism has become a fact of international life with varied levels of frequency, many of the patterns of intra- and interstate behavior have already been changed, or are in the process of being changed.

Yet, on the level of research and policy analysis as well as teaching, the study of terrorism has remained a surprisingly poor cousin to the traditional subfields of international relations. "This is almost a nonsubject," wrote a leading American behavioral scientist a few years ago. "It is not being examined in education, the media, in government or business and certainly not in the broad community." Accordingly, there have been few, if any, comprehensive or systematic investigations of the political sources, methods, and effects of terrorism; only a few cases have been studied in depth; and insufficient efforts have been made to learn from the errors of the past in order to develop a coherent, operational U.S. policy on terrorism, on the management of political crises caused by terrorist acts or threats, or on the prospects and methods of effective international cooperation aimed at defeating or containing the threat.

The papers collected in this volume are published by the Johns Hopkins Foreign Policy Institute (FPI) in order to increase public understanding of the sources and purposes of terrorism. Each paper presents a case study of terrorism in a specific state or region and examines the varied purposes which terrorist methods have been made to serve; as a whole, the collection is concerned with examining the motives and effectiveness of the state and non-state actors who utilize terror as a means of achieving specific political ends. In presenting terror as a method of choice, the authors debunk popular misconceptions about the sources of terrorism and help explain why, despite terrorism's limited effectiveness as a political tool, it is likely to remain a harrowing feature of the political landscape for some time to come.

The Politics of Terrorism: Terror as a State and Revolutionary Strategy is the first of a series of studies focusing on different aspects of international terrorism. Future volumes will examine, among other issues, the range and effectiveness of different policy responses and the potential impact of new technologies on the terrorist threat. The FPI's Program for the Study of International Terrorism is directed by FPI Fellow Barry Rubin. Funding has been provided by the Ford and Lynde and Harry Bradley Foundations; we gratefully acknowledge their support.

Simon Serfaty
Executive Director
The Johns Hopkins Foreign
Policy Institute

PREFACE

Terrorism is a political phenomenon that inspires far more publicity and emotion than analysis and research. The papers in this volume seek to redress this imbalance by examining the variety of purposes terrorism has been used to serve in different areas of the world.

The authors look at cases where terrorism has been used as a tool for revolution, an instrument of repression, or a means of furthering the interests of sponsoring states. Too often, the sources of terrorism have been traced either to an irrational impulse embedded in the human psyche or to long-standing social or political injustices. The first view neglects the very rational basis of terrorism as a political strategy while the latter cannot explain why many of the worst cases of injustice have failed to evoke a terrorist response. In truth, terrorism is but one of many strategies—violent as well as nonviolent—open to those seeking to advance or protect specific social and political ends. The diverse essays herein, then, seek to analyze the specific material, historical and political reasons why certain groups and countries *choose* terrorism as a strategy.

As the authors convincingly demonstrate, governments sponsor terrorism as a way to achieve well-defined objectives, including the destruction of opposition movements abroad, the intimidation and weakening of rivals, and the deterrence of political or diplomatic actions they oppose. Dictatorships use terroristic means of repression at home in order to stay in power under certain conditions. Revolutionary or nationalist movements employ terror because they have no hope of gaining a broad base of support (as in Western Europe or the United States), as part of a guerrilla strategy, or simply to destroy physically an opposing ethnic group. The very nature of terrorism—its special techniques and requirements—makes it unlikely that those who employ it will be democratic in either temperament or inspiration.

If the origins and uses of terrorism are often misunderstood, its real or potential achievements—particularly as a revolutionary method—have often been exaggerated. Those who are unable to build mass-based movements or organize an effective armed insurgency find terrorism a convenient alternative. After all, terrorism implies hitting "soft" targets—that is, unarmed civilians who are unable to defend themselves. By the same token, however, terrorist attacks—hijackings, assassinations, bombings— are ineffective against a strong government. Most often, terrorist methods will be rejected by many who might otherwise be won over by the revolutionary cause. Even in the rare situation where terror is used successfully to fuel ethnic fears and hatreds, terrorists must exploit certain unusual historical and cultural circumstances.

The papers in this book deal with these broader issues by looking at specific cases. Mark Falcoff describes Argentina's 1970s crisis stemming from the actions of revolutionary terrorists and the military's retaliatory terrorist repression. The revolutionaries never came close to victory; yet the junta—supported by middle class elements fearful of anarchy—killed thousands. Falcoff analyzes how in Argentina terrorism proved to be a more effective repressive than revolutionary strategy.

Barry Rubin writes about the political uses of terrorism in the Middle East, stressing the growing employment of these methods to serve the interests of particular states. Rubin explains why dictatorial regimes, particularly in Iran, Libya, and Syria, have found terrorism to be helpful in pursuing their broader objectives.

Ami Ayalon considers the various forms of terrorism in Egypt—as a tactic of extremist Islamic fundamentalists, as the supreme weapon of leftist insurgents, and as a convenient lever for foreign states seeking to undermine the Egyptian government. Ayalon shows how the various targets and methods of the different groups reflects their distinctive backgrounds and ideologies.

Joseph Kostiner examines the efforts of both Iran and Iraq to foment revolution abroad by providing support to terrorist and insurgent groups. Under the exigencies of war, Kostiner argues, both sides in the Iran-Iraq conflict were forced to reduce their ambitions; when support for terror and insurgency conflicted with more immediate and compelling state interests, both sides attempted to restrain client groups.

David Scott Palmer and Herbert Howe discuss the use of terror as a revolutionary tool in Peru and South Africa. Palmer highlights the unique conditions leading to the centrality of terrorism in the strategy of the Peruvian *Sendero Luminoso*. In a sense, he argues, the government forces in Peru represent a Spanish-speaking and European nation—separate from that of the Indians. The radical organization attempts to exploit this ethnic antipathy. Yet terrorism has served to limit as well as strengthen *Sendero Luminoso's* support among the Indian population.

Howe argues that the African National Congress in South Africa has rejected terrorism in an effort to define acceptable peaceful and violent means of protest. He also details the ways in which the government has used terrorism as a relatively effective means of repression. In the concluding essay, Cecilia Albin surveys the current state and variety of terrorist movements around the world, drawing a number of conclusions about their efficacy and future prospects.

It is hoped that this collection will deepen the debate about the sources and role of terrorism in international politics and that it will be of interest to those following specific regional issues and movements.

Barry Rubin

1

BETWEEN TWO FIRES: TERRORISM AND COUNTERTERRORISM IN ARGENTINA, 1970–1983

Mark Falcoff

Between 1970 and 1983, Argentina—one of the most refined and civilized countries in the world—experienced a sharp regression towards barbarism, the likes of which had not been seen since the Second World War. During those years uncounted thousands of persons were abducted, tortured and killed by revolutionary and counterrevolutionary forces, both regular and paramilitary, in conjunction with or with the approval of members of the clergy, judiciary, press, business and intellectual and labor communities.

In broadest outline, the events were these: between 1970 and 1973, armed formations loyal to former President Juan Perón engaged in an urban guerrilla war against a de facto military government. The characteristic methods were kidnapping and outright assassination; the ultimate purpose was to undermine the morale of the armed forces and compel it to call elections so that Perón, the leader of the largest political party in Argentina who had been expelled in 1955, could return to power.

The strategy eventually bore fruit. In 1973, the generals decided that discretion was the better part of valor; elections were held; and the Peronist party in fact returned to government. However, acts of terrorist violence—this time against a government that terrorists had

1

once sought to establish—continued until 1976, when the armed forces once again seized power and initiated blanket repression. In 1983, having been defeated in a humiliating war with Great Britain over the Malvinas (Falkland) Islands in the South Atlantic, the armed forces were compelled to step down; elections were again held; and Argentina passed into a rare period of democratic rule.

To say anything more than this is to enter immediately into a polemical minefield. To put matters simply, virtually every aspect of the problem is fraught with ideological implications; both sides of the civil war continue to struggle over the writing of recent history. There is, in the first place, absolutely no agreement on the number of victims of either terrorism or counterterrorism. The U. S. government, reporting to Congress in early 1977 on the state of human rights in Argentina, found that some 2,000 Argentines died between 1973 and 1976.[1] In contrast, the National Commission of Disappeared Persons (CONADEP), appointed by President Alfonsín in 1983, found only 600 such instances prior to the March 1976 coup.[2]

Nor is there any consensus on the number of victims of counterterrorism, or state repression. Prior to the collapse of the military government in 1983, estimates ranged widely; the Argentine Permanent Assembly on Human Rights (APDH), an organization known to be close to the Communist party, claimed 6,500 such cases (1976–1979). A special commission of the New York City Bar Association that visited Argentina in 1979 put the

---

[1]*Human Rights Practices in Countries Receiving U. S. Security Assistance*, 95th Congress, First Session (Washington, D.C., 1977), 101.

[2]*Nunca Más* (London, 1986), 10. It should be noted that this report has inspired a response, entitled *Definitivamente—Nunca Más: La Otra Cara del Informe de la CONADEP* (Buenos Aires, 1985). Unfortunately, it was not available at the Library of Congress at the time this paper was being prepared.

number at 10,000. Amnesty International preferred an estimate running between 15,000 and 20,000.[3] After Argentina's return to civilian government, the National Commission on Disappeared Persons was given extensive facilities to pursue its investigation; as its report explains, it sent representatives to interview victims, relatives, or witnesses not only throughout Argentina, but in Mexico, Western Europe, and the United States. In the end it documented just slightly less than 9,000 individual cases. It was not, however, satisfied to leave matters there. As its report explains, "We have reason to believe that the true figure is much higher. Many families were reluctant to report a disappearance for fear of reprisals." CONADEP's final report speaks somewhat cavalierly of "tens of thousands" of victims.[4]

The matter is further complicated by the fact that both terrorism and counterterrorism overlap administrations. Between 1970 and 1973, the principal perpetrators were armed formations of the Peronist Left attacking a de facto military dictatorship. But between 1973 and 1976 there were three kinds of violence—between the terrorists and an elected government they had helped to install but found they could not control; between the terrorists and the armed forces and police; and between paramilitary formations and parallel organizations of the police loyal to the Peróns' Social Welfare Minister, José López Rega. After the 1976 coup, some Peronists fell victim to outright military repression and suddenly discovered the virtues of human rights. Others, however, did not; instead, they took advantage of the military sweep to collaborate in the dispatching of their rivals. Thus, while individual Peronists may clamor for justice, the party as a whole has

---

[3]*Country Reports on Human Rights Practices for 1979*, 96th Congress, Second Session, Joint Committee Print (Washington, D.C., 1980), 239.
[4]*Nunca Más*, 5, 10.

no particular reason to look too closely into the events which occurred in the two years prior to the military coup.

Finally, there is no agreement on the sources of strategy and political doctrine which inspired so much political violence. The terrorists of the early 1970s had evidently drunk deeply at the wells of Marxist ideology. Yet the report of the National Commission on Disappeared Persons has nothing whatever to say about this; in fact, it denied that its job was to "look into the crimes committed by those terrorists," which in any event, it argued, were adequately documented by the military government and by the press of the period.[5]

It was less reticent about the doctrinal sources of counterterror, which it placed at the hands of the United States and France, particularly the former. In an appendix to its report, by cleverly stitching together various quotations from U.S. and Argentine officials, it blurs crucial differences between the counterinsurgency doctrine of the Kennedy and Johnson administrations and the actual conduct of the Argentine armed forces a decade later. The report thus serves two needs at once: to transfer all responsibility to the United States and to discount completely any linkage between Marxism and the conduct of terrorists who undermined civilian political institutions in Argentina in 1973–76.

The result is that any evaluation of the Argentine experience must be provisional and tentative. In this paper we propose to examine the setting and context; the personalities and doctrines; and the implications for the future course of Argentine society. But we make no pretense to offering more than a cursory exploration into a very complex and difficult subject which by its very nature eludes rigorous analysis.

---

[5]Ibid., 6.

The Setting and Context: Why Argentina?

All societies display certain political pathologies; not all of them, however, experience terrorism. The United States, for example, is thought to be a violent country, and in fact is so, if we base our judgment wholly on the number of violent crimes committed annually, adjusted proportionally to population. Yet the United States has suffered relatively little from political terrorism, in spite of the presence of diverse national, cultural and religious groups within its boundaries, some of which harbor serious grievances against authority, or at any rate, against the resident representatives of foreign powers (the Soviet Union, Turkey, Great Britain, and so forth).

Conversely, countries with a more "peaceful" social environment (the United Kingdom, France, Italy) have been primary victims of terrorism in recent years. This paradox should warn those searching for simple explanations of complex problems. It is possible to find within any society reasons why terrorism occurs, without the presence of those factors effectively explaining anything. This much said, there are certain features of Argentine life which cannot be ignored in any discussion of the subject; in considering them, however, we leave open the question of how important (or unimportant) each might have been.

Lack of legitimacy in the political system. Argentina led South America in political development before the First World War, electing its first truly representative chief executive in 1916. Since 1930, however, at least a significant minority of citizens have felt disenfranchised most of the time. In 1930 the military seized power and deposed President Hipólito Yrigoyen. Though new elections were held in 1932, fraud and exclusion prevented the majoritarian Radical party from registering its true strength. The same was true in 1938; the 1944 elections were never held.

A military coup in 1943 radically shifted the direction of Argentine politics by introducing a new alliance between the armed forces and the labor movement. Its leader was Colonel Juan Perón, who combined nationalism, populism and personalism to capture a solid majority of voters in new elections convoked in 1946. While some fraud and intimidation seems to have occurred, Perón's real problem was his governing style, which confused loyalty to the leader and his movement with loyalty to the Argentine nation. Exploiting class and regional resentments, Perón purposely polarized Argentina into Peronist and anti-Peronist camps; it became impossible for anyone to remain neutral on the subject of his person or policies. The anti–Peronist front was extremely broad—stretching from the Communists on the Left to the Conservatives on the Right; in its totality it supported the coup which brought the president down in September 1955.

Perón's flight into exile did not bring Argentines closer together, nor impart greater legitimacy to the political system. The victors and the vanquished merely changed places, with the important difference that the former fell to quarreling among themselves over the way to deal with Perón's followers. One group, led by the armed forces (particularly the navy) and seconded by the conservative political and business community, favored a thorough purge of Argentine society, hoping to extinguish Peronism as a political force. The other, made up of sections of the Radical party and the Left, sought to coopt Perón's followers and harness them to a new majority. Thus the leading Radical politician of the 1950s, Arturo Frondizi, struck a deal with the exiled Perón to re-legalize his party if the latter supported his presidential bid in 1958. For keeping his promise in 1962, however, Frondizi was deposed by the armed forces.

The following year new elections were held in which political exclusions were so complete that Dr. Arturo Illia, a Radical from a more rigidly anti-Peronist branch of the party, limped into office with a mere 23 percent of the vote. When he was deposed in 1966 by a military coup, many Peronists and anti-Peronists joined hands to applaud. On the other hand, the new military regime, the so-called Argentine Revolution, quickly divided between "liberals" (that is, conservatives) and "nationalists" (that is, fascistoid Catholics and their military allies). Meanwhile, the vast majority of Argentines—Peronist, Radical, and independent—went unrepresented.

Between 1966 and 1973 Argentine society underwent what can only be called "re-Peronization." The causes were several. Economic deterioration, which actually began in the late Perón period, but accelerated sharply in the 1960s, led many Argentines to confuse the earlier Peronist era with better days, which in fact they were, since they coincided with high agricultural prices following World War II. A new student generation emerged which had no memory of the Peronist period and which, not unnaturally, linked the lack of popular representation with the poor performance of the economy. And the exiled leader—now in Madrid—demonstrated a remarkable capacity to be all things to all people. In general, by the early 1970s Perón subsumed all of the anti-status quo elements in the country: to Catholics he represented opposition to the increasing secularization of society; to conservatives, the last, best hope to restore order and greatness to Argentina; to the young, particularly the youthful left, the Argentine version of a socialist revolution.

Quite obviously, Perón could not possibly be all of these things simultaneously—except in exile. By 1972–73 the military recognized that sooner rather than later elections would have to be held, and though they designed the rules to prevent Perón from presenting a candidacy of his own, he outmaneuvered them by naming a loyal subordinate, Héctor Cámpora, to stand in for him. Shortly after his victory, Cámpora resigned; new elections were held; and Perón was elected president of Argentina for the third time with sixty percent of the vote.

Perón's final period of power (1973–74) was brief and turbulent, characterized by growing difficulties between the aging chief executive and the left wing of his own party, which had already begun to mesh with the guerrilla movement. After his death, his spouse María Estela ("Isabel"), who had been elected with him as his vice-president, assumed the presidential office, but was increasingly dependent upon sinister advisers. Moreover, she lacked Perón's magic, so that as both internal security and the economy deteriorated rapidly she became the object of considerable popular discontent. Her overthrow by the armed forces two years later was widely supported.

The "process of national reorganization," as the military government of 1976–83 was known, immediately turned its attentions to a full scale counterguerrilla war, which enjoyed considerable popular support. This, combined with an economic policy which vastly overvalued the peso, led to a period of free spending on imported goods and foreign travel which neutralized much potential opposition to the regime. By 1982, however, the economy began to show signs of serious deterioration, leading President Gen. Roberto Galtieri to embark upon a military adventure in the South Atlantic—the recuperation of the Malvinas, an archipelago of islands seized from Argentina by the British in the early nineteenth century and thereafter more widely known as the Falklands.

The reconquest of the Malvinas temporarily rescued the government's popularity; Galtieri overnight became the idol of Argentines, and his regime suddenly reacquired all of the quasi-legitimacy it had enjoyed in its first days. But the defeat of the Argentine armed forces by a hastily assembled British expeditionary force suddenly turned the political tables, and the same crowds which had been wildly cheering the dictator now demanded his resignation. The defeat in the Malvinas war without doubt deprived the military of its will to continue in power, and, in new elections convoked in November 1983, Dr. Raul Alfonsín, a Radical sternly critical of the military, was elected by a strong popular majority.

From this cursory recital of names, dates, and events, two somber facts stand out. First, all military governments in Argentina have enjoyed a kind of quasi-legitimacy in their first days of power, but all have rapidly lost them. Second, no Argentine government was legitimate in the conventional, democratic sense of the term between 1928 and 1946; none were accepted as fully legitimate by most Argentines between 1928 and 1973; and Alfonsín is the first civilian since Hipólito Yrigoyen to come to power by elections in which there were no exclusions.

The prolonged crisis of legitimacy not merely encouraged some to resort to terrorism; it deprived others of the moral resources to extinguish it once it had appeared. Thus, during the government of President Gen. Alejandro Lanusse, an entire legal apparatus was put into place to deal with the terrorist problem; had the administration been democratically elected, such mechanisms could have been employed with minimal damage to civil liberties, as in the case of Italy. As it was, however, the new Peronist government, which came into power in May 1973 through the first free elections in a decade, felt obligated to reverse all acts of its predecessor. Not only was the counterterrorist machinery dismantled, but a blanket amnesty released from Argentine jails many perpetrators of terrorism who resumed their activities almost immediately.

Cosmopolitanism and provincialism. Argentina is a "European" country in social customs, structure, and aspirations.

It is also a melting pot of nationalities—particularly Italian and Spanish, but also French, British, Irish, and Russian Jewish. Unlike the United States, however, these groups do not fully identify with their country of birth and residence, but hold on to what links, however tenuous, they can claim with their ultimate country of origin.[6] An extraordinary number of Argentines continue to maintain family and other ties with the old country, and many young people have studied and traveled there—particularly since the advent of jet travel in the 1960s. There are, of course, many Europes. Like all colonial or quasi-colonial peoples, Argentines have been selective in their adaptation. In general the more positive Western European trends since 1945—political liberalism, market economics, educational reform—have appealed far less than the surviving remnants of prewar culture (Franco Spain or Gaullist France for the Right), or the revolutionary effervescence associated with the 1968 movement in France, Italy and West Germany (for the Left). In particular, young Argentines studying in Western Europe during the 1960s tended to come under the influence of Marxism, and those who spent time in Italy were exposed to one of the most creative and energetic terrorist movements of modern times.[7]

The relationship between Argentine and European terrorism is something more than literary and platonic;

---

[6]This includes the Argentine Jewish community, which is more actively Zionist than its American counterpart. This was obviously not the case with those Jews who—somewhat out of proportion to their actual numbers—participated in the terrorist movement; like their predecessors in czarist Russia, they saw revolutionary Marxism as a larger identity within which they could finally belong to the Argentine national community.

[7]It is perhaps worth noting here that a small number of students from right-wing and Catholic homes went to Spain on scholarships from Franco's *Instituto de Cultura Hispánica*. According to one informant, they came back "vomiting stupidities about the church, the army, and tradition." Some of course eventually ended up working as civilians in the military government of 1976–83, providing a gloss of ideology to the entire repressive sweep.

as Claire Sterling has pointed out, both the *Montoneros* and the People's Revolutionary Army (ERP) had extensive overseas connections. As early as 1971 the ERP was represented at a terrorist conference held in a Jesuit college in Florence, which included representatives of sixteen movements including the Irish Republican Army, the Basque ETA, and the Palestinians.[8] Five years later police in Argentina raided one of the ERP's safehouses and discovered a document revealing a plan to launch a "Europe Brigade" in order to recycle Argentine terrorism at one of the points of origin. For their part, the *Montoneros* were trained by the Basque ETA, who landed in Cuba in the early 1970s and later fanned out to South America.[9] At times the *Montonero* leadership operated from abroad— shifting headquarters from Rome, to Madrid, Mexico City, and Havana, and then back.[10]

It is entirely possible that even without these linkages Argentine terrorism would have assumed much the same configuration as it did. Certainly the *Montoneros* and the ERP were *sui generis* in inspiration and ideology, perhaps taking from foreigners certain techniques, but not answering in any way to foreign control. Yet the more pathological features of European society fit neatly into Argentina precisely because the country experienced little institutional development after the 1930s. Indeed, many visitors to the country in the 1960s and 1970s noted that obsolete issues that once agitated prewar Europe (political pluralism, the rights of religious and racial minorities, secularization of education and women's rights) had miraculously survived in Argentina. Similarly, it was the Italy of the 1930s, not the 1960s, which the Argentine authorities ultimately copied to suppress terrorism, sacrificing in the

---

[8]*The Terror Network* (New York, 1981), 44.
[9]Ibid., 98.
[10]Pablo Guissiani, *Montoneros: La Soberbia Armada* (Buenos Aires, 1984), 67.

11

process representative political institutions and an independent judiciary. At the same time, the terrorist Left operated on assumptions about the accessibility of state power that would have been more appropriate to anarchists and anarcho-syndicalists in Barcelona or Madrid during the mid-1930s, and eschewed the gradualism that characterized the Spanish transition in the 1970s. Thus it is at least possible that had Argentine political development not been frozen in 1939–40, the society would have been open to cosmopolitan influences of a more wholesome sort.

Confusion between left and right. The lack of democratic continuity in Argentine political development and the evident illegitimacy of most governments since 1930 bred a culture of resentful populism, whose principal themes were xenophobia, anti-intellectualism, and the conviction that constitutions, courts and the republican system were a conspiracy to prevent the "real" will of the people from being represented. Of course, this was technically true for much of the time.

Exclusion and alienation were the twin points at which all kinds of political ideologies crossed and met. Right-wing Catholics at times shared with left-wing revolutionaries the notion that all foreign influences in Argentine culture and education (most of them from democratic countries) were corrupting. The same, of course, could be said for foreign investment, so that left- and right-wing "anti-imperialism" overlapped. The centrality of the Peronist movement—which in a certain way was a populism, if not a fascism, of left, right, and center all at the same time—meant that antidemocratic currents could meet within the same broad church.[11] Finally, the culture of

---

[11] One *Montonero* intellectual once told Pablo Guissiani that "the Germans, after all, were not far wrong in voting for Hitler, since Hitler, after all, raised genuinely popular banners." *Montoneros: La Soberbia Armada,* 151.

violence itself tended to blur ideological distinctions in the maelstrom of praxis.

There seems also to have been a process whereby many young men and women trained at Catholic private schools—presumably in the doctrines of sword and cross, if not throne and altar—made the passage from right to left with no perceptible difficulty. Juan José Sebreli, a remarkable Argentine sociologist, points out that the lines between Catholic left and Catholic right became blurred during the 1960s; one characteristic personality, Father Carlos Mujica, "divided his time more or less equally between slum towns where he preached the social Christian revolution and the most elegant circles of the oligarchy, to which he belonged by birth, parentage, and association." Above all, Sebreli notes, Catholicism left indelible marks on the *Montoneros*, "which endured well into their Marxist phase: irrationality, sectarianism, asceticism, the cult of individual sacrifice for the greater good, a preference for absolutes, a near-longing for death and martyrdom."[12]

The peculiarly urban nature of Argentine society. During the early 1960s, the Cuban revolution was the dominant model for revolutionary forces in Argentina as it was elsewhere in Latin America. However, unlike Cuba (or Bolivia, Peru or Guatemala), Argentina possessed no peasant class, which, according to the theories of Che Guevara, was the "motor" of a social revolution in Latin America.[13] The earliest attempts by the guerilla leader Ricardo Masetti to replicate the Cuban revolution in the province of Salta, near the Bolivian border, ended in disaster. By 1970, however, the revolutionary Left was looking elsewhere for theoretical sustenance: to the writings of

---

[12]*Los Deseos Imaginarios del Peronismo* (Buenos Aires, 1983), 170.
[13]In *Guerrilla Warfare*, Brian Loveman and Thomas M. Davies, Jr., eds. (Lincoln, Neb., 1985).

Abraham Guillén, a veteran of the Spanish civil war who had settled in Argentina, and to the writings of Alberto Methol Ferré, the "theoretician" of the *Tupamaros* in neighboring Uruguay.

Argentina is not merely an urban society, but a metropolitan one as well—approximately a third of the country resides in and around Buenos Aires. This made the capital a perfect setting for urban terrorism, in which the guerrillas were indistinguishable from the population as a whole,[14] and could take advantage of the anonymity provided by population density. However, the urban setting also made counterterrorism a matter of systematic police dragnets, rather than endless days slogging in an inhospitable countryside, and deprived the guerrillas of one of their traditional advantages.

The overproduction of intellectuals. Higher education in Argentina is provided free of charge by the state, and in an immigrant or immigrant-descended society many families look to the university degree as the logical avenue of social mobility. The result has been huge enrollments at public institutions; during the 1960s, for example, the University of Buenos Aires carried more than 80,000 students on its rolls.

A heavy emphasis on liberal arts and the social sciences (introduced during the Frondizi presidency) resulted in bumper crops of sociologists, social psychologists, and psychoanalysts—most with no conceivable outlet for their talents. The combination of a highly theoretical education, with a heavy Marxist bias, and lack of employment opportunities generated immense frustration. Over time,

---

[14]Costa-Gavras' motion picture *State of Siege* (1970), based on the Uruguayan experience but obviously similar in many ways to Argentina, emphasizes the "ordinariness" of the *Tupamaros*. In one unforgettable scene we are shown block wardens of the movement, who include not only students and intellectuals but also housewives and even an Army officer.

increasing numbers of university graduates sought an out-let in either individual or collective liberation. Many young professionals underwent psychoanalysis, and in fact Argentina in the 1970s had the largest per capita number of practitioners of any country in the world. Others went on, with or without analysis, to terrorism and direct action.

A strong bias against intellectual independence. Historically pluralism has ranked low in the hierarchy of Argentine virtues. Power is respected above all things. All govern-ments enjoy a supportive *oficialista* press. Political move-ments aspire to complete hegemony, including democratic parties like the Radical Civic Union. The lonely dissenter enjoys little respect in a society in which the practical out-come between success and failure is so enormous.

Among other things, this means that Argentines dis-play a "herd instinct" that pushes them from one position to the other almost overnight, with no apparent contradic-tion. It explains how so many of the same people could favor the government of the Peróns, its overthrow by the military three years later, the counterterrorist campaign, the war in the South Atlantic, and the return to democracy in 1983. It also accounts for the fact that so much of the human rights movement in that country comes from po-litical forces which historically have been somewhat out-side the mainstream.

Who Were the Terrorists?

Origins. There were five large terrorist groupings active in Argentina from 1970. They included the People's Revo-lutionary Army (ERP); the Armed Forces of Liberation (FAL); the Peronist Armed Forces (FAP); the Revolutionary Armed Forces (FAR); and the *Montoneros.* The ERP was vaguely related to the Fourth (Trotskyist) International;

the FAL was Marxist-Leninist and not (initially) Peronist, a schismatic offshoot of the Revolutionary Communist party, one of the many factions into which the Argentine party had divided in the 1960s. Some members of these organizations were trained in Cuba; others were trained by those who had taken courses there. The *Montoneros* were actually an outgrowth of militant Catholic youth groups, particularly Tacuara, a fascistoid organization active in the early 1960s that later merged imperceptibly with a "revolutionary" Catholic left. By 1973, all of these groups except the ERP had merged with the *Montoneros*, subsuming their individual doctrinal identities in a praxis of violence which took on a logic of its own.

Whatever their initial ideological orientation, most of the leaders of Argentine terrorism came from mainstream political backgrounds. Fernando Vaca Narvaja's father was deputy governor of Córdoba province in the 1950s; Juan and Julio Storni were related to one of the principal figures of the "Liberating Revolution" of 1955—the Catholic nationalist movement which overthrew Perón. Raul Mende was the son of a Peronist minister, while Domingo Sosa Barber's father was a provincial minister during the Radical administration of Arturo Illia. Pablo Maria and Sebastian Llorens came from a similar background, while Sergio Paz Berlin was the son of a wealthy industrialist. Diego Muñiz Barreto, a landowner and Peronist deputy (1973–76) friendly to the *Montoneros*, had been a technical adviser to the military dictatorship of Juan Carlos Onganía. In effect, then, all of the pathologies of Argentine politics—left, right and center, traditional and avant-garde—met and coexisted in this movement.

Methods. The earliest urban terrorist organizations in Argentina probably received some resources from abroad, but by the early 1970s they were entirely self-sufficient, usually financed by bank robberies or kidnappings of

Argentine or foreign businessmen who were ransomed for huge sums. For example, the Born brothers, heirs to the vast Bunge y Born cereal fortune, yielded their abductors $60 million, the largest single ransom ever paid anywhere in the world. In short order the *Montoneros* were generating so much income that they had their own brokers investing on Wall Street, with interest payments from their accounts averaging as much as $130,000 a month.[15] It has been rumored as well that David Graiver, an Argentine financier who disappeared in a mysterious plane crash in Mexico in 1980, was the "banker" for the *Montoneros* in New York and Brussels.

While some of the resources generated by ransom were used periodically to distribute (with great flourish) food, clothing and medicine in the slums of Buenos Aires and other Argentine cities, most of the money raised by ransom was invested in overtly political activities. For example, in 1973 the long-defunct Argentine daily *El Mundo* was revived by ERP financiers. The *Montoneros* owned *Noticias*, and it is even possible that they held a major interest in the most serious Argentine newspaper of them all, *La Opinión*, unbeknownst to its publisher, Jacobo Timerman, whose business partner was David Graiver.

Between 1970 and 1973 the *Montoneros* and the ERP were known largely for what Timerman has rightly called "the eroticism of violence."[16] First, there was the murder of individuals thought to be standing in the way of a truly "revolutionary" trend within the Peronist movement, such as union leaders Augusto Vandor (1969), José Alonso

---

[15]Richard Gillespie, *Soldiers of Perón: Argentina's Montoneros* (Oxford, 1982), 180–83, 252. See Moyano Martin, *supra*, from which the citation is derived.
[16]*Prisoner Without a Name, Cell Without a Number*, Toby Talbot, tr. (New York, 1981), 14. "We had to do it," a guerrilla leader confessed to a friend after the assassination of labor leader José Rucci. "Our people were going soft in their office jobs. From time to time they have to be rescued by putting them back into military action." Guissiani, *Montoneros: La Soberbia Armada*, 49.

(1970), and José Rucci (1973). Second, there were "executions" of individuals for shock or symbolic value, most notably former President Pedro Eugenio Aramburu (1970). Third, there were attacks on members of the military establishment or their families, intended to undermine their morale and willingness to bear the costs of remaining in power. For example, the wife of the paraplegic son of President Gen. Alejandro Lanusse (1970–73) perished through a letter bomb. Fourth, foreign diplomats were abducted and military establishments or prisons temporarily seized in order to obtain the release of incarcerated comrades. Fifth, bombs were planted in public places where the well-to-do tended to gather, an updated version of the earlier Russian anarchist doctrine of "the propaganda of the deed." Finally, the guerrillas sought direct confrontation with the armed forces, convinced that by selective encounters and assassinations they could destroy the latter's capacity to sustain the political structure.

In retrospect it seems remarkable that a movement which probably never amounted to more than four to six thousand persons (even this number is controversial) could seriously entertain thoughts of seizing political power in its own right. Nonetheless, in 1972 and 1973 it acted as if this was only a matter of willpower, directly assaulting army and navy installations, killing officers and enlisted men in the process. The *Montoneros* were particularly active in the northern province of Tucumán, a part of which it succeeded in actively controlling for more than a year.[17]

Moreover, for a few weeks in mid-1973, when Dr. Héctor Cámpora was serving as a presidential stand-in for Juan Perón, it was possible to contemplate taking over the government by infiltrating existing institutions. Cámpora's interior minister Esteban Righli was widely

---

[17]Tucumán was subsequently the scene of "Operation Independence," the bloodiest example of repression anywhere in Argentina after 1976.

rumored to have close ties to the *Montoneros*; one of his first acts was to declare a blanket amnesty for convicted terrorists then serving sentences in Argentine prisons. At the same time, the state-controlled national television network evidently came under the control of the revolutionary Left, and it appeared that the national school system might do so as well. Once Perón himself returned to Argentina and to power, this trend was immediately reversed, leading to an open break between Perón and the *Montonero* leadership in 1974; a new round of terrorist violence followed in the weeks and months after the president's death and the shaky succession of his widow.

One final point. By mid-1975 many people had become afraid to go out at night in Buenos Aires and other major Argentine cities. The sense of insecurity was overwhelming; trust in major government institutions and particularly in the security forces was at an all-time low, since many perceived (not inaccurately) that the military was deliberately allowing things to get out of hand so that when it returned to power it would be with broad popular support. In this sense, the terrorists succeeded in half of their agenda—undermining an elected, civilian government, however incompetent and corrupt. But their assumption that the military's reluctance to move against them with full force was due to fear or even supposed ideological affinities proved to be a grave error. Once Isabel Perón was placed under house arrest, they felt the full blast of forces the army had kept in reserve.

Who Were the Counterterrorists?

Origins. The counterterrorist offensive was, as one might expect, initially the responsibility of the armed forces and federal police. What made the Argentine case unusual was the fact that there was no apparent centralization of effort; instead, the country was divided into geographical and functional "security zones," each under the command of a different branch of the service. Among other things, this meant that different policies prevailed in different zones; there was considerable interservice rivalry; some victims were spared because they (or their family) had contacts within the particular branch which conducted sweeps in their zone, while others perished for the lack of them.

In addition, during the presidency of Juan and Isabel Perón, the ministry of interior, the labor unions, and the ministry of social welfare were involved in antiterrorist activity, which necessarily overlapped with other agendas favored by the "traditionalist" leadership of the Peronist party. These included elimination of left-wing and dissident Peronists within the movement, particularly within the Peronist Youth. Since some of these were, in fact, actively involved with urban guerrilla activities, two tasks were accomplished at once.

To add to the confusion, over the years the interior ministry and police periodically recurred to "parallel" (that is, extra-official) formations of the police. Some of these overlapped imperceptibly with Argentina's criminal underworld; others with labor unions or shady business operations; others with extreme right-wing political groups. Since not much is known about these except for the fact of their existence, it is difficult to say how important a role they played during either the Perón government (1973–76) or the "process" (1976–83). The important point is that it was never possible to demarcate clearly areas of responsibility, even when the counterterrorist offensive was in full tilt.

Methods. Perhaps the most important feature of the antiterrorist sweep, or "dirty war" (1974–1979), was its covert nature. The Argentine military were much impressed with the international ostracism to which their Chilean counterparts had been subjected after the coup in that country in 1973 and sought to avoid the same fate by proceeding in secret. As the report of the National Commission notes, "no kidnapping was ever stopped, not a single detention center was ever located, there was never news of those responsible being punished for any of the crimes." Argentina was "engulfed by an ominous silence."[18]

This was made possible in large part by the conduct of the Argentine press, which, with the exception of the English-language Buenos Aires *Herald*, exercised rigorous self-censorship, and by widespread public complacency. Many Argentines—not wholly without reason—regarded the repression as distasteful but inevitable and necessary.[19] Though thousands of families were affected by "disappearances," the matter never became a burning public issue until after the military had been humiliated on the field of battle. In fact, public opinion surveys throughout the period showed that only a small minority of Argentines regarded human rights as an important issue, even within those sectors of the population disproportionately affected by "disappearances"—students and labor.

In an environment in which there were no restraints—either on the part of the judiciary or public opinion—what started out as a counterterrorist drive inevitably acquired wider dimensions. Some military and police officials took advantage of the situation to enrich themselves with the property of their victims. Others saw the campaign as an opportunity to eliminate not merely terrorists but people who happened to figure in their address books. The line disappeared not merely between suspicion and guilt, but between presumed guilt and presumed guilt by association.

---

[18]*Nunca Más*, 3.
[19]M. E. Aftilión et al., *¿Qué Nos Pasa a los Argentinos?* (Buenos Aires, 1985), 83–84.

In addition, the counterguerrilla offensive made it possible to settle outstanding political and cultural scores. As James Neilson, editor of the Buenos Aires *Herald* has written, "Many [victims], it is clear, were merely people in such suspect professions as journalism, psychology, or university education—people whom the men in charge of the government's antiterrorist squads believed, at a time of high hysteria, were the 'intellectual authors of terrorism.' "[20] These suffered far out of proportion to the actual number of their colleagues who actually participated in various action groups, impoverishing still further a country whose intellectual capital had been depleted by decades of military rule, Peronist anti-intellectualism, and budgetary neglect.

In a certain sense, the "dirty war" was the final installment of a long campaign the Argentine conservative community and military have waged against their adversaries since at least 1930. But whereas earlier military coups were concerned with overthrowing specific civilian governments (Yrigoyen, Frondizi, Illia), the "process" was intended to alter permanently Argentina's political and cultural landscape. In spite of the allegations of the National Commission on Disappeared Persons, and even of some of the army officers cited in its report, it is clear that no counterrevolutionary doctrine needed to be imported. What is more, had the armed forces met with greater success either in the management of the Argentine economy or the recuperation of the Malvinas Islands, it is likely that they would have succeeded in transforming the nation's political foundations.

Just what Argentina might have looked like under those circumstances is as difficult to say as what it might have resembled had the *Montoneros* or the ERP seized power. Even within the armed forces and their civilian

---

[20]"Argentina: The Process and the Puzzle," *Encounter,* January 1981.

allies there was (and is) no agreement on the kind of country Argentina should be—whether "liberal," that is, open to the world as a partner in the Western community, or "nationalist," that is, withdrawn behind a spiteful curtain of self-absorption.[21] As it was, the country had to pass through a crucible of both terrorism and counterterrorism before any democratic synthesis was possible. In any event, it is difficult to see how it might have otherwise occurred.

Long-term Implications for Argentine Politics

From the very beginning, Argentina's military government (1976–83) was faced with a dilemma entirely of its own making. Because it proceeded against terrorism without the slightest reference to the rule of law, a graceful exit from power at some future date was utterly impossible.[22] This explains why, at a moment when the economy was rapidly deteriorating and serious discussions with the opposition should have been the order of the day, President Gen. Leopoldo Galtieri chose instead to embark on a military expedition in the South Atlantic. Had Great Britain possessed a different prime minister, the gamble might have worked. As it was, what appeared to be one of the strongest military governments in Latin America collapsed within a matter of days. Nonetheless, some of the problems created by Argentina's bloody decade have survived into the current period of democratic government.

---

[21]See James Neilson's reflections on this point, loc. cit.

[22]Dr. Angel Robledo, defense minister in the last cabinet of President Juan Perón, remarked to me in 1983 that in 1978 he told some of his high-ranking contacts in the military that the moment was opportune to promulgate a blanket amnesty for both sides—terrorist and counterterrorist. "Instead," he remarked, "intoxicated with the arrogance of power, they chose to put the matter off. And now you see where they are."

In the first place, it has not been possible to fix full moral and personal responsibility for the events. Though the present government is Radical, the Peronist party remains the largest single political force in the country, and its cooperation is essential if democratic institutions are to survive. For their part, the Peronists obviously have no great interest in looking too closely into events which occurred on their watch (1973–76), nor in exploring the relationship between the armed forces, the trade unions, and other agencies who worked together in the past.

Nor is the matter much simpler with regard to the armed forces themselves. Though the Alfonsín government has brought the commanders-in-chief of the armed forces to justice, it cannot go much further short of dismantling the military establishment itself. This explains why it proposed "full-stop" legislation to the Congress, setting an early terminal date for victims and relatives of victims to file charges in the federal courts. As it is, there have been several minor military uprisings, including some promoted by younger officers—many of them combat veterans of the Malvinas war—who oppose the allegedly supine attitude of their superiors toward the government.

For its part, the Argentine human rights community and its allies abroad have no particular interest in closing out investigations and further judicial action on past abuses. Quite apart from the fact that so far only a tiny fraction of the guilty have even been brought to trial, this is the only conceivable issue which the Argentine left can hope to use to advance its other agendas. Given the constraints of the political system and of military-civilian relations, it is likely that the issue of "disappearances" will continue to bedevil Argentine politics and whichever party wins the 1989 elections.

Finally, an important minority of Argentines—perhaps 20 percent—view with a certain cynicism the human rights policies of the present Argentine government, since it has brought to trial only one terrorist, *Montonero* leader Mario Firmenich, extradited from Brazil in 1984.[23] A new organization, Families and Friends of the Victims of Terrorism, has placed frequent advertisements in the press to protest what it regards as a one-sided approach by the government and, particularly, by the National Commission on Disappeared Persons. The latter attempted to finesse this charge in its report by asserting that "it was not our task to look into the crimes committed by those terrorists," and that, in any event, "none of the relatives of the victims of that earlier terror approached us, because those people were killed rather than 'disappeared.' "[24]

On balance, then, the Argentine experience with terror and counterterror has inflicted wounds upon that society which will take many years to heal. Nonetheless, something positive must be said about the capacity of the political system to face up to this legacy, in however limited a fashion.[25] Without doubt it has reversed a long-standing tendency for political forces in Argentina to seek an understanding with the military rather than bargain frankly with their rivals and counterparts. It has convinced a younger generation of Argentines that anything is better than military dictatorship. It has strengthened the country's prestige and credibility internationally. And it has set the stage for a serious revival of the republican tradition, one which once distinguished Argentina among Latin American nations, and may yet do so again.

---

[23]At this writing (fall 1988) Fernando Vaca Narvaja is awaiting sentencing.
[24]*Nunca Más*, 6.
[25]We can never be reminded too often that the Nuremburg precedent is not wholly applicable here, since the Argentine authorities were not liberated from their responsibilities by invading armies, but were forced to confront the issue *motu propio*.

2

THE POLITICAL USES OF TERRORISM IN THE MIDDLE EAST

Barry Rubin

Terrorism, like a firecracker, makes a loud noise that stirs panic but causes little damage. Still, while terrorism may be the most overrated political phenomenon of our time, its origin and nature reveal much about the mechanics of Middle East politics and the paradoxes of U.S. involvement there.

Around the world, an estimated 639 people were killed and 833 wounded in 1985 while 398 were killed and 574 wounded in 1986 by terrorist attacks. Only one-quarter of these incidents originated in the Middle East and many of them actually took place in Western Europe. Each case was a tragedy but the sum is scarcely impressive on a global scale compared to the annual toll of war, disease, and accident that provokes far less commentary and attention. The situation is further put in perspective when one considers that a significant portion of these statistics arises from the disintegration of a single country—Lebanon—and a single event—a bomb placed by Sikh extremists in a passenger plane or the truck-bomb attack on the U.S. Marine barracks in Beirut.

Terrorism is not some inevitable, natural outgrowth of desperation or suffering. Many nations and groups throughout history have faced great deprivation without resorting to deliberate murder or kidnapping of passers-by, bombing public places, hijacking airplanes, or similar deeds. Rather, an organization's choice of terrorism as a central strategy both reflects its goals and shapes its nature. When terrorists glorify the purposeful killing of children as heroic revolutionary acts, this suggests that these are not groups capable of compromise, peaceful coexistence, or building a democratic state. Such behavior inculcates brutal and totalitarian attitudes into their members.

Any movement adopting terrorism, unless it would remain a tiny sect of a few dozen people, must sense that terrorism is culturally acceptable to its audience. Latin American death squads expect support from large elements of the upper and middle classes fearful of leftist revolution. Islamic fundamentalists, Irish extremists, Tamil nationalists in Sri Lanka, and Palestinian radicals extend no respect or tolerance to the human beings they would kill because they know that a sizable proportion of their countrymen share that view. In most of Western Europe, by contrast, terrorist groups are marginal cliques of a few dozen people who hire themselves out to state sponsors or fade away because they lack any possibility of gaining support within their own society.

Systematic terrorism is ordered by powerful leaders; it does not arise from the spontaneous action of misguided youths. It is not a way to lobby for reform, peaceful diplomatic bargaining, or concessions from one's enemies; on the contrary, terrorism is designed to polarize. Terrorists seek to intensify hatred among the movement's supporters and strengthen their devotion to the goal of destroying those targeted. Terrorism is a natural weapon of dictatorships that can keep their involvements relatively secret, are not constrained by public opinion, and are sufficiently ruthless.

Algeria backs the Polisario movement against Morocco. Libya uses terrorists against Egypt; the Arabs back Palestinian terrorists against Israel; Jordan for a time helped the Moslem Brotherhood against Syria; radical Syria and monarchist (later Islamic) Iran aided the Kurds against Iraq; Syria stood behind Armenian and Kurdish groups against Turkey; and so on. As for the Palestine Liberation Organization (PLO), its entire strategy (publicity, base-building, competition among different groups, elimination of critics, and planning for the destruction of Israel) and structure (armed groups organized around cross-border raids usually intended to hit civilian targets) were organized around terrorist activities.

In short, terrorism is innately suited to extremist ends and terror is a logical means for those with such aims. A few acts of incidental terrorism can be found in most nationalist movements or in the deeds of marginal elements. But terrorism becomes a nationalist movement's central strategy when the aim is to delegitimatize and eliminate—at least as a political entity—an entire class of people, whether it be Jews in Israel, Alawites in Syria, Sunnis in Iraq, Protestants in Ireland, or Sinhalese in Sri Lanka. For such groups, terrorism is not a public relations error but a manifestation of the intended revolution's ethical content.

An ideology justifying massive terrorism against civilian bystanders is not the kind of political thought that tends toward democracy. Those fighting to install a dictatorship cannot be called "freedom fighters" and the cause of those seeking to erect a repressive regime can hardly be considered just. Islamic fundamentalists justify terrorism by proclaiming their own societies to be in a state of idolatry and their enemies to be heretics; Marxists claim that the society is deformed by capitalism and imperialism while their enemies are whole classes in addition to those individuals described as counterrevolutionaries or puppets of foreigners. If everyone but the terrorists' few supporters is degraded and if only the extremists' doctrine is proper, elections are downright counterproductive. The people, terrorist leaders claim, have no right to choose what is wrong.

A movement is also likely to choose terrorism in response to its own political and military weakness. Here terrorism burgeons not as an expression of the masses' desperation but of the radicals' own failures. After all, terrorism has generally proven to be an unsuccessful method for sparking a revolution over the last two centuries. When extremists in Europe, Latin America, or the Middle East have failed to activate the masses—even when they have enjoyed passive approval—or develop full-scale guerrilla warfare to battle an army, they have turned instead to sporadic, well-publicized attacks against relatively undefended targets. In military terms, the PLO was a miserable failure beginning with its inglorious debacle in seeking to launch a guerilla-style "people's war" on the West Bank in the 1967–70 period. It found it far easier to terrorize Jordanians, hijack airliners, and shoot civilians. But for every terrorist attack that succeeded anywhere, a dozen were foiled with the death or capture of the terrorists. In September 1970 the Jordanian government recaptured control over its own country by defeating and expelling the PLO forces.

Ineffective as a revolutionary strategy, terrorism has proved to be an effective way to gain publicity, intimidate opponents, and achieve some limited aims. PLO groups commit or fabricate terrorist acts in competing for popular and state support, recruits, and the elimination of rivals. Such opportunities led Libya, Iran, Syria and Iraq to foster and manipulate terrorism. It is no coincidence that these governments are all ruthless dictatorships with no scruples about terrorizing their own citizens. International terrorism is merely an extension of their domestic policies.

For radical movements or states, terrorism provides a convenient low-cost means of waging war. They can strike at a time and place of their choosing knowing that those victimized cannot easily deter or punish phantoms whose connections are shadowy. When they wish, those responsible can hide behind front groups. The PLO used "Black September" and other pseudonyms while Abu Nidal employed such aliases as the "Arab Revolutionary Cells" (in the April 1986 Syrian-backed bombing of a TWA airliner), the "Revolutionary Organization of Socialist Moslems" (in attacks on British targets), and the "Arab Revolutionary Organization" (in the June 1985 bombing at Frankfurt airport). Syrian-controlled *al-Saiqa* bombed Jewish community centers, stores, and restaurants in France as the "Eagles of the Palestinian Revolution." Iran's minions are called "Islamic Jihad," "Guardians of the Islamic Revolution," or "Organization of the Oppressed on Earth"; Libyan surrogates have used "Egypt's Revolution" among other names. This method gives states double insulation—behind both a fictional group and the actual terrorists—allowing their covert operations to be disguised as deeds of protest.

Retaliation by the United States or West European governments is usually constrained by domestic opinion, international disapproval, or the threat of more terrorism. France, highly prizing its reputation as a land of refuge— and eager to avoid terrorism on its own soil—has been willing to make major concessions. In January 1977, for example, it refused to hold Palestinian terrorist leader Abu Daoud for extradition and allowed terrorists to move or function freely as long as they did not operate violently on its territory. Yugoslavia would not detain the terrorist "Carlos." The killers of the U.S. Ambassador Cleo Noel and Deputy Chief of Mission George Moore (Sudan in 1973), Ambassador Rodger Davies (Cyprus in 1974), Ambassador Francis Meloy Jr., and U.S. diplomat Robert Waring (Lebanon in 1976) and Arnold Klinghoffer (Egypt in 1985) were either released by those countries or never prosecuted though their identities were known. The United States, most vocal in declaring a policy of refusing to make political concessions to terrorists holding hostages, has done so on several occasions.

The terrorists' weakness is thus turned into a remarkable strength. By exploiting the media, a single gunman may confound a superpower and divide its allies. Even more astonishing, the terrorist may win no matter what happens so long as his action breeds fear in some and stirs uneasy consciences for others: passivity or concessions shows the victims' nation as a paper tiger; retaliation will brand it as a bully.

Sponsoring governments give terrorists money, safe haven, logistical help, training, and weapons; secure rear areas; extend diplomatic support; and provide protection against retaliation. The ability to obtain genuine passports, ship arms and explosives via official diplomatic pouches, and enjoy lavish financing allows Middle East terrorists to operate in a more frequent and deadly manner.

When more than fifty American diplomats and private citizens were held hostage for fifteen months by Iran in 1979–80, the Carter administration's inability to secure their release damaged its political standing. Angry and humiliated, Americans concluded that the Iranian government's behavior stemmed from its belief that the United States was too weak to do anything about it.

But holding U.S. hostages turned out to be an extremely profitable act for the Islamic radicals in Iran. They used the ensuing crisis to displace moderates in the leadership, unite the country around themselves, and destroy relations with the United States. Carter's efforts to conciliate post-Shah Tehran only made the radicals more suspicious that Washington was seeking to undermine or dilute the revolution. This situation provides an archetypal case study of the uselessness of concessions in coping with terrorism.[1]

---

[1]This issue is discussed in more detail in the author's *Paved with Good Intentions* (New York, 1980).

Ronald Reagan's strong antiterrorist stand gained him votes in the 1980 election, but it proved difficult to implement once he was in the White House. Everyone opposed terrorism but did not necessarily welcome dramatic operations that might end with hostages and rescuers killed or an international crisis.

Ironically, Reagan stumbled over softness rather than toughness on the question. He became obsessed over his own inability to free a handful of American hostages in Lebanon. In the search for a solution, Lt. Col. Oliver North not only sold Iran arms, he also dealt with Libya, Abu Nidal, *Hizb Allah*, and the PLO to try to free hostages. Nothing could have more effectively told terrorists and their sponsors that kidnapping could have an almost unlimited impact on the Americans.

The despicable murder of an elderly, handicapped American on the *Achille Lauro* by PLO gunmen, combined with the revelations about Iran, marked a turning point in U.S. public opinion as decisive as the Iran hostage crisis. Ironically, revelation of the Reagan administration's violation of its stated principles in the Iran arms sales did more than anything else to mobilize support for its original policy of no concessions to terrorists, while the bombing raid on Libya showed that such actions could be effective in deterring radical states from supporting terrorism. Americans became more disgusted at the idea of making concessions to terrorism and its backers, which, they recognized, encouraged more terrorist attacks.

Implicitly, this new American attitude recognizes that terrorism is neither a random plague nor a cry of anguish, but a coldly calculated political strategy. Foreign hostages in Lebanon were rarely killed. Most were held for long periods of time, were released in exchange for concessions, or died of illness or injury from their mistreatment in captivity. They were too valuable to sacrifice lightly. Sometimes, of course, violence is used to settle personal scores. Abu Nidal reportedly killed his Jordanian brother-in-law because he failed to sell a building the terrorist owned in Amman and would not buy it himself.[2] Relatives of George Abdullah, a Lebanese terrorist imprisoned in France, planted bombs in Paris to force his release. In January 1987 two West Germans were abducted in Beirut by Abbas Ali Hamadi to prevent the extradition by the Federal Republic of Germany of his brother, Mohamed Ali Hamadi, to the United States for air piracy and murder in the TWA case. The ploy worked in preventing the extradition, though Abbas himself was later caught and tried by West German authorities.

But free-lancers are relatively rare. Middle East terrorism has increasingly become a tool of radical states. Syria played a critical role in the mid-1960s in initiating Palestinian terrorism, but this did not stop Damascus from using terrorism against Palestinians when it suited the national interest. And Syria also uses Kurdish, Armenian, and Turkish groups to strike covertly at Iran and Turkey. The Syrian-backed assassination of Lebanese President-elect Bashir Gemayel in 1982 removed the strongest opponent to their hegemony there. Syrian forces in Lebanon recruited suicide bombers to attack the Israelis and allowed Iranian-backed forces to operate freely in attacking the U.S. embassy and Marines in Beirut.

When it appeared possible that Jordan might find a way to negotiate with Israel in 1965, Syria organized numerous attacks on Jordanian diplomats and airline offices to deter the peace process. As soon as King Hussein gave up the idea, the assaults ceased. A British court discovered that a man captured trying to place a bomb on an El Al plane in April 1986—a deed that would have killed nearly 400 people—was directed by the head of

---

[2]*Jordan Times*, November 28–9, 1985, in Foreign Broadcast Information Service (FBIS), November 29, 1985.

Syrian air force intelligence, traveled to London on a special passport issued to Syrian government employees, and received the sophisticated explosive device directly from the Syrian embassy there.

Similarly, an Iranian-backed terrorist offensive against Kuwait in December 1983 was a warning to that country to stop helping Iraq in the war. A great deal of hostage-taking and terrorism ensued in the attempt to free seventeen Shiites imprisoned for these crimes in Kuwait. Other Iranian surrogates took French hostages in Lebanon to stop Paris from giving asylum to Iranian rebels and to gain repayment of a Shah-era loan, a plan that finally succeeded in 1988.

In early 1985, a Libyan intelligence officer and a Palestinian terrorist working for Abu Nidal met in Rome to discuss how a truck-bomb carrying 200 pounds of explosives might be set off outside the U.S. embassy in Cairo. The Libyans offered $500,000 for the operation. The contact man went to Syria for training, picked up the explosives in Lebanon, and took them to Cairo. Fortunately, an informant tipped off the Egyptians who rounded up the conspirators just before they executed their plan on May 22, 1985.[3]

U.S. intelligence found a similar trail in the bombing of a disco frequented by American servicemen in West Berlin in March 1986 and in the murder of American hostage Peter Kilburn in Beirut the next month shortly after the U.S. reprisal raid on Libya. A Libyan military attaché in Syria arranged for a Libyan-financed group to purchase Kilburn from his kidnappers and then kill him.

There is, then, much more political method than madness in terrorism. Most Middle Eastern terrorism is directed by ambitious leaders pursuing well-defined

---

[3]Ihsan Hijazi, "Terror: Americans as Targets," *New York Times*, November 26, 1985.

political objectives: to overthrow or intimidate governments and to expel Western influence. These are not objectives that can be achieved by mutual compromise nor
are they the result of American mistakes or misdeeds. In
short, terrorists usually attack American targets not
because the United States is doing something wrong but
because it is doing something right.

This is a difficult idea for Americans to accept. "We
are the most hated nation in the world and rightfully so,"
an American wrote her senator during the TWA hijacking in June 1985 and such sentiments are held by many
in the United States. Much as ancient peoples thought
a plague was the result of their sins (and perhaps had a
shiver of satisfaction that their punishment was deserved),
the contemporary American view is that terrorism is
punishment for political sins. More than one commen-
tator has claimed that actions against Americans in Lebanon were retribution for U.S. shelling of Lebanese
villages. But they did not realize, for example, that villages hit accidentally by shells from U.S. ships (aimed at
antiaircraft emplacements) were Druze, while anti-
American terrorism emanated from the Shiites.

The guilt theory is supplemented by another piece
of pseudo-wisdom, one of the most pernicious, philosoph-
ically fascistic notions in contemporary circulation: "One
man's terrorist is another man's freedom fighter." This
degraded notion, posing as sophistication, implies that
all actions are morally equal and that a rhetorically elevat-
ed end can justify any means. Yet on the contrary, the
twentieth century has shown that people can be as pas-
sionately loyal to bad causes as to good ones, even more
so since fanaticism banishes restraint and self-doubt. It
could be equally well said that Germans thought Nazi con-
centration camp guards defenders of the nation or that
Russians believed Stalin's gulag torturers were the embodiment of working class rule and harbingers of egalitarian

socialism. The idea that large numbers of people may approve of terrorism by their own rulers or movements they support is no new discovery; the suggestion that this fact justifies deliberate atrocities represents a fantastic lapse of moral sense.

There is something equally perverse about the idea that terrorism against Americans should make Americans more understanding or accepting of the terrorists' motives. Why should the savage beating and cold-blooded murder of an American serviceman traveling on an international flight win sympathy for the terrorists' cause? Similarly, it is difficult to understand why Syria, which allows terrorists to act freely in killing American diplomats and Marines in Lebanon, should deserve gratitude when it helps release an American hostage or two.

The romantic view of terrorism also neglects its commercial aspects. Abu Nidal and others have run what is, in essence, a rent-a-terrorist service. Kidnapping in Lebanon is carried out for ransom by criminal gangs; one escaped hostage, Charles Glass, discovered that his nominally Islamic fundamentalist captors talked about girls, rock music, and cars. "They were ordinary Lebanese teenagers with no commitment at all."[4] Even suicide bombers were often hired from people desperate to obtain money for their families.

Ironically, Syria and Iran have also suffered from opponents who set off bombs and assassinate officials. Compared to the conscience-bound hesitancy of their victims abroad, the dictators willingly meet terror with terror: Iraq deported over 200,000 ethnic Persians and shot about 600 clerics and activists including the popular Ayatollah Bakr Sadr and his sister. Iran tortured and executed thousands. Its ambassador to the United Nations put the matter bluntly: "Our opponents have a right to try to assassinate

[4]*Washington Post*, October 15, 1987.

us," he said with a big smile, "and we have a right to get them first." Syria destroyed large parts of its own city of Hama and killed thousands of civilians to wipe out a few Sunni fundamentalists.

Those advocating terrorism are bitter at such treatment. Showing marks of torture on his body when he was on trial in 1965, the Egyptian fundamentalist theoretician Sayyid Qutb noted sarcastically, "The principles of the (Nasserist) revolution have indeed been applied to us, Muslim Brethren, in jail." An underground Syrian fundamentalist publication proclaimed, "How miserable you are, oh Syria! The Mongols invaded you, followed by the French, killing, devastating and spoliating. Then a worse disaster befell you: the Alawites infiltrated the regime and started to shed blood, seize property, and violate taboos."[5]

Yet those revolutionaries are not fighting for democracy but to put into place an equivalent or even worse Islamic or Marxist tyranny. And it is certainly not the ruthless modern dictatorships—which are often their sponsors—that anti-American terrorists seek to displace, but far more moderate regimes and the American culture and influence seen as threatening Arab or Islamic authenticity. The United States is targeted more for its power and cultural influence than for specific policies; its "crime" is not only the support of Israel but also aiding Egypt, Saudi Arabia, Jordan, and other forces that block the ambitions of the terrorists and their sponsors.

The romantic view of terrorism in Western intellectual and journalistic circles is that terrible oppression drives average people to commit horrendous acts. Still, even when other kinds of resistance are quite comprehensible, the leap to terrorism cannot be understood without considering the psychological factors, suspension of

---

[5]Emmanuel Sivan, *Radical Islam: Medieval Theology and Modern Politics* (New Haven, 1985), 42.

ethical constraints, and frustrated revolutionary fantasies that produce the choice of such a strategy. A member of a terrorist band under such conditions achieves high status and material benefits. Gunmen are well-paid in Lebanon; the PLO's ranks include mercenaries who may not be Palestinians or even Arabs.

Those killed, even after committing the most brutal murders, become glorified martyrs, a particularly comforting thought for Shiite fundamentalists. Relatively few, though, are called on to risk their lives, those captured may well believe they will soon be released by some new terrorist action.

International terrorism is less and less the work of crazies—those driven to distraction by unbearable grievances—and more and more the product of careful political calculation. Most international terrorism in the Middle East functions as an adjunct of Libyan, Syrian, or Iranian foreign policy. It is designed to achieve very specific aims: isolate Israel, encourage antagonism toward the United States, and intimidate the sponsoring state's real or potential enemies. Yet this very goal-oriented quality of terrorism also makes its backers vulnerable to deterrence and discouragement.

Three myths about anti-terrorist policy must be abandoned:

First, strong action against those committing terrorism is not useless just because it does not completely end terrorism. There are many problems in the world that can only be ameliorated, not eliminated. Applying diplomatic and economic pressure or a judicious amount of force—enough to hurt terrorist groups and their supporters but not so much as to produce a war—can reduce the number and effectiveness of terrorist attacks. The U.S. attack on Libya did cut down the number of incidents by reducing Qadhafi's enthusiasm for fomenting terrorism.

Second, the apparently logical belief that the eradication of terrorism can be obtained by addressing its root causes is thrown into question when one considers the identity of these "causes" which include: Libya's efforts to lead the Arab world and to overthrow all moderate regimes; Syria's attempt to control Lebanon, subordinate Iraq, and prevent Jordan from making peace with Israel; Iran's goals of sparking Islamic fundamentalist revolutions and gaining hegemony over the Persian Gulf; radical efforts to wipe out any moderate Palestinians; and the PLO's effort to destroy Israel. All these forces want to eliminate U.S. influence in the region; Syria, Libya, and the PLO are allied with the USSR. Obviously, it is not desirable for the West to surrender to these demands.

Finally, the view that only dramatic progress on Middle East peace can stop terrorism is fallacious because all the main sponsors of international terrorism—the PLO, Libya, Syria, and Iran—have consistently opposed serious negotiations on the Arab-Israeli conflict. Progress toward a diplomatic settlement, whatever its own merits, will *increase* terrorism as hardliners try to stop these initiatives, as when Syria launched its bloody murder campaign against Jordanian diplomats in 1985 to discourage King Hussein from entering the peace process.

No country has been more affected by systematic terrorism than has Lebanon in a cycle of blood feud, atrocity, and revenge among the indigenous Maronite Christian, Shiite Moslem, Druze, and Palestinian refugees. Loyalty to family and religious community have broken any empathy with other groups. The Palestinians massacred Christians at Damour; the Christians massacred Palestinians at Tel al-Zatar.

Yet even here, international terrorism was not an altogether "natural" process. The civil war itself spawned *Amal*; it was Iranian intervention that gave rise to *Hizb Allah*. Faced with the threat from *Hizb Allah*, the relatively moderate *Amal* had to prove itself equally tough and anti-Western to compete for the community's allegiance. When radicals hijacked a TWA plane to Beirut in June 1985, *Amal* seized control of the action to win credit for gaining the release of Shiites captured by Israel in southern Lebanon. Once terrorism is granted legitimacy within a community, competition among groups will escalate its use.[6]

This aspect of terrorism is demonstrated by Yasir Arafat's reaction to a spectacular attack on Israel by a rival, Syrian-backed group using motorized hang-gliders in December 1987.[7] Feigning ignorance, Arafat responded, "Can you tell me what operation you refer to?"

> Interviewer: "The operation which the Palestinians carried out inside Israel recently."
> Arafat: "Every day the Palestinians. . . ."
> Interviewer (interrupting): "No, the major operation, the Qibyah operation in Upper Galilee."
> Arafat: "Hardly a day passes without. . . If there is a news blackout, we hope that you do not participate in it." Arafat pretends that the PLO stages numerous successful attacks on Israel every day but the media simply does not report them.
> Interviewer: "No, never."
> Arafat: "May God forgive you in any case. There are operations every day. There are operations in Gaza, the West Bank, the Negev, and the Galilee, and everywhere. There are operations also in southern Lebanon. What operation do you mean?"
> Interviewer: "The Qibyah operation in Upper Galilee which was carried out by two gliders."
> Arafat: "Oh yes, the glider operation. I consider this a message to Israeli arrogance. We are telling them that there is no army that can stand against the fedayeen from the Palestinian-Lebanese joint forces. There are no obstacles, resolutions, security forces,

---

[6]David Hirst, "The Other Hostage in Beirut," *Guardian* weekly edition, vol. 132, no. 26 (June 30, 1985): 7.
[7]Radio Monte Carlo, FBIS, December 1, 1987.

or radars that can stand in the face of a fedayeen who has made up his mind to sacrifice his life for his people and nation. The Israeli rulers and those behind them should understand that this Palestinian revolution is here to stay and to emerge victorious."

Interviewer: "This operation was carried out by the joint Palestinian-Lebanese forces?" He knows that, despite Arafat's pretense, his organization had nothing to do with the attack.

Arafat: "You should remember that every Palestinian fighter is still part of the joint Lebanese-Palestinian forces, regardless of whether all of them are Palestinian or all of them are Lebanese. You should know that so far there is nothing that can prevent or stop this blood from flowing together. This united blood, this solidarity, this revolutionary cohesion is unparalleled. The Lebanese brothers shared with us our pains. Therefore, I salute them from the bottom of my heart."

There are several interesting points in the exchange. Arafat intimidates the reporter, who would not dare appear so unpatriotic as to challenge such a powerful and dangerous man. Arafat also tries to appropriate "credit" for the attack, exaggerates his group's activities, and ignores the bitter anti-PLO attitudes of so many Lebanese. He maintains the myth of Arab unity and support for the PLO at a time when *Amal* is attacking Palestinian camps.

Shiite terrorism in Lebanon is a decentralized movement: Islamic Jihad is a cover name used in operations by Iranian intelligence using Shiites from Lebanon or other countries; Islamic Amal operates in the Biqa' valley; and the Islamic Resistance is the name used in the south. The name *Hizb Allah* is most often used by groups in the Beirut area. While *Amal* simply seeks more patronage and benefits for Lebanese Shiites, *Hizb Allah* wants an Islamic state in Lebanon and beyond. *Amal* merely wants outsiders (both the PLO and Israel) to leave the Shiite turf alone and is willing to eschew anti-Israel terrorism in exchange. *Hizb Allah* carries out terrorist attacks against Israel as a top priority, indifferent to reprisals.

The problem is simple, explains *Hizb Allah's* mentor, Mohammad Fadlallah. If an Islamic fundamentalist spirit replaced the present "defeatist mentality" then "there would be no major problem regarding the objective of finishing Israel off." This same kind of simplistic confusion of ideology and reality, in its nationalist version, has brought one debacle after another to the Arab states and the PLO.[8]

Hizb Allah is also far less representative of its community and Arab sentiments than it tries to seem. Fadlallah, unlike his more naive colleagues who blindly follow Iranian doctrine, knows the poor prospects for imposing an Islamic state on Lebanon, despite the passionate commitment of *Hizb Allah's* followers. A movement cannot triumph if potential recruits are limited and its growth will only unite its enemies. All the groups in Lebanon face this problem that makes it impossible for anyone to win the civil war. *Hizb Allah* has not even gained hegemony over *Amal* in the Shiite community. If *Hizb Allah* became stronger, the Maronites, Druze, and Syria would probably put aside their own quarrels and cooperate against it. And Damascus does not share the West's moral compunctions about using an iron fist. When the Syrian army entered West Beirut in 1987, it did not hesitate to attack *Hizb Allah's* office and shoot the two dozen members present.

The USSR's response on the rare occasions when it has been subjected to terrorist attack has been more complex. In September 1985, when the Syrian army was

---

[8]Interview in *Al-Nahar Al-Arabi wa al-Duwali*, March 18–24, 1985, in FBIS, March 21, 1985, 64. See also Peyman Pejman, "Hezbollah: Iran's Splintered Ally," *Washington Post*, August 1, 1985.

besieging the city of Tripoli in northern Lebanon, fundamentalists in Beirut, probably associated with *Hizb Allah*,
kidnapped four Soviet diplomats in Beirut and demanded
that Moscow pressure Syria to lift the siege. Almost immediately, the terrorists killed one hostage. The Russians then
swiftly evacuated most of their 150 personnel and depen-
dents from Beirut in broad daylight and openly pressured
Syria to end the siege. So eager were the Soviets to com-
municate compliance that their ambassador in Damascus
held a press conference to announce the request. The Syrians complied (although they attacked again, this time successfully, over a year later). At the same time, Moscow
showed unprecedented interest in supporting UN resolu-
tions unconditionally condemning terrorism.

But the Soviets avoided the reputation of yielding
easily to terrorism because they were able to avoid international media coverage, had a reputation for toughness,
and enjoyed the protection of close relations with almost
all of terrorism's sponsors. Many terrorists, particularly but
not exclusively Palestinian ones, learned their skills in Eastern Europe or from Soviet bloc advisers in training camps
in Libya and elsewhere in the Middle East. Middle East terrorist groups thus ignore Soviet oppression in Afghanistan
or other specific policies of Moscow. Shaykh Subhi al-
Tufayli, a *Hizb Allah* leader, laconically commented that the
hostage-taking ran "counter to Islamic interests in the region. This is not because the Soviets are supporting the
Muslims; they basically support the existence of Israel and
ensure its security."[9]

---

[9]One article reported that the KGB kidnapped, tortured, and shot a relative
of a *Hizb Allah* leader to obtain the release of the remaining Soviet hostages.
Although this story has been repeated often, there is simply no evidence to
confirm it and one suspects its accuracy. Since it is widely believed in the region, however, the rumor makes it less likely that Soviets will be kidnapped.
Ian Black, "The KGB Way with Terrorists," *Guardian*, weekly edition, vol. 134,
no. 2 (January 12, 1986): 6; *Al-Safir*, October 24, 1985, in FBIS, October 29,
1984, 61.

Needless to say, the paucity of anti-government terrorism against the USSR is not a result of the Soviet Union changing its policies or acting in a just manner. The support which the USSR provides to terrorists and their sponsors, rather than its overall policy, purchases immunity.

If Soviet behavior has been brutal, American behavior has been objectively ridiculous. Small groups of Lebanese terrorists had taken hostage a handful of Americans who, despite all obvious danger and warning, insisted on staying in Beirut. The taking of American hostages attracted worldwide publicity, elicited endless interviews with the hostage's families, and placed incredible emotional pressure on the president. Humanitarian concern and the political calculation that failure to free the hostages would damage his public standing persuaded Reagan to abandon some of his most cherished policies. Even the extraordinary efforts which nearly wrecked his administration succeeded in freeing only three hostages. In the meantime the terrorists' success encouraged them to seize more Americans. The whole affair showed the incredible leverage that small and essentially irrelevant deeds could have on U.S. psychology and policy.

It is harder, however, to use terrorism as a means of gaining power or diplomatic leverage. Thus, while gaining a great deal of publicity for the organization, the PLO has been unable to use terrorism to win military victory, much less Palestinian self-rule or even a diplomatic role in the Middle East peace process. Up to a point, terrorism helped publicize the PLO's cause and won some Western concessions, especially in Europe. But ultimately the terrorist strategy has damaged the group's standing in the United States and Western Europe while making Israel adamant in refusing to negotiate with the PLO, skeptical of Arab intentions, and more unwilling to yield territory that might be used as a base by terrorists. Terrorism thus provides mixed political benefits for the PLO. It helps

Arafat maintain a posture of leadership, activism, and success while simultaneously contributing to his inability to negotiate or persuade others to make concessions to him.

The *Achille Lauro* incident and its denouement illustrates this paradox. On October 7, 1985, four Palestinian gunmen seized the 23,000-ton Italian cruise ship off Egypt's coast and took hostage its 344 crew and 201 passengers. The liner was on an eleven-day cruise whose stops included an Israeli port. Agents of Abu Abbas's Palestine Liberation Front, one of the PLO's constituent groups, had spent ten months preparing the operation, but the terrorists were discovered before reaching Israel and took over the ship. The PLO's rationale was to have been that kidnapping or murder of passengers in Israeli waters was justifiable. In the event, however, the terrorists shot a sixty-nine-year-old wheelchair-bound American and threw his body overboard. The PLO later claimed he died of natural causes and Farouk Khaddumi, often referred to as the organization's foreign minister, suggested the man's wife might have pushed him overboard for the insurance money.

When Hani al-Hassan and Abu Abbas arrived to try to salvage something on the public relations front, the gunmen quickly "surrendered" to their own leaders. The speed of this decision may have been due, American intelligence officials later said, to the fact that Egypt leaked word to the terrorists that U.S. forces were about to launch a rescue. The PLO then falsely promised Egypt that it would try the men in Tunis and Egypt's President Mubarak announced that the hijackers had left the country when they were actually at an Egyptian military base. But when Abu Abbas and his men flew out on an Egyptian military transport, four U.S. Navy fighter planes intercepted it and forced it to land at the Signoella air base in Sicily. The passengers were seized by Italian authorities.

The Italians, however, wanted no political conflict with Arafat. The prime minister decided to ignore a U.S.

request to arrest Abu Abbas, at that moment sitting in the Egyptian Academy building in Rome, and prosecutors were not even permitted to question him. An Italian arrest warrant was issued only after Abu Abbas was safely outside the country. A court ultimately sentenced the four remaining gunmen and a captured henchman to four to nine years in prison.[10]

In Cairo, violent demonstrations condemned the U.S. insult to Egyptian "honor." But, despite the usual claims that the American action would damage bilateral relations, the furor soon died away. A few months later when an Egyptian airliner was hijacked to Cyprus by Abu Nidal's men, Cairo asked for U.S. logistical and intelligence assistance.

Transcripts of communications between the mediators and the terrorists clearly indicate the complicity of Abu Abbas and Arafat, but the Palestinians denied all involvement since the incident embarrassed Egypt and proved so damaging. Arafat took a similar tack toward the deeds of the PLO's front group Black September— most active in the 1971–73 period when it murdered Israeli athletes at the Munich Olympic Games and U.S. diplomats in Sudan—and in the murder of three Israeli tourists on Cyprus in September 1988 by al-Fatah's Force-17 unit. Abu Abbas merely kept a low profile after the *Achille Lauro* incident for a few months and was then given a warm personal welcome by Arafat on his return to active participation on the PLO executive committee.

After the *Achille Lauro* debacle, Arafat promised Mubarak to confine future attacks to Israel and the occupied territories. The issue was not one of terrorism per se, but the choice of victims. Iran, Syria, and Libya follow similar patterns, directing terrorist campaigns for particular purposes during difficult periods of time and

---

[10]*La Republica,* October 22, 1985; *La Stampa,* November 13, 1985.

selecting targets in relation to political objectives. Of course, it is often not easy to micro-manage terrorism, but the sponsoring regimes seem satisfied with the system.

Iran first employed terrorism spectacularly, if non-lethally, with the holding of American diplomats as hostages in 1979. The Americans, Khomeini claimed, were the real terrorists who directed the Shah's regime to torture and execute opponents. The Khomeini regime, however, continued and even expanded these long-standing Iranian practices.

As early as September 1980, an Iranian-sponsored group fired rocket grenades at the U.S. embassy in Beirut. Tehran wanted to send Revolutionary Guard units to Lebanon to encourage the Shiites there to launch a revolution but the Syrians at first refused to allow it. Soon, however, Tehran's agents developed a network there. In December 1981 the Iraqi embassy was bombed as part of Iran's war effort against Baghdad. Thirty people including the ambassador died. Iranian-backed Islamic Jihad bombed the French embassy in May 1982, even though Lebanese Shiites had no particular quarrel with France. France was being punished for selling arms to Iraq, Iran's enemy. The U.S. embassy was attacked in April 1983 as the Great Satan's local headquarters from which plots were launched to oppose Iran and an Islamic revolution in Lebanon and to support Israel and the Lebanese government. Iranian-trained and financed groups used suicide bombers with devastating effect against the U.S. Marine and French camps in Beirut in October 1983 and the Israeli headquarters in Tyre in November 1983.

On the Gulf front, Iran used terrorism to extend its war against Iraq and to strike at neutrals helping it. Kuwait gave vital transport and financial help to Baghdad. On December 11, 1983, Iranian-based Islamic Jihad terrorists used truck-bombs or explosives triggered by remote control at the U.S. embassy, a foreign residential

complex, the airport, an industrial park, and a power station in Kuwait city. Evidence indicated that the explosives
for all the bombings in Kuwait and Lebanon were fur-
nished by Iran and moved through Syria.[11] Kuwait's imprisonment of Shiite Moslem terrorists led to a series of
new kidnappings and attacks.

In May 1985, Iranian-backed terrorists even dared
try to assassinate the Emir of Kuwait. Six bystanders died.
On May 17, 1986, Islamic Jihad attacked the al-Ahmadi
and Mukawwa oil refineries, installations later targeted
by Iran's more sophisticated technology of Silkworm missiles.[12] In July 1987 two Kuwaiti Shiites were killed while
trying to place bombs in a shopping area. The men had
disappeared nine months earlier while fishing in the Gulf
and told authorities on their return that they had been
picked up and held by the Iranian navy. Actually, they
had been trained as saboteurs.[13]

The Iranians never used their own nationals but
rather employed Lebanese, Iraqi, or Kuwaiti Shiites to
cloak their involvement. Victimized countries were unwilling to probe too deep lest they be forced to confront
Iran. Even U.S. Secretary of Defense Caspar Weinberger
quickly said, when an escorted U.S.-flag tanker hit a mine
in the Gulf in the summer of 1987, "We don't know who
put the mines there."

Iran's minions also murdered opponents overseas. In
July 1980, an anti-Khomeini activist, Ali Akhbar Tabatabai,
was killed in a Washington, D.C. suburb and shortly thereafter an unsuccessful attempt was made against ex-Premier
Shahpour Bakhtiar in Paris. In 1987 alone, eight anti-
Khomeini activists were assassinated in Pakistan, West Germany, Britain, Turkey, and Switzerland. Syria has also used

---

[11]See, for example, *New York Times,* October 5, 1984.
[12]*Al-Dustur* (Amman), "The Tuesday Fires," vol. 16, no. 435 (June 30, 1986):
16–17.
[13]*Arab Times* (Kuwait), July 18, 1987, 1.

terrorism against dissidents or critics overseas as it does at home.

Of course, the United States counted on Iran's strong links to Lebanese terrorists to free American hostages during the secret negotiations of 1984–85. France negotiated directly with Iran also for the release of its citizens held hostage in Lebanon. It repaid $330 million of a Shah-era loan, allowed an Iranian embassy official wanted for questioning about his involvement in terrorism to leave the country, and expelled anti-Khomeini activists. In exchange, Iran quickly arranged for two French hostages to be released in Lebanon.[14]

While Iranian-backed terrorism has not brought Islamic fundamentalist regimes to the Gulf or Lebanon, destroyed Israel, or defeated Iraq, it has benefitted Tehran. Iran has gained a foothold and weakened Western influence in Lebanon; Gulf Arabs have been intimidated; and Iran has regained assets in the United States and France. In Tehran, at least, it appears that the Islamic republic has confronted great powers on an equal basis, raised its prestige in the Islamic world, and foiled plots against it. Terrorism has been successfully integrated into Iranian foreign policy.

Syria employed terrorism with even better results and at less cost than the other major purveyors of international terrorism—Libya, the PLO, and Iran—because it followed several important rules. First, it used terrorism for limited, well-defined goals: maximizing its influence in Lebanon, destroying U.S. and Israeli leverage there, discouraging Jordan from making peace with Israel, constraining any PLO action contrary to Syrian objectives, and blackmailing wealthy Arab oil-producing states.

Second, it used terrorism as part of a broader strategy incorporating diplomatic and military leverage. In

---

[14]*Washington Post*, December 1, 1987.

Lebanon, such attacks were used as an adjunct to the Syrian army's presence and to President Hafez al-Assad's clever manipulation of internal politics there. Against the PLO, assassinations complemented political maneuvering and bribes used to help split the organization.

Third, although it has made some serious errors, Syria was far more cautious than Libya or Iran in covering its tracks, avoiding publicity and refraining from boasting about its involvement in terrorism. Since it is difficult to find ironclad proof of responsibility for terrorist acts, this policy discouraged Western states from applying sanctions.

Finally, Syria was strong enough in its own right and close enough to the USSR to deter military retaliation. Iran and Libya were not under Moscow's protection to the same degree. More important, as the Soviet's sole important ally in the Middle East, Syria has been able to resist Soviet pressure.

Syria learned these lessons from hard experience. President Hafez al-Assad's adventurous predecessors' open, energetic support for Palestinian attacks on Israel was a major factor precipitating the disastrous 1967 war. Three years after the defeat, Assad, then commander of the air force, blocked Syrian intervention into Jordan to save the PLO from a beating at the hands of King Hussein's army.

Lebanon provided the first test for Syria's strategic use of state-sponsored terrorism. The Syrian army entered Lebanon in 1975 and easily overpowered the indigenous militia engaged in civil war. But Assad realized that Lebanon was too fragmented to permit total Syrian control except at a very high cost.

Instead, Damascus's policy developed three kinds of relationships: it sponsored surrogate groups that could be counted on to carry out its will, supported indigenous clients that generally shared its goals, and intimidated

opponents (or even independent-minded allies) into compliance. The surrogates included the Syrian Social National Party (SSNP), the small Tripoli Alawite militia,
along with the Palestinian *al-Saiqa*, Abu Nidal, and Ahmad
Jibril's Popular Front for the Liberation of Palestine
General Command. After 1983 a number of Palestinian
groups including the Abu Musa splinter faction were
added to this assortment. The most prominent clients
were the Druze militia, the Shiite *Amal*, and some smaller
Christian groups.

Determined to maximize its influence in Lebanon,
Syria followed the classic strategy of divide and conquer.
No faction was to be allowed sufficient strength either
to win the civil war or provide a challenge to Syrian
authority. Lebanese leaders were allowed to choose only
between accepting Syrian subsidies and running the risk
of being assassinated by Damascus's minions. Compliance
also brought with it a supply of arms and the ability to
operate in or pass through the sizable portion of Lebanon occupied by the Syrian army.

Terror played a large part in this system. Damascus
apparently ordered the murder of Kemal Jumblatt, the
most impressive and independent of the "radical" leaders, in 1976 because he was seeking a total victory. Similarly Syria killed President Bashir Gemayel in 1982
because of his dynamism, determination to produce a
Christian military triumph, and connections with Israel.
Bashir's replacement as president, his brother Amin, was
a far weaker figure often willing to bend to Syrian
demands.

The general populace was also frightened into acquiescence. According to a Beirut witticism, a man complained to the police, "A Swiss soldier just stole my Syrian
watch." "Don't you mean," asked a policeman, "a Syrian
soldier stole your Swiss watch?" The victim answered,
"You said it, I didn't."

To avoid coverage of Syrian corruption and repression at home or in Lebanon, Damascus agents terrorized Arab and Western journalists. Seven Lebanese newspapers were closed by Syria. In 1980, one of the most outspoken emigré editors, Salim al-Lawzi, was kidnapped and murdered during a visit to Lebanon. He had moved his newspaper, *Al-Hawadess,* from Beirut to London to escape censorship and published columns critical of Syrian leaders. His body showed signs of horrible torture. Evidence from other unsolved killings and attempts also points to Syria.

On April 22, 1982, for example, a car bomb in front of the offices of *Al-Watan al-Arabi* in Paris left two people dead and sixty-two wounded. The French expelled two Syrian diplomats—one of them Assad's nephew—who, evidence showed, were involved in the attack.

The most important use of Syrian-sponsored terrorism in Lebanon was to force the withdrawal of Israeli troops and U.S. Marines in the 1982–84 period. Although the dirty work was performed by Iranian-backed Islamic fundamentalist groups, Syria allowed them a free hand to train in and operate from Syrian-held territory. Despite the anarchic conditions in Lebanon, these activities would have been impossible without Syrian knowledge and assistance.

Having forced a U.S. pull-out, Syrian intelligence then turned its attention to southern Lebanon. Certainly, much of the guerrilla and terrorist activity there was organized by Shiite extremist groups tied to Iran. At the same time, however, Damascus assisted Palestinian factions it controlled in striking against Israel. Its immediate objective was to destroy the May 1983 Lebanon-Israel peace agreement but these operations were also intended to demonstrate that the pro-Syrian groups were more successful than those of Yasir Arafat's PLO.

Some suicide bombers were even more closely tied to Syria. In July 1985, for example, a twenty-three-year-old

Lebanese named Haytham Abbas blew up himself and his car at a checkpoint of the Israeli-backed South Lebanese army. The previous day, Abbas had given a television interview praising Assad (whose picture could be seen on the table and wall) calling him "the symbol of resistance in the Arab homeland and the first struggler." He was a member of the Lebanese branch of Syria's ruling Ba'th party. Other suicide terrorists belonged to the Syrian-controlled Syrian Social National Party.[15] After the successful series of operations in Lebanon, Syria's main goal was to wipe out any PLO members who advocated serious negotiations with Israel or alliance with Jordan.

It is a myth that Syria rejects Arab-Israeli negotiations merely because it wants to ensure return of the Golan Heights or seeks better terms. Damascus's rejectionism runs very deep. On the one hand, Syria maintains that Lebanon, Jordan, and Palestine (both Israel and the West Bank) are all part of a "Greater Syria" that are rightfully Damscus's sphere of influence. Since Damascus views both Israel and the West Bank as "southern Syria" and as part of the pan-Arab patrimony, Assad argues that Arafat has no right to make any decisions that contradict Syria's views. On the other hand, any diplomatic solution is likely to strengthen Jordan's hand over the Palestinian question, increase U.S. influence (favoring Egypt, Israel, Jordan, and even Iraq over Syria), loosen Syrian influence on the PLO, and allow Israel to be legitimized (and hence become a stronger regional rival and a likely ally of Egypt and Jordan against Syrian ambitions). In short, peace would turn Syria into a second-rate power and almost any conceivable solution is anathema to the Syrian government.

Another myth is that a heightened Western effort to promote Arab-Israeli negotiations would decrease terrorism. The main supporters of terrorism—Iran, Syria, and

---

[15]Damascus radio, July 16, 1985, in FBIS, July 16, 1985.

Libya and the most actively terroristic Palestinian groups—all oppose any serious negotiations. For them, terrorism is not a cry of outrage against Western failure to pursue peace but is an attempt to block diplomacy altogether.

During 1983–87 and 1985–86, respectively, King Hussein pondered accepting the Reagan Plan and sought an alignment with the PLO to pursue negotiations. In both cases, these efforts broke down due in part to Syrian pressure through terrorism. In April 1983, PLO moderate Issam Sartawi was murdered in Portugal by Abu Nidal. In October, the Jordanian ambassadors to India and Italy were wounded. The following month, a Jordanian security man in Athens was killed and another embassy employee was wounded. In December, an attack in Spain killed one and wounded another Jordanian diplomat. And as all this occurred, the possibility of similar sanctions being applied against them kept Saudi Arabia and Kuwait generously subsidizing Syria.

At the same time, the Syrians wanted to eliminate relatively moderate PLO officials and demonstrate that Jordan could not protect Palestinians from its wrath. In December 1984, former West Bank mayor and PLO executive committee member Fahd Kawasmeh, who took a relatively softer line on cooperation with Jordan, was killed in Amman. In April 1985, a rocket was fired at a Jordanian airliner taking off from Athens. In July the Jordanian airline's office in Madrid was attacked and a diplomat was killed in Ankara. In September a Jordanian publisher was murdered in Athens. The 1986 murders of Palestinian moderate Aziz Shehadeh in Ramallah and Nablus Mayor Zafir al-Masri, on good terms with both Hussein and Arafat, were traced to PFLP operations in Damascus.

The perpetrators in these cases were from Abu Nidal's group, the Syrian-sponsored PLO splinters led by Abu Musa, and the Damascus-based PFLP. After al-Masri's murder, Arafat pledged to revenge him, but barely a year later the PLO leader was again allied to the PFLP whose gunmen carried out the killing. Abu Nidal, Assad's most energetic triggerman, was recruited despite a record of anti-Syrian terrorism during his years in Baghdad before 1980. In 1985, Abu Nidal moved from Syria to Libya but continued to cooperate with Damascus.

Syria's long history of supporting terrorism against Israel is due to a number of factors. Obviously, Damascus considers itself an Arab nationalist state playing a leading role in the anti-Zionist struggle. But in practical terms, Syria is also a regional power desirous of undercutting Israeli strength without becoming directly involved in a losing confrontation with Israel. Consequently, Syria has been careful not to strike directly against Israel through the Golan Heights since this might prompt direct Israeli retaliation. Instead, it has routed operations through Lebanon, Jordan, or even Europe.

An attempted bombing in April 1986 against an El Al passenger plane in London was another in this series of operations. Nizar Hindawi convinced his pregnant, unwitting Irish girlfriend to carry the suitcase which contained a bomb that would have killed nearly 400 people. Fortunately, an Israeli security man discovered the false bottom. Hindawi had entered England on a Syrian government employee's passport. His bomb was similar to those employed in 1983 bomb attempts against El Al and an explosion that killed four Americans on a TWA plane over Greece.

Hindawi's confession directly implicated the Syrian ambassador to Britain, two other Syrian diplomats, and the deputy director of Syrian air force intelligence. London expelled all three and severed ties with Syria.[16]

One can surmise that Syrian-controlled Palestinian groups would have wished to claim responsibility for the

---

[16]David Ottoway, "Syrian Connection to Terrorism Probed," *Washington Post,* June 1, 1986.

action, gaining a major victory in the terrorist competition that dominates Palestinian politics. Facing the worst economic crisis in memory, Assad may have thought that a bit of tension with Israel would focus the people's anger against an external enemy rather than their own government and would force Arab oil producers to increase subsidies. If the sabotage had succeeded, however, it could very well have led to a Syrian-Israeli war and a defeat for Damascus.

The balance sheet for Syrian terrorism, despite some failures, is relatively profitable: primary influence over Lebanon, intimidation of Jordan, a splintered and constrained PLO, the elimination of key opponents, the continued flow of large subsidies (protection money) from Arab oil producers, and the discouragement of Arab-Israeli peace negotiations. Syria has suffered little for this terrorism; the West has been far more willing to forgive and forget Syrian transgressions than those of Libya or Iran. Syria is the state, after all, that Reagan profusely thanked for helping to free the TWA hostages in 1985, despite evidence of Syrian involvement in Beirut car-bombings that killed close to 300 Americans and U.S. embassy employees.

Washington Post correspondent Jim Hoagland once compared the remarkable tolerance of Syrian behavior to the swings of fashion: "International terrorism is out of vogue here in the Syrian capital, somewhat in the way long hemlines are disappearing in Paris. . . . But the respite . . . will not last long. . . . Assad has paid a minimal price for improved relations with the West." Assad's temporary shut-down of Abu Nidal's operation brought back the U.S. ambassador, withdrawn in solidarity with Britain after the Hindawi trial. The United States did not investigate too closely evidence that Damascus airport was used by Abu Nidal as a staging point for a September 1986 attack on a Pan American airliner in Karachi, Pakistan, and in other cases. After all, if Syria were implicated, Washington would have to react.[17] Ironically, the most strategically devastating terrorist action in recent Middle East history was an assassination attempt carried out by Iraqi agents that led to a major Syrian defeat. Nawaf Rosan, an Iraqi intelligence colonel who also served as Abu Nidal's deputy, led a three-man hit team against Israeli Ambassador Shlomo Argov in London on June 3, 1987. The ambassador was paralyzed by his wounds. Three days later, Israel invaded Lebanon, and four days after that Iraq offered a unilateral cease-fire in the Gulf war arguing that the Arabs and Iranians should unite against Israel.

The attack on Argov was deliberately designed to provoke an Israeli attack on Syrian forces in Lebanon. Syria, Iraq's enemy and an ally of Iran, would suffer directly while the new crisis gave Baghdad a good excuse to demand that Iran end the fighting. Although Iraq's fondest hopes were not realized, Syria did suffer a major defeat.

Rosan, leader in the attack on Argov, was a Jordanian—not a Palestinian—who served in his country's air force until he was recruited by Iraqi intelligence. In London, his group reconnoitered and was prepared to attack the embassies of the United Arab Emirates, Jordan, Saudi Arabia, Egypt, and Kuwait if Iraqi interests so dictated.

Iraq has long used terrorism against the opponents of the Saddam Hussein regime abroad. Iraqi dissidents have been murdered in South Yemen, Kuwait, and Sudan. The British expelled eleven members of the Iraqi embassy staff in 1978 after an exiled Iraqi prime minister was shot. They also suspected that Baghdad trained the Iranian Arabs who seized the Iranian embassy in London in May 1980. The British Foreign Office did nothing in response to the attempt on Argov. The U.S. State Department,

---

[17]Jim Hoagland, "A Clean State for Syria?" *Washington Post,* September 19, 1987.

then struggling to keep Iraq off the list of "nations supporting terrorism," also refused to take action.[18]

As brazen as ever, Syria offered a new definition of terrorism to the United Nations in 1987. Violence by "national liberation movements" was to be deemed acceptable while violence—even in self-defense—by "racist" and "colonial" states was terrorism. Presumably, Damascus did not intend this definition to apply to the Islamic fundamentalists in Hama or the Iraqi-directed "freedom fighters" in London.

Compared to Syria, Libya's Muammar Qadhafi has been a bumbler in his use of terrorism. He has ranged far outside the Middle East, providing a wide variety of terrorists with training, weapons, and facilities. He has openly campaigned to murder opponents abroad, telling students in a May 1980 speech that such emigrés, "should be physically liquidated."[19] Eleven emigré dissidents were killed in 1980–81 and five such assassination attempts occurred in 1985. In March 1984, a bomb planted against Libyan emigrés injured twenty-four people in England. The following month, Libyans fired from the embassy building in London at a peaceful demonstration by exiles. A British policewoman was killed and eleven exiles were wounded. Due to Libyan pressure, the suspects were allowed to leave the country.

After Libyan attempts to murder exiles in Egypt, the Egyptians pretended that the second one had succeeded. In November 1984, phony pictures of the bloody "victim" were turned over to Libyan agents. As soon as this information was received in Libya, the official media celebrated the murder only to be confronted with Egyptian audiovisual tapes and confessions from four arrested

---

[18]Ian Black, "Iraqi Intelligence Colonel Led Terrorists in Bid to Kill Envoy," *Guardian*, March 7, 1983.
[19]Amnesty International, *Political Killings by Governments* (London, 1983).

Libyan agents. Another Libyan-backed hit team planning to kill Mubarak and others, including U.S. diplomats, was captured in Cairo in November 1985.

Abu Nidal also counted Libya among his patrons. On December 27, 1985, Palestinian terrorists launched simultaneous attacks at the airports of Rome, where twelve persons were killed (including five Americans) and seventy-four wounded, and Vienna, where two were killed and more than forty wounded. The official Libyan news agency praised the murders as "heroic." Tunisia reported that the Tunisian passports used by the Vienna terrorists had been confiscated by the Libyan regime from workers expelled earlier that year.

But Qadhafi's use of terrorism, like his other foreign initiatives, was too grandiose and too unfocused to yield results. He simultaneously sought Arab unity, mergers with other Arab states, and the fomenting of coups in a half-dozen places at once. In contrast to Syria and to a lesser extent Iran, Libya tried to use terrorism to foment revolution rather than to achieve more modest strategic goals. While Qadhafi had large economic resources, his strategic and political armory could not compare with those of the Iranians and Syrians.

Qadhafi was vulnerable and the direct attacks on American citizens made the Reagan administration eager to confront him. "By providing material support to terrorist groups which attack U.S. citizens," Reagan said after the Rome and Vienna shootings, "Libya has engaged in armed aggression against the United States under established principles of international law, just as if he had used its own armed forces. We have urged repeatedly that the world community act decisively and in concert to exact from Qadhafi a high price for his support and encouragement of terrorism...."[20]

---

[20]Text in *Washington Post,* January 8, 1986.

On April 15, 1986, an American air aid retaliated for Libyan involvement—proved by communications intercepts—in the bombing of a West Berlin discotheque where an American serviceman and a Turkish woman were killed and 230 people were injured. The raid was wildly popular in the United States. Polls showed that 76 percent of Americans supported it and would endorse additional attacks. Reagan's popularity soared.[21]

Predictions that the attack on Libya would unite the Arabs against U.S. interests in the region were once again proven false. "Revenge and Anger Resound in Arab World," said a headline in *U.S. News and World Report* on April 28, 1986. Yet while Arab governments made ritual, rhetorical criticisms of the U.S. raid, none of them did anything to help Qadhafi. They were unable even to agree on an agenda or site for a Libyan-proposed Arab summit to discuss the issue. OPEC rejected Qadhafi's call for an oil boycott; Algeria did not even postpone sending a high-level delegation to Washington to discuss improving bilateral relations. Egypt allowed a U.S. aircraft carrier to transit the Suez Canal and, as did other states, quietly signaled approval. If the Arabs criticized any aspect of U.S. Libyan policy, it was that highlighting Qadhafi exaggerated his importance. Understanding his own isolation, Qadhafi stopped supporting terrorist attacks for about two years. The U.S. bombing of Libya was clearly a success.

Middle East terrorism is less the work of those made desperate by unbearable grievances and more the product of careful political calculation. It often functions as an adjunct of Libyan, Syrian, or Iranian foreign policy designed to achieve very specific aims: isolate Israel,

---

[21]See for example, *Gallup Report,* "Americans Sanction More Raids if Libyan Terrorism Continues," no. 247 (April 1986): 2–11; *Washington Post,* April 30, 1986, A43.

encourage antagonism toward the United States, and intimidate the sponsoring state's current or potential rivals. Yet this very goal-oriented quality of terrorism also makes it sponsors and facilitators vulnerable to deterrence and discouragement.

Consequently, the application of international pressure, sanctions, or appropriate force can weaken terrorist groups, raise the costs of sponsoring them, and reduce the number and effectiveness of terrorist attacks. An action like the U.S. attack on Libya does not reduce terrorism to zero but it does cut down on the number of incidents, saves lives, and makes it harder for terrorists to act or escape punishment afterwards. No one suggests that a medicine be abandoned merely because not all patients are cured. In retrospect, it was clear that the effect of the U.S. raid was to reduce drastically the number of incidents and casualties resulting from terrorism during the next eighteen months.

Israel's air attack on the PLO's offices in Tunisia in 1985 was decried at the time as futile. Nonetheless, the result was the expulsion of PLO training bases and terrorist operatives from Tunisia, Jordan, and North Yemen. Again, attacks on Israel have not disappeared entirely but they have been greatly reduced. The overwhelming majority of terrorist plans have been completely foiled. The streets of Jerusalem are far safer at night than those of most American cities.

The argument that only dramatic progress on Middle East peace can stop terrorism is also fallacious because all the main sponsors of international terrorism—the PLO, Libya, Syria, and Iran—have consistently opposed any diplomatic settlement. More efforts or progress on negotiations, whatever its own merits, will lead to an *increase* in terrorism as the hardliners try to stop these initiatives. For example, Syria has carried out a massive murder campaign against Jordan and its diplomats over seas since 1983 in order to prevent King Hussein from entering the peace process.

Finally, there is the notion that the root causes of terrorism must be addressed to deal with the problem. But the root causes of terrorism are, respectively: Libyan efforts to dominate the Arab world and to overthrow all moderate regimes; Syrian attempts to dominate Lebanon and prevent Jordan from making peace with Israel; Iranian ambitions of sparking Islamic fundamentalist revolutions and gaining hegemony over the Persian Gulf; PLO objectives of destroying Israel, mobilizing support for its intransigent policy, and wiping out any independent-minded Palestinians. All these forces want to eliminate U.S. influence in the region; Syria, Libya, and the PLO are closely allied with Soviet regional interests. Obviously, it is very difficult for the West to compromise with these motivations.

But while the United States rejects the idea of surrender to terrorism, it frequently makes important concessions. The Europeans are even more yielding. Britain reopened relations with Libya only a year after Libyan "diplomats" murdered a British policewoman. Despite the Reagan administration's verbal attacks on Libya, the United States was still buying 40 percent of Libya's oil production until a boycott was proclaimed in March 1982. As late as 1985 U.S. exports to Libya (including service contracts) ran between $800 million and $1 billion.[22]

In 1981, shortly after his inauguration, President Reagan welcomed home American hostages from Iran, proclaiming, "Let terrorists be aware that when the rules of international behavior are violated, our policy will be one of swift and effective retribution." But compared to

---

[22]*Times* (London), June 9, 1986; *Congressional Quarterly*, "Reagan Tightens Economic Sanctions on Libya," January 11, 1986, 59.

the administration's practice, the president's words rang hollow.

After the April 1983 bombing of the U.S. embassy in Beirut, he warned, "Those who directed this atrocity must be dealt justice. And they will be." And a half-year later, he declared following the attack on the Marine barracks, "Every effort will be made to find the criminals responsible. . . so this despicable act of terrorism will not go unpunished."

The *Achille Lauro* incident and the disgust over the covert Iran arms sales seem to have changed the American public's attitude toward hostages and terrorism by early 1987. Agreeing with President Reagan's declared policy of refusing to surrender to terrorists or granting their demands, both liberals and conservatives criticized him when he deviated from it. The terrorists' manipulation of the democratic system and the media had reached intolerable levels. While sympathetic to the hostages and their families, Americans seemed to believe that these private tragedies should not dictate U.S. policy.

The American people disagreed with what Reagan did thereafter, but agreed with what he said about terrorism in June 1985: "America will never make concessions to terrorists. . . . To do so would only invite more terrorism. Nor will we ask nor pressure any other government to do so. Once we head down that path, there will be no end to it—no end to the suffering of innocent people, no end to the ransom all civilized nations must pay."

Even more compelling, however, would be to question the exaggerated importance assigned to terrorism. The terrorists, after all, hardly have the United States or the West over a barrel. Countries can ignore or apply judicious pressure to them and their sponsors. The relatively sporadic incidents and small number of hostages pose no real peril to the West's overall interests or the security of the mass of their citizens. Moreover, terrorism is unable to achieve the more inflated aims attributed to it. There was no hint that terrorist groups were anywhere near overthrowing a single government or fomenting revolution anywhere in the Middle East. Compared to Western nightmares, it was terrorism that was the real paper tiger.

3

REGIME OPPOSITION AND TERRORISM IN EGYPT

Ami Ayalon

When President Anwar Sadat saw his assassins rushing to the reviewing stand with their automatic guns firing, he reportedly stood up and muttered: "Impossible, impossible. . ." He was disproved. Seconds later he lay on the ground, mortally wounded.

Should Sadat have been shocked? Just one month earlier, he had ordered the arrest of 1,500 Muslim radicals whom he had described as "very dangerous elements." Four years earlier these dangerous elements had demonstrated their capability for violence when they abducted and murdered the minister of religious endowments, Shaykh al-Dhahbi. There was no reason to believe that their rage had abated. If anything, it had intensified. And Sadat's assassination was not the final word in terror. For weeks after the assassination, Egyptian security forces confronted terrorist groups that attacked targets in Cairo, Asyut, and other locations. In 1984, 1985, and 1986 terrorists killed two Israeli diplomats and wounded a third. In 1986, thousands of Central Security Force members rose in violent revolt, killing several people, destroying property, and spreading havoc in the Egyptian capital. And in 1987, a wave of terror again swept the country; this time it was directed against former cabinet ministers, U.S. diplomats, and a senior Egyptian editor.

Is Egypt a violent country? Is terror an accepted form of political behavior? The answer is no. To the extent that the communal character of a society can be defined, the Egyptian political culture is not one of violence. Sadat's assassination shocked both his critics and his supporters. The assassination like most other acts of terror in Egypt was met with widespread revulsion. Violence is the exception in Egypt; many other communities in the Middle East—including some with more abundant material resources—are more prone to violence than are the Egyptians.

Egyptian realities are indeed harsh. For many years the country has endured a severe economic and cultural crisis, which has proved increasingly difficult for the government to manage. The regime has yielded ground in perpetual strife with an ever-expanding array of opposition forces. The government's foreign relations strategy, problematic as it has been especially during the last decade or so, has complicated matters further, generating more opposition pressures from within and without. These circumstances are directly relevant to the issue of terror. Most, if not all, incidents of violence in recent years may be ascribed directly to them.

In this chapter, the causes of opposition to the regime in Egypt are examined first. Then, the ways that the government handles opposition pressures and evaluates their effectiveness are explored. Finally, the forces that, uncontrolled by the state, resort to violence and terror are examined. This last discussion is covered under three headings: Islamic terrorism, terrorism of the Left, and international terrorism in Egypt.

The Crisis

Egypt is one of the poorest countries in the world. Its only natural resources are the 4 percent of its land that is fertile (the rest is desert) and a relatively small quantity of oil. The fertile area is already cultivated and half of the oil is consumed domestically. It has a population of some 52 million, which increases by 1 million every nine months. Egypt imports more than half of its staples from abroad and has thus accumulated a total debt of $40 billion. Food, housing, and employment are in short supply and public services are ineffective. Conditions have deteriorated steadily in recent years, and most experts predict a continued decline in the economy.[1]

These circumstances affect every Egyptian in some way. Even the wealthiest citizens cannot escape the frustration of, for example, crossing public streets flooded by refuse and waste whenever the sewage system collapses. More important than the exasperation of the wealthy, however, is the plight of the poor—the great majority of the population—especially those who live in the cities. These city dwellers suffer not only because they are poor, often abysmally so, but also because they witness the luxury that the new economic policy of the government has brought into the country to be enjoyed only by the few. An "open door" economic policy launched by Sadat and continued by President Hosni Mubarak was supposed to relieve the burden of the poor, but so far it has failed. In the process, it has not merely broadened the gap between the poor and the wealthy, but it has also made extravagance permissible, allowing the wealthy to display their wealth openly, to the anguish of others. A palpably deteriorating economy and an ever-widening socioeconomic gap have led many to lose faith in the system. A growing number of Egyptians have become desperate.

---

[1]For a more detailed survey see Gudrum Krämer, "In Search of Normalization: Egypt Under Mubarak's First Term of Office," *Aussenpolitik* (English edition), vol. 38 (1987), 378–89.

Material distress is but one part of the prolonged crisis. Another part is spiritual and ideological disorientation, a crisis of communal identity. For centuries Islam provided ready answers to all questions and resolved all the inherent tensions of society. However, exposure to modern Western ideas and technology brought problems that Islam could not solve. As Egyptian society evolved during the last hundred years, traditional values were supplemented or supplanted by new ones. Islam was reformed and secular nationalism, liberalism, constitutionalism, Pan-Arabism, and Arab socialism were imported from abroad. These imports have proved unsatisfactory and disappointing, and Egyptian society still finds itself wavering between traditionalism and modern beliefs, and between Islamic, Arab, and Egyptian identities. In recent years political developments—more in the region at large than within Egypt—and particularly the conflict with Israel lent this search for identity special urgency and, indeed, has turned it into a crisis. Egypt's defeat in the 1967 war with Israel, perhaps more than any other event, demonstrated the barrenness of its imported ideologies and slogans. A decade later the Egyptian leadership embarked on the unexpected course of peace with Israel, designed, among other things, to relieve or resolve the problem of orientation. It did neither; instead, this joining of hands with the archenemy of the past generated confusion rather than relief. Arab and Israeli moves after Camp David further exacerbated the frustrations.

The solutions formulated by Nasser and Sadat, exciting though they once had been, have lost most of their attraction. Sadat's successor, whether because of sober skepticism about available ideologies or because of his inability to produce a new vision, does not offer his countrymen light at the end of the tunnel. The most that Mubarak is prepared to say is that the tunnel is not as dark as it looks and that the train is probably moving in the right direction. For him, the only way to confront the crisis is through blood, sweat, and tears (especially sweat) and through scientific planning, hard work, and devotion, which he applies rigorously in the way that he runs the government. With Mubarak, it is not merely the present that is gloomy: he resents "unrealistic optimism" and frequently presents a depressing vision of the country's future. To the discontented and certainly the desperate, he hardly offers any relief.

The Egyptian people are optimistic and patient by nature. Still profoundly religious despite recent developments, they have withstood a great deal of pain without loosing hope or faith. Their endless optimism in the face of the harshest of circumstances never fails to amaze foreigners. Yet, there are limits to the patience of even the most hardy people. No one can be certain that the persistence and worsening of problems will not eventually erode the people's readiness to endure further hardship with equanimity, especially if they begin to suspect that those in power are partly responsible for their suffering. And there are always those who feel the effects of privation more than others do and who are less willing to suffer in silence. As frustration increases, the potential for violence certainly grows.

The Political Rules: Authoritarian Regime and Assertive Opposition

Egypt is governed by a relatively small group of leaders whose authority is upheld by the armed and security forces and who claim public legitimacy as inheritors and preservers of the July Revolution—the revolution that replaced the corrupt order of the past with one more just and efficient. In Egypt, authoritarian government is not imposed on the people against their wishes: regardless of changes in values and concepts brought about by modernization, Egyptians still uphold, for the most part, the traditional approach to relations between rulers and ruled. The people expect their leader to navigate the ship with a firm hand. Except for a small group of westernized intellectuals, few Egyptians have expressed a desire to take part in the decisionmaking. (This is not to say, of course, that they refrain from criticizing their leader.) The government responds with an equally traditional approach: its first concern is to keep the army and the police happy and loyal. It also ensures that the civilian bureaucracy is fully dependent on and hence eager to support the government.

For over a decade, Egypt has experimented with political pluralism. Opposition parties are permitted to organize, publish their own newspapers, criticize the regime, and compete with each other and against the regime's own National Democratic party in parliamentary elections. Although there are profound differences between this system and Western-style democracy, the degree of freedom—particularly freedom of expression—in Egypt is truly impressive. No other Arab state is as open or competitive. More important, the multiparty system provides a release valve for the regime's opposition. Because the government holds pluralism within well-defined limits, it is able to channel and contain dissent. The process of expanding democratization has, of course, the potential of undermining an authoritarian government. Presently, however, the Egyptian regime has no real problem with its legally organized opposition.[2]

This last point is, perhaps, the reason that opposition parties are insufficient channels of action for some discontented elements. They are insufficient because of

---

[2]See further in 'Ali al-Din Hilal, *Al-tatawwur al-dimuqrati fi misr* (Cairo, 1986); Gudrun Krämer, "The Change of Paradigm—Political Pluralism in Contemporary Egypt," *Peuples Méditerranées*, nos. 41–42 (October 1987–March 1988), 283–302.

the limited role assigned to them in the political arena. More important, most Egyptians have more suspicion of them than faith in them. Egyptians, sensibly enough, find it hard to believe that the regime truly intends to compromise its complete authority and share it with others whom it invites into the arena. Those who oppose the government and are not satisfied with simply expressing their opposition verbally or who do not know how to express their opposition seek other channels. They turn to popular movements such as the Muslim Brothers and various smaller Islamic societies, spend their opposition energy on university campuses if they are students, or go underground.

Clandestine activity both of a political and of a terrorist nature is basically from two sources: (1) radical Islamic groups, which express their opposition to the regime in religious terms and seek to replace it with an "Islamic state" through forceful revolution, and (2) secular-minded leftist-Nasserite elements, which are critical of the government's policies, especially in foreign matters, and which organize secretly to act against those policies. A third source of antigovernment terrorism is groups sent or financed by foreign governments in the region that seek to destabilize the Egyptian regime and perhaps bring it down.

Islamic Terrorism

The recent emergence of Islamic radicalism in Egypt and elsewhere has been a subject of intense public and scholarly concern. The literature examining it has already reached vast proportions;[3] therefore, an extensive analysis

---

[3]For a recent, thought-provoking study on the subject see Emmanuel Sivan, *Radical Islam* (New Haven, 1985); also Bruno Etienne, *l'Islamisme Radical* (Paris, 1987).

of the phenomenon is not needed here. A brief discussion of its sources and aims is sufficient.

The growing influence of religion in Egypt's political and cultural life may be viewed as part of a universal trend. It has comparable expressions in other societies, reflecting increasing skepticism about the ability of technological civilization to produce a happier world. In Egypt, of course, it also has specific material and ideological roots. In the eyes of the leaders of the Islamic movement, the secular philosophy borrowed from the West, the imported alien values and institutions of Europe, and the association with and inevitable dependence on foreign powers are responsible for the malaise of the Muslims. Egyptian society has exposed itself to all these negative forces and has been greatly affected by them. It therefore needs to return to its old ways and the shelter of the eternal truth of Allah. The Muslims, these leaders recall, once acquired a vast empire while adhering to Allah's message, sent through his prophet; such adherence is sure to bring them more grandeur in the future. The basic approach of this movement toward greater religious influence is, thus, to look backward and to advocate a formula from the past as a model for the future. Rather than a state that pays lip service to Islam's true spirit while straying far from it in practice, a true Islamic state should be established, modeled on that of the Prophet and the early caliphs.

How will this goal be achieved? Muslim fundamentalists have developed at least three distinctive approaches to the goal of recreating an Islamic state. The first approach may be considered moderate because it seeks to attain the goal through education, the propagation of ideas, and a political struggle within the existing system rather than through violent opposition to it. The backbone of the movement representing this approach is the Muslim Brothers, the oldest Egyptian fundamentalist body. A long history of violent confrontation with the government and long periods of incarceration of its leaders have caused the movement to give up violence—at least for the moment—and adhere to other means of action, while concentrating on expanding its popular base and infrastructure. From the perspective of the government, the Muslim Brothers are presently being incorporated into the political system. Even though this process of incorporation is not problem free, the Muslim Brothers do not pose an immediate security threat.

The other two approaches are of more interest; both reflect more radical and more militant strategies than the moderate approach of the Muslim Brothers. The first of these has been adopted by the Islamic groups *(al-jama'at al-Islamiyya)* and their movement which began to organize in the early 1970s with President Sadat's blessing. Sadat sought to use them as a counterweight to the leftist and Nasserite opposition, active especially on university campuses. These groups, however, soon grew into a force far more dangerous than the leftists; they represented an impatient, violent version of Islamic fundamentalism. They mainly attracted young men in their twenties and thirties who were students, university graduates, and young professionals at the beginning of their careers. As has been shown in numerous studies, they are the chief victims of the country's socioeconomic crisis; they find it increasingly difficult to obtain housing (and hence, often, to get married), to find employment, and to fulfill their expectations for socioeconomic upward mobility befitting their education. Forming a part of the intelligentsia, they also suffer more than the undereducated majority from the crisis of national identity. These frustrated, angry young men seek refuge from the ills of the present by attempting to replace the existing regime with another, more just, Islamic state. To them, slow, gradual progress to an Islamic state is unsatisfactory: they struggle for a revolutionary change attained either by clandestine or open use of force.

Out of this trend springs the most radical and militant Egyptian fundamentalist movement. It consists of messianic-millenarian groups that are not only opposed to the existing regime and its policies, but also reject, without reservation, the entire sociopolitical and cultural order. In their view, Egyptian society has deteriorated to a state of disbelief, *jahiliyya* (that is, pre-Islamic darkness). Hence, they seek to dissociate themselves from contemporary society, to establish their own true Islamic order, and then to impose their order on the rest of society, just as the Prophet did in the seventh century. Like the Islamic groups, they view force and violence as necessary means to attain their goal. The membership of the millenarian groups is drawn basically from the same social circles as the Islamic groups and is similarly motivated: they are mostly young men, often associated with the universities, who are the primary victims of the country's problems. Sometimes accidental circumstances and at other times personal proclivities determine which kind of group an individual will join. The most well-known millenarian groups are *al-Jihad* (literally "Holy War," a name often mistakenly applied to the entire class of fundamentalists) and *al-Takfir wal-Hijra* ("disbelief and flight," a title that epitomizes the group's philosophy). Recently, another such group, calling itself *al-Najun min al-Nar* (those saved from [hell] fire), made headlines; it was responsible for some of the 1987 terrorist attacks. Other smaller organizations that share this kind of philosophy and strategy have also formed.

The distinction between the two latter types of groups—those who want to introduce Islamic values through violence and those seeking to destroy the entire order—is not always clear. The Islamic groups often operate in the open, forcefully taking control of mosques, clashing with university campus guards, and distributing propaganda. They sometimes also organize underground, as do the millenarians. This clandestine organization consists of a network of cells on the campuses, in the quarters and suburbs of Cairo, in towns of Upper Egypt, and in the delta countryside. There is a hierarchy of command with a control system that assumes total obedience to the local head *(amir)* and the supreme leader *(al-amir al-'amm)*. These organizations accumulate weapons and explosives, train their members to use the weapons and explosives, and prepare operational plans to implement their strategy. Often they rob and steal to finance their organizational needs.

Whether dealing with an impatient group seeking to impose its views by force or a nihilist organization at war with the whole system, the response from the government has been the same: terrorism from any source is fought uncompromisingly. Both act against the same targets and use the same methods. And the government employs the same tactics used by these groups to confront them.

The targets chosen by the Islamic militants vary. They include everything from President Mubarak to liquor stores. The president has been repeatedly "sentenced to death" by the radicals, and group members apprehended by the police have confirmed that Mubarak has long been on their lists. The successful attack on Sadat in October 1981 has surely served to encourage them in this goal. Thus far, however, they have been unable to come close to a serious attempt on Mubarak's life. Other top state officials, especially past and present ministers of the interior who command or have commanded the police and thus are or have been in charge of fighting the Islamic groups, are also targets. Significantly for the radicals, ministers of the interior are also responsible for the torture that their members allegedly suffer in prison. All of these ministers since Sadat's death have at some point been targets of assassination attempts by the Islamic militants. Two of them, Hasan Abu Basha and Mohammad Nabawi Ismail, were attacked in May and August 1987 respectively. The former was seriously wounded. The assault on the latter, who escaped unhurt, attests to the long memory of the group. Nabawi Ismail left his ministerial post five years before the assassination attempt.

Other potential targets for terrorist attacks have been journalists, in particular those who take a firm antifundamentalist line. One of them, the editor of *al-Musawar*, Makram Mohammad Ahmad, was slightly wounded one evening in June 1987 while driving his car in the heart of Cairo. After their arrests, members of the group responsible for the attack *(al-Najun min al-Nar)* provided a list of five other journalists and twenty-nine public figures targeted for assassination.[4]

Installations belonging to official institutions (regarded by radicals as part of the regime's control system) are also potential targets. For example, in March 1985 an attempt was made by a fundamentalist terrorist squad to blow up the headquarters of the State Security Investigation Administration. In December of that year, arson was attempted in the radio and television broadcasting building in Cairo. And, a plot to attack the broadcasting building in Alexandria was exposed in October 1986. Since mid–1986, nightclubs, theaters, videotape rental shops, liquor stores, and similar "places of corruption" have become favorite targets of the fundamentalists. These establishments have been broken into or set on fire on many occasions. To Muslim radicals, such targets are so obvious that one wonders why they have not been targeted sooner or more frequently.

---

[4]See *al-Qabas* (Kuwait), international edition, September 4, 1987; *al-Siyasa* (Kuwait), September 7, 1987. Unless otherwise specified, newspapers referred to in the notes are published in Cairo.

Israeli and U.S. diplomats and other citizens are significantly absent from this list of targets. To be sure, the objection of the radicals to cooperation with "Zionism and imperialism" is unequivocal, and they pronounce their objection daily in the most forceful terms. Yet, they have not attacked Israeli and U.S. officials, installations, or citizens (although the latter are not given any special protection in Egypt). This policy may be explained by the fundamentalist belief that the chief enemy is the one from within—the un-Islamic government, tyrannical rule, and corrupt social and cultural institutions. It is the government that commits evil while cooperating with the forces of darkness outside; therefore, it is the government, not the outside forces, that should be brought to account as a first priority.

The fundamentalists employ terrorism on different levels. There is terror by threat and warning without the actual use of force. This level, combined with occasional more direct acts of violence, has been rather effective judging by the palpable fear prevailing in some parts of the country. Yet the most immediate threat is posed by more violent types of terrorism. During Sadat's presidency, there were three major operations by Muslim radicals that showed careful planning and were quite successful: an attack on the military technical academy in Cairo in 1974,[5] the abduction of al-Dhahbi in 1977,[6] and Sadat's assassination. Other contemplated or attempted operations during that period were foiled by the police before they were executed. Then, for the next five years, nothing spectacular happened: the radicals needed time to recover from the shock of confrontations with the states

---

[5]See Saad Eddin Ibrahim, "Anatomy of Egypt's Militant Islamic Groups: Methodological Note and Preliminary Findings," *International Journal of Middle East Studies*, vol. 12 (1980), 423–53.

[6]For details see *Middle East Contemporary Survey, 1976–77*, vol. 1 (New York, 1978), 296–7.

and time to regroup. They continued, however, to engage in small-scale terrorism, in acts that were devoid of imagination—mostly hit-and-run arson. Many such contemplated acts were exposed before they could be implemented. Their most remarkable achievement was the series of successful assaults on videotape rental shops and theaters in 1986. These assaults were not particularly sophisticated in planning or performance.

The series of operations in mid–1987, however, was far more imaginative and courageous, readily betraying the work of a new mind. The assailants attacked their victims from rapidly moving cars, hit them in two out of three cases, and left the scene swiftly without a trace. They used stolen cars whose color and license plates were changed after each operation and a second vehicle for cover in each case. These operations involved careful preplanning, including a study of the victims' routines; effective coordination between all parties involved, from the man who stole rifles from the army to the one who repainted the cars; and a high degree of skill in executing the attacks themselves.[7] It was also remarkable that three such operations were carried out within a three-month period, during which the police had no information on the identities of the perpetrators.

When the mystery was solved, in late August 1987, everything about the perpetrators seemed to fit with the organizational patterns of similar groups uncovered before. The group, *al-Najun min al-Nar*, had split from the larger *al-Jihad* organization. Its leader—the mastermind behind its operations—was Majdi al-Safty, a twenty-eight-year-old pediatrician, who told his loyal followers that he could bring down the regime with a hundred highly

---

[7]For details see *al-Ahram*, August 25, 30, 1987; *al-Jumhuriyya, al-Akhbar*, August 30, 1987; *Akhir Sa'a*, September 2, 1987; *al-Siyasa* (Kuwait), September 7, November 16, 1987.

trained men at his disposal. Thirty-three group members were apprehended and stood trial; the prosecutor demanded the death penalty for fifteen of them and imprisonment with hard labor for the others. Majdi al-Safty managed to escape. A year later, he was still at large.

Terrorism of the Left

Opposition from the leftist-Nasserite groups became a problem for the Egyptian regime by the time Sadat was halfway through his presidency. "Leftist" here does not mean Communist: Communism has always been anathema to Egyptian governments and most of the people and has remained a small movement with limited political weight. Once or twice a year, the police expose groups labeled as Communist, and their members stand trial. Communist opposition is thus not a serious problem for the regime. Far more important is the opposition that may be defined loosely as Nasserite. It consists of people, mostly from the intelligentsia, who are disappointed that the dream of Egyptian grandeur that Nasser articulated is gone. Frustrated with the country's present condition, they seek to restore what they remember (rather selectively) as Egypt's glory during the Nasser era. In this sense, like the fundamentalists, they look to the past as a desired model for the future. Some of them also propound a Marxist philosophy that is comfortably compatible with Nasserism. This opposition was born with Sadat's policy of de-Nasserization in the mid-1970s. Sadat gradually detached himself from the teachings of his predecessor and devised new lines in his domestic, socio-economic strategy and, more importantly, in his foreign policy: an alliance with the United States and peace with Israel, two principles that are totally objectionable and even repulsive to the Nasserites. Since Mubarak has subscribed to Sadat's philosophy on domestic and foreign policies, the Nasserite opposition has remained quite active.

Nasserite opposition is an amorphous notion in Egypt. Many of those who may be identified as Nasserites express their views in the establishment press (notably, but not solely, in *Ruz al-Yusuf*) and in the licensed organs of opposition parties. Since 1986, they have also had their own weekly, *Sawt al-'Arab*. Still having difficulties in establishing their own party, many of them are active in existing opposition party life, participate in demonstrations, and sign statements of political protest. In recent years, some of them have become involved in terrorism.

Reference to the existence of Marxist terrorism in Egypt has been made occasionally by officials in charge of domestic security. As early as February 1984, Minister of the Interior Abu Basha disclosed that the police had a great deal of information on a "radical leftist-Marxist trend that seeks to resort to terror in order to fulfill its aims."[8] Four months later, a group adhering to this trend struck: early in June, an Israeli diplomat, on his way home from the Israeli embassy, was shot and wounded. The attacks featured some new elements, which appeared in later incidents. The selection of an Israeli official for a target was one innovation. Also, the methods employed in the attack and its highly professional execution were new: having studied the victim's daily schedule, the assailants arrived in a car, blocked his way, shot him at close range and disappeared. Finally, the most significant innovation was the statement left to identify the perpetrators: a written statement left at the scene was signed by the hitherto unknown "Egyptian Revolution" *(Thawrat Misr)* organization. The group, the statement said, was committed to fighting "the Zionist and imperialist

---

[8]*Al-Ahram,* February 6, 1984.

invasion of Egypt." The organization pledged to kill more Israelis and Americans, "until Egypt is rid of this shame."

Having struck, Egyptian Revolution went back underground, leaving behind a wave of rumors. At this stage, authorities could do little more than speculate. The organization was silent for a year and then struck again in August 1985, blocking an Israeli vehicle in the same manner as the previous assault and killing an Israeli diplomat. The assailants left no clues, except for a statement claiming responsibility and promising to return. Again, there was a long period of silence. Then, in March 1986, an Israeli embassy employee was killed and two others were wounded when they were attacked near the Israeli pavilion at the Cairo International Trade Fair. After another long interval, the organization launched another operation in May 1987, this time against U.S. diplomats traveling from their homes to the U.S. embassy. Two men were wounded. In all of these attacks, the assailants opened fire from moving cars and fled.

After executing each operation, the organization took time to prepare carefully for the next. Its leadership preferred to proceed cautiously, gradually expanding its membership and logistical infrastructure. Information that came to light after the group was uncovered revealed a well-organized body with ample financial resources and impressive quantities of arms and other equipment. It had a network of highly devoted members both in Egypt and abroad, some of whom were charged with gathering essential intelligence on the movements of Israelis and Americans in Egypt.[9] Its ability to remain unexposed for over three years was a remarkable achievement in itself. By the middle of 1987, the Egyptian security forces had

---

[9]See especially *al-Ittihad* (Abu Dhabi), January 7, 1988; *al-Ahram*, February 19, 21, 1988; *Sawt al-'Arab*, February 21, 1988. See also the interview with a group member residing in Kuwait in *al-Qabas* (Kuwait), March 27, 1986.

firm ideas on the organization's aims and methods of operations but hardly a clue on the identity of its leaders and members. "All I can say," admitted the Egyptian director of public security, "is that our findings show that these incidents are not the making of individuals; undoubtedly, there is some kind of organization behind them."[10]

A quarrel between the group's leader and his brother eventually led to its exposure in September 1987. The latter showed up in the U.S. embassy in Cairo and provided a detailed report on Egyptian Revolution. Soon afterward, scores of its members were arrested, along with other Nasserites. What the authorities discovered about the organization must have shocked them. Its head was Mahmud Nur al-Din, an ex-colonel in military intelligence. There were also several other former senior officers in the group. Still more perplexing was the fact that the group turned out to be Nasserite, indeed, for one of its leaders was Nasser's son, Khalid abd al-Nasser. Khalid, a thirty-eight-year-old engineer, was in charge of the group's finances. Another member of the Nasser family, the late president's nephew, Jamal Shawqi Abd al-Nasser, was also involved in the group. Khalid, whose role in the group soon became a subject of sensational media headlines, was quietly allowed to leave the country. It was much more convenient for the government to try him in absentia; the public prosecutor demanded the death penalty.

Egyptian authorities have encouraged the belief that Egyptian Revolution has been eliminated, but there are many signs to indicate that the organization has remained alive and active. It would be surprising if it had not. Soon after the arrest of its leaders, a statement was issued on behalf of the organization, signed by a "Colonel Rihan,"

---

[10]Major General Muhammad 'Abd al-Halim Musa, interviewed in *al-Sharq al-Awsat* (London), June 21, 1987.

announcing that the group was "suspending" its operations for six months to "reorganize its ranks."[11] At about
the same time, another group, calling itself the "Crescent
Revolutionary Organization" *(Munassamat al-Hilal al-
Thawri)*, made itself known and pledged to "destroy the
U.S. and Israeli embassies in Cairo" and to "kill all Israelis
in Egypt."[12] Whether the pledge was real or fake, its an-
nouncement indicated that Nasserite sentiments were still
very strong. In January 1988, more evidence of leftist-
Nasserite opposition was offered when an explosion took
place behind the U.S. consulate in Alexandria. A group
calling itself the National Front for the Liberation of
Egypt claimed responsibility and vowed to "persist in its
armed struggle against Zionist and American interests"
in the country.[13]

Leftist-Nasserite terrorism is patently still a fact of
life in Egypt. The political and ideological bases for it
still exist and will probably be around for some time to
come. One may realistically expect to see more unhappy
Nasserites translating their rage into violent actions.

International Terrorism in Egypt

Egypt also has to contend with what security officials
call "export terrorism." For many years, Egypt's international relations have changed like a kaleidoscope, with
rivalries and accords alternating frequently. In the last
decade, however, the situation has stabilized; presently,
when trouble comes from the outside, its potential sources
are relatively easy to identify. Three states in the Middle
East are hostile to the Egyptian regime: Libya, Syria, and
Iran. Each has its particular reasons for enmity, but they

---

[11]Quoted in *al-Nashra,* January 11, 1988.
[12]*Al-Nahar* (Beirut), October 3, 1987.
[13]*Al-Ahali,* January 13, 1988.

all share a desire to punish the present Egyptian government, which, in their view, treacherously adheres to a line of policy that brings shame on the Arab and Islamic world. All three, therefore, export terror to Egypt. In addition, Egypt sometimes finds itself the direct or indirect victim of Palestinian terrorism.

Relations between Libya and Egypt have long been strained. Tension began to develop after the death of Nasser, Qadhafi's idol. Sadat's determination to revise Egypt's foreign policy strategy upset the Libyan leader. Attempts to persuade Cairo to reconsider its policies, through temptation and threat, including an attempt to impose on it unity with Libya through dramatic "marches of the Libyan masses" toward their common border (in 1973 and again in 1984), were of no avail. By the mid-1970s, a pattern of tense relations and mutual mistrust had evolved, which, among other things, resulted in the deployment of large numbers of military troops on both sides of the border. Libya offered shelter and assistance to Egyptian oppositionists in exile (General Sa'd al-Shadhili, for example) and to a variety of aggressive revolutionary elements for whom Egypt was sometimes a target (such as Abu Nidal's Palestinian organization). Egypt, for its part, provided asylum to Libyan political fugitives, among them leading personalities who had lost favor with Qadhafi, much to the colonel's discomfit. The Libyan leader, a believer in terrorism as an effective instrument of policy—as he has often demonstrated elsewhere—began to employ this tool in his policy toward Egypt.

In recent years, Libyan-sponsored attempts at terrorist operations have frequently been uncovered in Egypt. These attempts were particularly intensive in 1984 and 1985, but continued thereafter as well. Men sent or financed by Qadhafi to carry out such operations have sought either to kill Libyan political refugees residing in

Egypt or to punish the Egyptian government for its policies by attacking its leaders and public installations or
U.S. and Israeli interests in Egypt. Such terrorists do not
necessarily come from Libya; most are hired terrorists of
different nationalities (although they are predominantly Arabs and Europeans), whom Qadhafi provides with
funds, explosives, training, and instructions for operations. Attempts were even made to recruit Egyptians for
the purpose.[14]

While these attempts were still in the planning stages,
almost all of them were foiled by alert Egyptian security
units. There were, however, two major exceptions. In the
summer of 1984, Libyan vessels apparently placed mines
in the Red Sea, mainly along the Egyptian coast, seeking
to harm Egyptian economic interests. Twenty ships hit
the mines, navigation was interrupted, and a large-scale,
expensive effort was needed to clear the waters. In
November 1985, an even more spectacular operation was
carried out under Libyan instructions: an Egyptian airliner en route from Athens to Cairo was hijacked and
forced to land on Malta. After landing, the plane was
stormed by an Egyptian commando unit (flown in from
Cairo) that killed the hijackers and tragically killed fifty
passengers. The hijackers, four Palestinians and a Tunisian, were identified by Egyptian authorities as members
of a "Palestinian group opposed to the PLO [Palestine
Liberation Organization] which works for an Arab country notorious for its terrorist policies and aid to terrorists."[15] These two operations were exceptional both
in their dramatic scope and in their relative success.

Libyan involvement in subversive activities in Egypt
was exposed in later years, and there are periodic

---

[14]For example, *al-Ahram,* April 7, 1985; *al-Musawwar,* April 12, 1985.
[15]Radio Cairo, November 25, 1985, FBIS, *Daily Report* (Middle East and
Africa), November 25, 1985.

indications that the peril of Libyan terrorism remains. Qadhafi's goodwill declarations notwithstanding, Egypt has remained soundly suspicious. "If Qadhafi extends his hand to me," President Mubarak has said, "I would do the same—provided his hands are not full of explosives."[16]

Syrian-Egyptian relations have been in crisis since Sadat embarked on his peace initiative toward Israel. Syria has consistently refused to accept Egypt's regional policy and has unflinchingly fought against it on political and diplomatic levels in all inter-Arab, pan-Islamic, and international forums. Although Syria shares Libya's total rejection of Egyptian behavior, it has not been as eager to express its rejection through terror; President Assad, a shrewd strategist, has elected to be more cautious.

Nevertheless, Syria has been involved in anti-Egyptian terrorism, at least indirectly. It has allowed Abu Nidal to base his headquarters in Damascus, to train his men there, and to send his men on operations in Egypt, mostly in cooperation with Libya. It also backed and equipped the dissident Palestinian commander Abu Musa who, having split with his men from the Palestine Liberation Organization's main body because of Arafat's "cowardly" leadership, has proved instrumental in translating Syrian anger with its foes into aggressive action. During April to May 1985, a plot to blow up the U.S. embassy in Cairo was exposed: the plot had been initiated by Qadhafi and operationally supervised by Abu Nidal and Abu Musa. The staging point for the operation was Damascus. Had the plan succeeded, the Egyptian daily al-Ahram suggested in abhorrence "the booby-trapped car [used for the operation] would have destroyed most of [the] Garden City [quarter in central Cairo], not just the embassy."[17] In June

---

[16]Radio Cairo, January 7, as reported by BBC, Summary of World Broadcasts (the Middle East and Africa), January 9, 1987.
[17]Radio Cairo, May 25, 1985, as reported by BBC, May 27, 1985; al-Ahram, May 25, 1985.

1986, Egyptian Minister of the Interior Badr reported that several sabotage operations "sponsored by Libya and Syria" had been foiled in Egypt during the previous three months.[18] For those in charge of domestic security, Syria had to be taken as a potential or actual partner—along with Libya and Iran—in the "tripartite hostile and terrorist axis" that the country was facing.[19]

Iranian involvement in anti-Egyptian terrorism has been far more direct and extensive than that of Syria. Moreover, in recent years, it has clearly been on the rise. In the eyes of Iran's revolutionary leadership, Egypt, like every other Muslim country, is a target for the export of the revolution. This mission has been pursued in many ways, including subversive ones. Iran also has more specific grievances with Egypt, which offered asylum to the deposed Shah and has long been a chief Arab supporter of Iraq in its war against Iran. Diplomatic relations between Egypt and Iran were cut after the Iranian revolution, although Iran continued to maintain a small interest office in the Swiss embassy in Cairo.

The involvement of individual Iranians in clandestine activities in Egypt had already been reported in the early 1980s. Security officials, referring to this involvement, sometimes hinted that such activity, far from being a personal initiative, was sponsored by the Iranian government. Iran was also a prime suspect, along with Libya, in the Red Sea mining affair of the summer of 1984. By mid-1987, a large-scale Iranian plot to destabilize the Egyptian regime was exposed: in that plot, a diplomat in the Iranian interests section extended financial and other support to fundamentalist terrorist groups. An Iranian citizen was found to have acted as a liaison between Tehran and the militant *al-Jihad*. The Egyptian government

---

[18]MENA, June 19, 1988—FBIS, *Daily Report,* June 20, 1986.
[19]Interior Minister Ahmad Rushdi, quoted by MENA, April 6, 1985.

hastened to expel the diplomat and to close down the Iranian office.

In later months, there were signs that Iranian subversion was continuing and even expanding. In the second half of 1987 and in early 1988, there was a spate of reports in the Arab press claiming that, beyond the ties of a single diplomat with a local Egyptian group, there was a master plan to exploit Egyptian fundamentalist sentiments to establish an Egyptian branch of the Iranian-backed *Hizb Allah* (which for several years had flourished in Lebanon).[20] One indication of this plan was the appearance of slogans signed by the *Hizb Allah* on walls in certain neighborhoods in Cairo.[21] Another sign was the reported reference, made by members of *al-Najun min al-Nar* when interrogated after their arrest, to Khomeini's revolution as the desirable model for Egypt.[22] Acting as a source of inspiration and of financial support to Egypt's militant fundamentalists, Khomeini's Iran has remained a source of great concern to the Egyptian security apparatus.

Finally, the Palestinian factor should be mentioned. The Palestinians have been angry with Egypt for reasons that need no elaboration here. However, these reasons have been greatly offset by Egyptian sympathy with and support for the Palestinians, especially since 1982. The Palestinian attitude toward Egypt has therefore been rather ambivalent; PLO leaders have been careful not to let relations deteriorate more than necessary. Although the focus of Palestinian terrorism has been elsewhere in the Middle East, it has never been very far from Egypt. There has always been a danger of such activity spilling over into Egypt, something to which the Egyptian security

---

[20]For example, *al-Tali'a al-'Arabiyya* (Paris), June 15, 1987; *al-Majalla* (London), September 9, 1987; *al-Muharrir* (Paris), January 23, 1988.

[21]*Ruz al-Yusuf,* September 21, 1987.

[22]See, for example, *al-Siyasa* (Kuwait), September 7, 1987.

forces have often alluded. Occasionally, individual Palestinians have been exposed in Egypt as members of terrorist groups. And Abu Nidal has been active in plotting and attempting terrorist attacks on Egypt, in collaboration with Libya and Syria.

The October 1985 hijacking of the Italian cruiser *Achille Lauro* demonstrated how Egypt can become an unintentional victim of Palestinian terrorism. The hijackers, four members of a splinter group within the PLO, apparently planned to use the ship to smuggle themselves and their weapons ashore to Israel and to attack targets there. Having been discovered while still in Egyptian waters, they changed their plans, seized the ship, and killed a U.S. citizen. Eventually, they surrendered to Egyptian authorities, but the terms of their surrender pact with Egypt and the fact that a U.S. citizen was murdered led to subsequent developments that resulted in an Egyptian-American rift, something that both countries regretted. PLO forces also used Egyptian territory on at least three occasions in 1987 to launch terrorist attacks on Israel through the Sinai Peninsula. Egypt's geostrategic position and political standing in this notoriously violent region has thus made it a potential target of terror, intentional and inadvertent.

Conclusion

Terrorism, aimed at the stability or very existence of the Egyptian regime, is a problem for the Egyptian authorities in the late 1980s. It may not be an acute problem requiring a national state of emergency (although a formal state of emergency has been in effect since Sadat's death), but it is surely more than a marginal nuisance. The most serious type of terrorism is domestic terrorism, especially that which is initiated by radical Muslims. It is most serious because it springs from real, deep-rooted socioeconomic and spiritual problems for which there is no immediate relief. The movement that Islamic terrorist groups represent seems to be expanding and is likely to continue to do so. Similarly, the leftist-Nasserite opposition reflects a sincere disaffection with the faulty philosophy of the regime at a time when the country desperately needs a clear vision. This movement, which expresses an authentic yearning for a rather idealized type of leadership (a type believed to have existed in the past), is also likely to remain on the political scene.

One way in which the regime can confront the challenge is through dialogue, especially with the relatively more moderate sectors in the spiritual leadership of the fundamentalist movement. Dialogue fits perfectly into Mubarak's style of government. But dialogue, even if persistent—or widely televised—cannot make terrorism disappear completely. The regime therefore relies primarily on a highly effective network of intelligence and security units: detailed accounts published after the exposure of terrorist plots attest (even when read critically, discounting the police's self-praise) to an impressive degree of sophistication and skill. Most clandestine groups have been uncovered before carrying out their terrorist plans. Others groups, which had succeeded in executing attacks, were caught thereafter. The wave of terrorism from May to August 1987 at first seemed insoluble, as did the series of rather successful attacks by Egyptian Revolution over a period of three years. The eventual resolution of both may perhaps signal potential terrorists that they will eventually be caught. Some terrorists, however, will not be deterred.

Export of international terrorism forms a challenge that is both more complex and more simple than that originating at home. It is more problematic in that it is directed by forces over which Egypt has little or no control. This lack of control, of course, limits the ability of the security forces to take precautions. However, this form of terrorism is also more simple because it has little to do with conditions at home or with the government's own performance; hence, the regime has no difficulty in formulating its response to it—uncompromising battle.

In the final account, an effective security and intelligence apparatus has proved to be the best response to terrorism in Egypt and elsewhere. To date, it has been more effective in Egypt than in many other places.

4

WAR, TERROR, REVOLUTION: THE IRAN-IRAQ CONFLICT

Joseph Kostiner

The outbreak of war between Iran and Iraq at first fueled, then complicated, and in the end served to discipline and restrain the efforts of both states to expand their influence in the region through revolutionary terrorism. Prior to the outbreak of the war, both nations had been involved in widespread efforts to promote revolution—left-wing, Arab nationalist on the part of Iraq, conservative Shi'i Islamic for Iran—throughout the Middle East. This chapter examines how, engaged in a war of survival, the two powers each sought to use terror as a weapon against the other, but were forced to limit their support for terrorism elsewhere in the Middle East as they searched for allies among their erstwhile targets.

For Teheran, there were serious contradictions between waging internal revolution, encouraging the spread of that revolution abroad, and fighting a full-scale war. The revolution required the construction of a new ruling group, ideology, and institutions.[1] In the words of

---

[1] Nathan Leites and Charles Wolf, Jr., *Rebellion and Authority* (Chicago, 1972); Charles Tilly, *From Mobilization to Revolution* (New York, 1978); Theda Skocpol, *States and Social Revolution* (Cambridge, 1979). Compare with Richard E. Rubenstein, *Alchemists of Revolution* (New York, 1987), particularly Part V. I wish to thank the following people for their helpful remarks: Shaul Bakhash, Patrick Clawson, Laurie Mylnoie, James Piscatori, and Robin Wright. I am particularly indebted to Barry Rubin for his advice and assistance.

Bernard Lewis, the revolution was "a mass movement with wide popular participation that resulted in a major shift in economic as well as political power and that inaugurated or, perhaps more accurately, continued a process of vast social transformation."[2] Yet the war demanded that all the country's resources and energies be devoted to defeating Iraq and to either stripping away or damaging Iraq's allies.

Iraq, too, had been a revolutionary society. But whereas Iran sought to promote an Islamic fundamentalist—particularly Shi'i—revolution, the post-1968 Ba'ath regime in Iraq was a leftist, Arab nationalist government. And, while Iran's support for Islamic fundamentalist revolution expanded in the 1980s, Iraq began to curtail its subversive efforts against the Arab monarchies of the Persian Gulf—the very regimes that Iran sought to overthrow because of their pro-Western, pro-Iraqi policies. In contrast to Iran, Iraq used the war to facilitate its shift from using terrorism against moderate forces in the Arab world to employing it as an instrument against Iran and its supporters.

This was quite different from the days when Iraq was attempting to be the spearhead of leftist Arab nationalism. Iraqi-backed groups, mainly the leftist Popular Front for the Liberation of Oman and the Arab Gulf (PFLOAG) tried to subvert Gulf states in the late 1960s and the 1970s. Similarly, by supporting factions in the Palestinian Liberation Organization (PLO) such as the Arab Liberation Front (ALF) and the Palestine Liberation Front (PFL), which joined the PLO in 1969, and Abu Nidal's group *(Sabri al-Banna)*, which broke away from the PLO in 1975, Baghdad had hoped to gain leverage both within the PLO and in the wider Arab world.[3]

---

[2] Bernard Lewis, "Islamic Revolution," *New York Review of Books,* January 17, 1987.
[3] Jillian Becker, *The PLO* (New York, 1984), 71, 73.

Iraq's failure to make strategic gains in the Gulf and its focus on economic development, facilitated by oil revenues, was a prime reason for the attenuation of Baghdad's support for leftist revolutionary activities. Iraq sought to diversify both its trade partners and arms suppliers, leading to a reduction in its trade and military ties with Moscow and to an expansion in links to France and other Western states.

The 1975 Algiers Conference—bringing an improvement in Iran-Iraq relations and a border agreement in exchange for Tehran's ceasing to support the Iraqi Kurds' rebellion—was a first sign of Iraq's readiness to improve relations with its neighbors. Since 1978, Iraq has ceased supporting revolutionary movements in the Gulf and sought to mend fences with Saudi Arabia and Kuwait.[4]

During the Baghdad summits of October 1978 and March 1979, when most of the Arab world condemned the Camp David Accords and Egypt's participation in them, Iraq emerged as the leader of a broad Arab front which rejected U.S. and Israeli policy. In seeking to play a central role as convener and mediator for this pan-Arab front, Iraq virtually abandoned its earlier efforts to subvert and revolutionize Arab societies. When the Iran-Iraq war broke out in September 1980, Baghdad's enthusiasm for revolution was nearly extinguished.

Iran's Islamic revolution created an alternative revolutionary axis, that of Islamic fundamentalism. Seeking to establish an authentic Islamic order in response to the widening social inequalities and dislocations generated by rapid modernization and Western influence, Islamic radicals aimed to replace existing Arab regimes with governments inclined toward Muslim fundamentalism.

---

[4]Anthony H. Cordesman, *The Gulf and the Search for Strategic Stability* (Boulder and London, 1984), 398–399.

While this aim appealed to some Sunni opposition groups in Egypt, Syria, Saudi Arabia and elsewhere, the Iranian call for fundamentalist revolution found greater resonance in the Shi'i communities in Iran, southern Iraq, and South Lebanon, where the Shi'a constituted a majority, as well as in the Gulf monarchies where they were only a minority. Certain Shi'i characteristics in particular fueled radical revolutionary Islam: a profound belief in martyrdom, the clergy's alienation from secular governments, and the Shi'a's own sense of being downtrodden.[5]

The new Islamic republic in Iran set out to establish what R. K. Ramazani called an "Islamic world order."[6] The Iranian government denied planning to export its brand of fundamentalism throughout the Islamic world. Violence, the government said, was justified only for the "defense of Islam." But since, in its view, true Islam had been suppressed in many areas of the Muslim world, it was the duty of faithful Muslims to encourage the elimination of oppressive regimes and the establishment of Islamic republics in their stead, even through the use of violence. Traditional Iranian state interests—such as the desire to dominate the Gulf—continued with Iran's new leadership and encouraged Iranian activity in the region.[7]

A revolutionary atmosphere was particularly apparent in two of the major Shi'i communities outside Iran: in Lebanon and Iraq. In Lebanon, the Shi'i communities started conducting sometimes violent anti-government activities in "the movement of the downtrodden" (*Harakat al-Mahrumin*), founded by Musa al-Sadr, a Lebanese clergyman of Iranian descent, in 1974. The movement derived

---

[5]On the breakdown of the Shi'i population, see Martin Kramer, ed., *Shi'ism, Resistance and Revolution* (Boulder and London, 1987), 10.
[6]Rouhollah K. Ramazani, *Revolutionary Iran* (Baltimore and London, 1988), 24–27.
[7]Ibid., 29–31; Shahran Chubin, "The Islamic Republic's Foreign Policy in the Gulf," in Martin Kramer, *Shi'ism*, 159–172.

from the sense of deprivation typical of the Shi'a in Lebanon, and also from the rise of a better-educated, salaried middle class of Shi'a. The latter infused ideas of unity and revivalism into Shi'i communities migrating from villages into the cities. Thus the Lebanese Shi'a became an organized force during the Lebanese civil war. Israel's Litani operation of March 1978 in South Lebanon and the disappearance of Musa al-Sadr during a visit to Libya in August 1978 (almost certainly murdered by the Libyan government) turned the Lebanese Shi'a into a radical militia, ready to fight for their interests in the state.

Led by a French-educated lawyer, Nabih Birri, these forces, the "groups of the Lebanese struggle" *(Afwaj al-Muqawama al-Lubnaniyya)* were also known by their abbreviation as the "movement of hope" *(Harakat al-Amal or simply Amal)*. Their links to Iran were strengthened in 1979 when a small number of Iranian "volunteers" arrived in Lebanon and enhanced personal contacts there. Muhammad Montazeri, the son of Ayatollah Ali Montazeri, and Mustafa Charman, the chairman of the Iranian Defense Council, were known as figures particularly close to *Amal*.[8] Moreover, the example set by the Iranian revolution as a successful manifestation of organized Shi'i activity definitely inspired the Lebanese Shi'a.[9]

In Iraq, Shi'a, who constitute 50 to 60 percent of the population, felt discriminated against both in their home area in the south and in poor urban neighborhoods, like Baghdad's al-Thawra district, to which they tended to migrate. A rising Shi'i middle class sought to change this

---

[8] *Al-Dustur*, July 1, 1985.
[9] On the evolution of Shi'i history in Lebanon, see Fouad Ajami, *The Vanished Imam* (Ithaca and London, 1986); Augustus R. Norton, *Amal and the Shi'a* (Austin, Texas, 1987), Chapters 1–5; Joseph Olmert, "The Shi'a and the Lebanese State" in Kramer, *Shi'ism*, 189–202; Marius Deeb, *Militant Islamic Movements in Lebanon: Origins, Social Basis and Ideology*, Georgetown University, Occasional Papers Series, Center for Arab Studies, Washington, D.C., November 1986.

situation. High Shi'i clerics such as Mahdi al-Hakim and Muhammad Baqir al-Sadr started preaching an activist line. They focused on transforming the Shi'i holy shrines of Najaf and Karbala in southern Iraq into scholarly centers and adopted an anti-government, anti-Ba'thi stance. Al-Sadr advocated establishing a "Muslim state." The "Call" organization, *al-Da'wa*, founded by Ayatollah Muhsin al-Hakim (Mahdi's father) in the early 1960s, became a center of opposition in the mid-1970s. In February 1977, following the execution of several clerics, *al-Da'wa* instigated an uprising of thousands of Shi'a in Najaf and Karbala which the government suppressed by force. The Ayatollah Ruhollah Khomeini's stay in Najaf and the subsequent triumph of the Iranian revolution again served to inspire the Iraqi Shi'a. Hence the leaders of *al-Da'wa* were entertained in Iran and their activities were encouraged. The appearance of the "warriors" *(Mujahidin)* organization in 1979 also bore the stamp of Iranian influence. Subsequent mass riots by Shi'a all over southern Iraq led the Iraqi government to detain Baqir al-Sadr and, in June 1980, to execute him.[10]

In the Gulf states, the situation was more equivocal. There, too, the Shi'a (about 5 percent of the population in Saudi Arabia, more than 20 percent in Kuwait, and more than 50 percent in Bahrain) had endured persecution and discrimination. Government policies in recent decades, however, were more attuned to their needs and rights, and a majority of those employed by the oil companies and other business enterprises in these states were

---

[10]On Iraq's Shi'a, see Elie Kedourie, "The Iraqi Shi'is and Their Fate" in Kramer, *Shi'ism*, 135–158; Hanna Batatu, "Iraq's Underground Shi'a Movements: Characteristic Causes and Prospects," *Middle East Journal*, Autumn 1981, 578–594; Marvin Zonis and Daniel Brumberg, *Khomeini, the Islamic Republic of Iran and the Arab World* (Cambridge, Mass.: Harvard Middle East Papers, Center for Middle Eastern Studies, Harvard University, 1987), 62–65; Ramazani, op. cit., 35–38.

Shi'i. Internal divisions in Gulf Shi'i communities also hampered the formation of an active opposition movement. Prior to 1978, families with Iranian backgrounds did not form cohesive bonds with Iraqi-Arab Shi'a who had arrived more recently. The Iranian revolution, however tipped the local balance here, too. Inspired by propaganda campaigns carried over the radio from Tehran, spread with Khomeini cassettes, and transmitted through a network of personal contacts with such influentials as the al-Muhri family in Kuwait and the al-Mudarrisi family in Bahrain, Shi'a began to participate in antigovernment riots. Harsh government retaliation, mass detentions and the deportation of Shi'i leaders such as 'Abbas Muhri and Taqi al-Mudarrisi, stimulated further Shi'i reactions. Ultimately, all these events crystallized a Shi'i communal identity manifested in mass demonstrations and in mounting demands for changes in economic and social policies. Riots occurred in Bahrain in August 1979 and April 1980 (following Baqir al-Sadar's detention), in Saudi Arabia in November 1979 (during the Shi'i Ashura ceremonies) and February 1980 (on the first anniversary of Iran's revolution), and in Kuwait in late November 1979 (following the capture of the Mosque in Mecca by a Sunni fundamentalist group).[11]

These developments demonstrate that before the Iran-Iraq war broke out, Iran had succeeded in contriving the beginning of a tangible revolutionary process in the region. Iran had tapped the feelings of the so-called deprived (*Mustaz'afin*, in Khomeini's parlance) and channeled them into some mass opposition. The Shi'i opposition was motivated by genuine communal grievances and an ambition to establish an Islamic republic, in Iraq

---

[11]On Gulf Shi'a, see Joseph Kostiner, "Shi'i Unrest in the Gulf" in Kramer, *Shi'ism*, 173–188; James Bill, "Islam, Politics and Shi'ism in the Gulf," *Middle East Insight* (January–February 1984), 3–12; Zonis and Brumberg, op. cit., 42–54; Ramazani, op. cit., 39–52.

and Bahrain, or at least governments receptive to Shi'i demands, in states like Saudi Arabia and Kuwait. A conference organized by Iran's main revolutionary propagators that took place in the Sinna Hotel in Tehran in February 1980 reportedly inaugurated a "supreme council for the world-wide Islamic revolution," a regional axis for export of the revolution.[12] Moreover, revolutionary Iran reached out to both Sunni leftists and fundamentalists to form a regional revolutionary wave. Iran's example also encouraged Sunni fundamentalists such as those who captured the Mosque in Mecca in November 1979, and fostered cooperation between the new Iranian leadership and leftist opposition elements in the Middle East—most notably the Palestine Liberation Organization (PLO) in 1979—which resulted in joint guerrilla training.[13]

The Impact of War on Iranian Support for Revolution

Although credible reports of Iran's decisionmaking processes are not available, there is some evidence indicating that war efforts have had an impact upon several spheres of Iranian public life and thus upon Iran's revolutionary initiatives. First, Iranian decisionmakers seem to have reconsidered their priorities. The reasons behind the establishment of a special brigade to "carry out unconventional warfare in enemy territory" are presented in a top secret document prepared for the Iranian leadership (probably dated May 5, 1984) and attest to these new priorities. Both the minister of guidance, Muhammad Khatami, who introduced the plan, and the designated commander of the brigade, tentatively identified as Mehdi Hashemi, insisted that their main concern was to achieve success in "this imposed war" and, apart from that, to

---

[12]*Al-Dustur*, July 1, 1985.
[13]*Al-Dustur*, August 27, 1984.

defeat "the enormous satanic forces" that encircle Iran and generate "thousands of other internal and external problems." Only a one-line remark by Khatami recalled the earlier commitment to revolution: "Apart from this [the major goals], as indicated by our beloved leader, we have a heavy duty to Islam."[14]

Under the exigencies of the war, Iran's leaders redefined strategy: Iraq was to be the primary target, and the "oppressors," "infidels," and other "satanic forces"—that is, the United States, Israel, and the states that assisted Iraq—were next in line. The priority was now placed on ensuring the regime's survival and legitimacy. Whatever the popular perception may have been, the "duty to Islam" became a secondary operational concern. Even the unconventional forces were to be dedicated to the immediate task of carrying the war to Iraq.

The scope of the war and the efforts it demanded affected Iran's policy by imposing on the original revolutionary considerations a variety of state interests. Hence, while the government deemed the maintenance of a revolutionary aura essential both for gaining internal legitimacy and boosting bonds with Shi'i brethren in the Arab world, the Iranian regime also needed a diplomatic, even friendly, face in order to obtain support or at least neutrality from other parties in the region.

In pursuit of this aim, Iran's foreign policy stance shifted noticeably. A department for foreign propaganda was formed in the ministry of information in February 1982 to propagate a more benign image for Iran. Iranian leaders tended in varying degrees to stress the "cultural and ideological" aspects of exporting revolution. Khomeini declared that Iran had no intention of forcing

---

[14]"Islamic Republic of Iran on the Creation of an Independent Brigade for Carrying Out Unconventional Warfare in Enemy Territory" in *State-Sponsored Terrorism*, Report prepared for the Subcommittee on Security and Terrorism for the use of the Committee on the Judiciary, United States Senate.

the revolution on others, a statement aimed particularly at allaying fears of Iran's neighbors, the Gulf Arab states.[15]

The contradictions generated by the war's intensity were also manifested in the vicissitudes of the process of post-revolutionary consolidation at home. The need to unify the state's political leadership coincided with the attempts by religious leaders to dominate government and eliminate all rivals, including their erstwhile revolutionary partners, notably the *Mujahidin Khalq*. The rise of the "Revolutionary Guards" *(Pasderan)* in August 1981, followed by persecution of the *Mujahidin* the next summer, signified the onset of this process.[16]

As internal factional struggle intensified, policy alternated sharply between periods of full government support for revolutionary activity abroad and periods of less intense meddling for partisan purposes. According to Western reports, a revolutionary council consisting of Hashemi, Ayatollahs Montazeri and Kho'ini, Revolutionary Guards Minister Muhsin Rafiqdust, and other "hardliners" were responsible for overall planning of revolutionary activities.[17] There were also Western and Gulf Arab reports about meetings between Iran's leading figures and representatives of various Islamic revolutionary bodies for the purpose of coordinating activities.[18] In addition, Iran launched continuous propaganda campaigns through radio stations, cassettes and written publications which were designed to spread Iran's gospel. These initiatives seem to have been opposed or at least restrained in part by a group of leaders, including Hashemi Rafsanjani, speaker of the *Majlis*, who favored

---

[15]Quoted by David Menashri in "Iran" *Middle East Contemporary Survey*, vol. 8 (1983–84), 428–459.
[16]Shaul Bakhash, *The Reign of the Ayatollahs* (New York, 1983), 218–225.
[17]*Liberation*, December 30, 1983; *International Herald Tribune*, January 22, 1984; *The Australian*, December 27, 1983.
[18]See for instance, *The Listener*, January 3, 1985.

pragmatic state interests over partisan revolutionary initiatives.

The war helped to attenuate another aspect of Tehran's revolutionary activity, namely, cooperation with Sunni counterparts. The PLO's neutrality over the war cooled the relationship between Tehran and its would-be Palestinian collaborators. According to a Palestinian account, it was the Iranian intention to subvert Arab governments that caused an initial breech in early 1980, and Tehran's coolness towards PLO attempts to mediate the dispute with Iraq finally set the parties apart.[19] While Tehran's version of the rift is unavailable, it is clear that the PLO's unwillingness to commit itself against Iraq precipitated the break between the parties. This break in turn, served to cool relations between leftist and Shi'i groups throughout the Gulf region.

Moreover, the clerical nature of the new Iranian government and the growing anti-Arab tone of Iranian war propaganda led Sunni elements away from Iran. The ousting of Bani Sadr and of the *Mujahidin* from Iran's elite chilled Tehran's relations with Arab leftists. Sunni fundamentalists *(Salafiyyun)* asserted that the Shi'i concept of the *imam* as a "heritage from the prophet" who is "incapable of error" was unacceptable.[20] Groups of Muslim Brethren in Kuwait then went on to bomb Iranian offices there and, in November 1981, a leading Saudi sage, 'Abd al-'Aziz bin Baz, issued a *fatwa* denouncing Iran's practice of celebrating the Prophet Mohammed's birthday, further highlighting the gap between Sunni and Shi'i fundamentalist streams.[21] Iran's ability to launch a regional revolutionary campaign thus diminished.

---

[19] *Al-Qabbas*, June 28, 1986.
[20] *The Middle East*, July 1980.
[21] *International Herald Tribune*, July 13, 1980; see Martin Kramer's discussion, "The Muslim Consensus Undone" in *Middle East Contemporary Survey*, vol. 6 (1981–82), 290–291.

Under the impact of the war, Iran modified its revolutionary activities in other spheres as well. In terms of target selection, Tehran had to take into account both its diverse state interests and its military priorities. In the operational sphere, the questions of physical access, the responses of both allies and target governments, and the impact of Iranian leadership disputes or unauthorized factional initiatives had to be factored in. Consequently, Iran became more flexible in its revolutionary activities and adapted its tactics to changing conditions prevalent in different arenas.

Iranian-backed Insurgency, 1981–87

The system by which Iranian revolutionary acts were executed after the outbreak of the war emulated what Regis Debray has called the *foco*. The term refers to a "center of guerrilla operations" or focus formed by a small group of dedicated revolutionaries who conduct a variety of limited terrorist or guerrilla activities but who also serve as an inspirational nucleus for a mass revolutionary movement.[22] The advantage of this technique is that it enables the sponsor to choose targets and tactics as conditions permit. A pro-Iranian Iraqi Shi'i pamphlet indeed stressed the tactical advantage of an alliance of such nuclear groups all enlisted to serve a common revolutionary cause.[23]

The creation and coordination of these various bodies has been maintained through lines of communication. One important link is in the personal and scholastic ties which bind some of the clerics in these groups. Martin Kramer has pointed to a "Najaf connection" in the

---

[22]John Gerassi, *Towards Revolution* (London, 1971), Vol. I, 16–17.
[23]*Durus fi Tafjir al-Thawra al-Islamiyya*, a publication of the Iraqi *Mujahidin* movement. No date, no publisher.

common learning experience of Shi'i clerics from all over the Muslim world who studied in this holy city during the 1950s and 1960s.[24] The school of thought so critical of materialistic, Westernized regimes in the Middle East first emerged there. Thus members of the al-Sadr and al-Hakim families—some of whom actually functioned as the great sages of the formative years—as well as the Lebanese cleric Fadlallah and Khomeini, himself, studied and taught at Najaf. Khomeini spent thirteen years in exile there, from 1965 to 1978. These figures both created the climate of radical Shi'i Islam in Najaf and drew inspiration from it. Moreover, their personal bonds and the similarity of their views produced a cohesive network of revolutionary activists. Family ties among Shi'i throughout the Muslim world reinforce the bonds of such Arab Shi'i leaders with Iranian leaders.

Iran's alliance with Syria, which assured Iran an influence in distant Lebanon, was obviously a marriage of convenience between the secular regime of the Syrian Ba'th party and Iran's clerics. Syria found in Iran a power that might extend Damascus's influence over the Lebanese Shi'a. Damascus also obtained 8.8 million tons of oil yearly at a cost below the OPEC benchmark. And as Iraq's opponent in the war, Iran posed an effective check on Syria's main rival in the Arab world. Iran, in turn, gained a strategic ally to provide weapons and political support in the Arab world, a collaborator to facilitate the flow of *Pasderan* to the Lebanese Biqa' region, arms for *Hizb Allah*, and tactical assistance for insurgency. There were historical precedents for this partnership: Shi'i-Iranian contacts and cooperation with Syrian 'Alawis in the past culminated in Musa al-Sadr's *fatwa* of July 1973,

---

[24]Martin Kramer, "The Structure of Shi'ite Terrorism" in Albert Kurtz, ed., *Contemporary Trends in World Terrorism* (New York, 1987), 43–52.

legitimizing the 'Alawis who dominated Syria's leadership as legitimate Twelver Shi'i Moslems.[25]

Iran's policy towards the Gulf states reflected a mix of revolutionary and conventional state interests. Iran's Islamic revolutionary impetus became part of the war effort as the government attempted to use revolutionary fundamentalists as tools to further Tehran's political and strategic interests in the Gulf.

Judging by the nature of operations (little other evidence concerning Iran's actual process of decisionmaking is available), the primary aim of Iran's policy in the Arab Gulf area must have been to reduce and, if possible, eliminate the support Iraq obtained from these states. A second, more far-reaching goal was to upset regional balances of power which appeared hostile from Tehran's perspective and to establish a more favorable power-structure in the Gulf basin.

Several strategic priorities followed from these goals. First, the supply lines from Arab Gulf states to Iraq had to be obstructed and local governments deterred from other anti-Iranian activity. Second, and more substantially, Arab Gulf governments had to be weakened or even toppled in order to pave the way for a revolutionary takeover by pro-Iranian forces. To achieve these goals, Iranian agents struck at specified and limited targets through sabotage, bombings and assassinations. Weary of government crackdowns on their ranks and leaders, some of the pro-Iranian groups in the Gulf also resorted to more direct "anti-government actions."[26]

Pro-Iranian organizations often exceeded the limits prescribed by Iranian officials as local revolutionaries pursued their own agendas. On the other hand, conciliatory diplomacy aimed at obtaining *rapprochement* with

---

[25]Zonis and Brumberg, 38–39; *New York Times,* January 11, 1984.
[26]*Durus fi Tafjir.*

Arab Gulf governments sometimes stalled pro-Iranian revolutionary activities and produced long periods of quiet in the region. The visit of Saudi Arabia's Foreign Minister Sa'ud al-Faysal to Tehran in May 1985, for example, was followed by an extended period of calm.

The counterinsurgency measures taken by Gulf governments also dampened Iranian and pro-Iranian revolutionary activities in the Gulf. Since forming the Gulf Cooperation Council (GCC) in May 1981, these small, wealthy states worked to remedy their natural vulnerability to insurgency. They quickly concluded an agreement on mutual cooperation over extradition, hot pursuit, and exchanges of criminal intelligence and counterinsurgency techniques. In addition, each of these states, notably Kuwait, invested heavily to reinforce their own intelligence, law enforcement, and control of foreigners' movements.[27]

The Iranian-inspired operations in the Gulf proceeded along several different paths. The *foco* organizations included the Islamic Front for the Liberation of Bahrain (IFLB). Its leader, Taqi al-Mudarrisi, a Shi'i activist from Iraq who resided in Bahrain, incited riots there as Khomeini's representative in 1979–80. After he was deported he moved to Tehran where he broadcast Iranian radio propaganda to the Gulf population. The IFLB worked closely with two local Bahraini groups, the 'Abbas Gathering *(Majmu 'at 'abbas)* and the Group of the Worship Place *(Husayniyya)*, called *Nur al-Islam*. Yet, with the IFLB's headquarters in Tehran, Iran was obviously in control.[28]

The *al-Da'wa* party became a second hub of Iranian revolutionary activity. Led from Tehran by Baqir al-Hakim

---

[27]For instance: summary of the United Arab Emirates–Saudi Arabia Security Agreement, signed on February 21, 1982, BBC, February 1, 1983; *al-Watan* (Kuwait), interview with a chief security official in Kuwait, March 28, 1985.
[28]Kostiner, op. cit.; *al-Dustur*, July 1, 1985.

(another scion of the sage Hakim's family) and committed to establishing a Khomeini-led Islamic Republic of Iraq, *al-Da'wa* had branches in every Gulf state. It was closely allied with the Iraqi Shi'i *Mujahidin*, the Islamic Action (*al-'Amal al-Islami*), and others. Tehran's influence over each of these groups was used to establish the Supreme Assembly of the Islamic Revolution of Iraq (SAIRI), an umbrella organization uniting all of these bodies, in November 1982.[29]

Pro-Iranian revolutionaries twice attempted to topple governments in the region. Bahrain seemed an especially vulnerable target—a large Shi'i population and Iran's historical claims to the island seemed to make this nation a logical site for the extension of Islamic revolution. Several squads of IFLB insurgents were dispatched on December 16, 1982, to Bahrain where they were supposed to capture strategic posts, then take over the government and establish an "Islamic republic" led by Mudarrisi. The teams were evidently trained in Iran. Bahrain has also accused Iran of supplying hovercraft loaded with troops and equipment to aid the conspirators. And it is widely believed that equipment smuggled through Iranian diplomatic channels was supplied to the conspirators, although the evidence of such active Iranian assistance has not been accepted by other sources. The Bahraini authorities foiled the coup and arrested the commandos.[30]

An equally bold operation was launched on May 25, 1985, when the car of Kuwait's ruler, Jabir al-Ahmad al-Sabah, was machine-gunned. The Amir was only slightly wounded. In this case, the trail led to *al-Da'wa*. As in 1981, the aim was to shatter the Kuwaiti government and reverse its support of Iraq. The perpetrators also sought to

---

[29]*Al-Mujtama'*, December 27, 1983; Zonis and Brumberg, 64–65.
[30]*Al-Siyasa*, December 23–24, 1981; *Al-Sharq al-Awsat*, December 15, 1981; *International Herald Tribune*, July 7, 1982; see also Kostiner in Kramer, *Shi'ism*.

pressure the Kuwaiti government to release *al-Da'wa* detainees held since late 1983 (see below).[31]

A second pattern of subversive activity involved mass sabotage—damaging strategic or public facilities and imposing heavy casualties. These activities were directed against Iraqi targets and parties who had assisted Iraq. Revolutionary terrorism was directed against targets in nations perceived as active enemies of Iran.[32]

In Kuwait, twelve different targets were blown up on December 12, 1983, including the French and American embassies and the Shu'ayba depot from which shipments to Iraq were sent. Twenty-five men who belonged to *al-Da'wa* (among them Iraqis, Lebanese and only three Kuwaitis) were arrested.[33] There were less precisely targeted attempts, such as the shooting at a café in Kuwait in July 1984, in which eleven people were killed, that was attributed to a supplementary group of *al-Da'wa* called "the Black Brigades," led by 'Abbas Muhri.[34] At about the same time, two bombs exploded in Riyadh, Saudi Arabia, killing one person. Behind the shadowy body called the "Islamic Jihad," which claimed responsibility for this and many other attacks, probably lurked *al-Da'wa*.[35] On January 19, 1987, just before the convening of the Islamic summit in Kuwait—which Iran boycotted and *al-Da'wa* had threatened to disrupt—two explosions damaged a Kuwaiti offshore oil rig. The eleven saboteurs arrested were Shi'i Kuwaitis of Iranian origin. An unknown group, the "Revolutionary Organization, Sons of the Prophet," took responsibility.[36] Three days later, a car exploded in front of the Meridian Hotel, which hosted journalists covering the summit.

---

[31]*New York Times*, May 28, 1985; *Washington Post*, May 26, 1985.
[32]*Al-Fath al-Islami*, 35, 1985.
[33]*Al-Ray Al-'Amm*, December 13–14, 1983; *Financial Times*, April 14, 1984.
[34]*Al-Dustur*, May 6, 1985.
[35]*Financial Times*, May 20, 1985.
[36]*New York Times*, February 1, 1987; *al-Qabbas*, February 4, 1987.

In 1987–88 there were more sabotage activities in the region.[37] There were explosions in Kuwait's gas installations on August 16, 1987. Cars exploded in front of the Pan American airlines offices in Kuwait on October 25, and in front of the Kuwaiti ministry of the interior on November 3, 1987. Following Saudi Arabia's rupture of relations with Iran, the offices of Sa'udiyya airlines in Kuwait exploded on April 28, 1988, causing one injury. Similar activities also occurred in several Iraqi locations.

The Iranian-backed Shi'i terrorist organizations have also been involved in aircraft hijacking. The main objective of the hijackers was to free their fellow perpetrators detained in Kuwait following the December 1983 bombing. This was a purpose Iran definitely endorsed, although it did not necessarily support the tactic of hijacking. A Kuwaiti airliner was hijacked to Iran on December 6, 1984, probably by an *al-Da'wa* group, to pressure the Kuwaitis to release these detainees. Iran freed the hostages but did not punish the perpetrators.

A TWA airliner hijacked en route to the United States from Athens on June 14, 1985, probably by *Hizb Allah* people or by an *Amal* renegade group, was brought to Beirut. The hijackers demanded the release of the *Da'wa* prisoners and of 700 Shi'a captured during Israel's intervention in Lebanon. The episode ended three weeks later with the release of the passengers through Syrian mediation. Behind the mediation lay an Iranian decision to halt the hijacking and to press those responsible to withdraw. The hijacking of a Kuwaiti airliner en route from the Far East on April 6, 1988, was once again aimed at focing the Kuwaitis to release the 1983 detainees. The airliner was released through Algerian mediation after three weeks during which several Kuwaiti passengers were

---

[37]The following facts are based on material accumulated by the data base of the Jaffe Center for Strategic Studies, at Tel Aviv University.

executed by the hijackers.[38] The hijackers disappeared, their identities unknown.

Still, these activities show that despite Iran's revolutionary rhetoric Tehran's support for revolution was in practice restricted to isolated terrorist actions which were increasingly constrained by Iran's state interests. First, in comparison to the operations launched in 1979–80, the aims of Iranian and pro-Iranian activities during the war with Iraq were scaled down markedly. Operationally, Iran abandoned the aim of establishing a mass-based movement with the goal of creating a region-wide revolutionary regime. Iran's agents were a handful of well-trained professionals; insurgency focused on limited, specific targets that provided no framework for a continuous, popularly based process. Revolutionary socialization through violent mass participation, a quality which has proven essential to the success of many revolutionary movements (including Iran's), was thus lacking in pro-Iranian insurgency in the Gulf. Moreover, with the exception of the group arrested attacking oil installations in January 1987, most other known or arrested saboteurs were foreign nationals trained outside Iran. In another respect, the activities under question were too limited in scope and too random to systematically subvert government institutions, or win over their people. In fact, Iranian- inspired activities in the Gulf during the war period were acts of simple terrorism—small-scale operations aimed at destruction and assassination and incapable of sparking a full-fledged revolutionary process.

Second, while the perpetrating organizations were basically followers of Khomeini's ideas and zealous advocates of an Islamic republic regime in their respective states, Iran could not maintain complete control over

---

[38]On the hijacking, see Robin Wright, *Sacred Rage* (New York, 1985); *Washington Post*, April 15, 1980.

their activities. In some cases, these organizations took advantage of Iranian support to pursue their own objectives, contrary to Iran's interests or desires. The hijacking series aimed at the release of the 1983 Kuwait prisoners seems to be such a case as no Iranian strategic interest was served, and indeed Iran used its influence to terminate the incidents. Similarly Martin Kramer has suggested that the attempt on the life of Kuwait's ruler was a similar autonomous act of *al-Da'wa* which Iran would not have condoned.[39] This seems logical in light of the conciliatory atmosphere dominating Iran's relationship with Gulf states after the visit of Saudi Arabia's Foreign Minister Sa'ud al-Faysal to Tehran in May 1985, just prior to the attempt on al-Sabah's life. The elimination of the Kuwaiti ruler, however, might have served an Iranian interest by destabilizing Iraq's main depot for war supplies.

Iranian Revolutionary Activities in Lebanon

Iran's other main arena of revolutionary activity in the Middle East has been Lebanon. The motives for Iran's activity there differed from those which loomed behind its actions in the Arab Gulf. Tehran had a strategic interest in Lebanon because of the availability of American and Israeli targets there. Israel's operation in Lebanon in the summer of 1982, and its attempts to aid a Christian-led government there, generated mounting antipathy among the Lebanese Shi'a. When, shortly afterward, U.S. forces arrived as part of an international peacekeeping force to support the new government, Lebanon became a theater in which Iran could strike directly at two of its most important and elusive enemies. Albeit peripheral to the Iran-Iraq war, the United States and Israel were

---

[39]Martin Kramer, "The Routine of Muslim Solidarity," in *Middle East Contemporary Survey*, vol. 9 (1984–85), 154.

perceived as two pillars of the anti-Iranian—and hence, "anti-Islamic"—forces in the region. A successful strike against American and Israeli influence would serve important strategic interests and also enhance the domestic prestige of the clerical regime.

Lebanon became important for another reason. As Iran was forced to limit its mass-oriented revolutionary activities in the Gulf region by more compelling war priorities, Lebanon provided the only regional outlet for a genuine revolutionary campaign. It had both a simmering Shi'i population and a totally ineffective government, making it an opportune target for externally inspired revolutionary insurgency. The strategy adopted combined specific terrorist action aimed at discrete, limited objectives with an effort to construct a mass-based revolutionary infrastructure among the Shi'a.

Iran's activities in Lebanon were conditional, moreover, on its ability to cooperate with its ally, Syria. Syria's degree of control over Lebanon and its ambition to dominate this country both helped and hindered Iran's attempts to influence events there.

The actions of the *foco* group which served as Iran's agent in Lebanon demonstrated the multifarious and convoluted purposes of Iran's support of terrorism and insurgency there. Following Israel's June 1982 invasion of Lebanon, the Party of God, *Hizb Allah*, became the main focus of Iran's activity. Its consultative council served as an umbrella for several groups with shared ideological and operational bonds. Prior to 1986, even members of Birri's organization, *Harakat al-Amal*, were reported to have been sympathizers of *Hizb Allah*. The vague identity of its membership ("we are all *Hizb Allah*") has often intrigued Western journalists.[40] The loose structure of the organization has made it possible to obscure the identity

---

[40]*Washington Post*, September 21, 1984.

and activities of its members and permitted *Hizb Allah* to function both as an ideological-political body and as an effective perpetrator of terrorism.

Yet certain things are known about *Hizb Allah*. Its ideology is shaped by the strong religious views of the renowned Shi'i clergyman, Muhammad Husayn Fadlallah, and other clergymen more closely tied to the organization, such as Subhi al-Tufayli and Ibrahim Amin. *Hizb Allah* seeks to eradicate atheistic Western influences and install an Iranian-style Islamic republic. In this respect, *Hizb Allah* parts company with the *Harakat al-Amal*, which seeks to reform rather than replace the secular Lebanese regime. *Hizb Allah* has incorporated smaller groups, such as the local *al-Da'wa* branch. An important body in the *Hizb Allah's* orbit, the Islamic Amal *(al-'Amal al-Islami)*, has reportedly carried out many of its military activities. It is led by a layman, Husayn al-Musawi, who was aligned with Birri until he was expelled from *Harakat Amal* in July 1982 after he objected to Birri's consent to the establishment of the Gemayel government. Ba'albak, where Musawi finally settled, has become a center for the revolutionary activities of Iran and *Hizb Allah*.[41]

Hizb Allah groups have been involved in a variety of terrorist activities. Sabotage and assassination were particularly popular in the early 1980s. A car bomb destroyed the Iraqi embassy, killing seventy-two people and the ambassador on December 15, 1981. Another Iraqi diplomat was killed on March 22, 1982. The American embassy in Beirut was destroyed in a suicide car incident on April 8, 1983. The same method was used to destroy the U.S. and Franch military units in Lebanon on October 23, 1983, and an Israeli army headquarters in Tyre was

---

[41]Martin Kramer, "The Divided House of Islam" in *Middle East Contemporary Survey*, vol. 7 (1982–1983), 241; Marius Deeb, op. cit.; *Christian Science Monitor* (by Robin Wright), May 10, 1984.

attacked in a similar fashion the following month. The death toll from these incidents amounted to hundreds. The Islamic Amal and Syrian intelligence were implicated.[42]

Another type of activity focused on spreading Iran's revolutionary gospel among Shi'i masses and on training Shi'i guerrilla fighters. *Hizb Allah* has engaged in such activities in the Biqa' in 1983, in West Beirut since 1984, and in South Lebanon since 1985, following Israel's withdrawal.[43]

Hizb Allah cadres have also been engaged in fighting the Israeli-backed South Lebanese Army (SLA) and in shelling Israeli targets across the Lebanese frontier. A major clash with SLA forces occurred in March 1987. The number of incidents in the Israeli "security strip" in South Lebanon rose from thirty-five in January 1987 to eighty-five in May 1988.[44] Israel's increased military activity in South Lebanon following a Palestinian glider attack in November 1988 prompted a fierce clash with *Hizb Allah* in April and May 1988.

Hizb Allah's activities also included the capture of a number of Western citizens as hostages. Although criticized by Fadlallah, *Hizb Allah*'s activists have found it convenient to hold such hostages as a way of both embarrassing Western states and making money.

In the Lebanese arena, Iran's compromises with necessity took a different form than in the Gulf. Here Iran's lack of control and initiative prevented Tehran from directing the pro-Iranian activities as it might have wanted. Iran's dependence on Syrian interests on one hand, and Lebanon's instability on the other, both made it difficult for Teheran to discipline the several pro-Iranian

---

[42]A.R. Norton, "Political Violence and Shi'a Factionalism in Lebanon," *Middle East Insight*, vol. 2, no. 2 (1973), 9–16; *Washington Post*, February 8, 1984.
[43]Wright, op. cit., 82–84, 95.
[44]*Washington Post*, May 14, 1988.

organizations. Each of these groups acted independently. Most important, Iran lacked control and organization at the operational and tactical level, as evidenced in the 1983 suicide bombing operations organized and carried out by agents of Syrian, Libyan, and the Popular Front for the Liberation of Palestine (PFLP) intelligence communities as well as Iranian participants.[45] The Iranian difficulties became more apparent after 1986 when a clear rift broke out between *Harakat al-Amal* and *Hizb Allah*. Allied with Syrian interests, *Amal* sought to consolidate its power in Lebanon without triggering an Israeli military response by declaring an Islamic republic. Fadlallah and his supporters, on the other hand, aimed to unite all Lebanese Shi'a, and *Hizb Allah* gained new ground and support among Shi'a. *Hizb Allah*, ignoring Syrian interests, sought to ignite a (holy) war with Israel and turn Lebanon into an Islamic republic.

Iran apparently has found it difficult to sort out the various factions in Lebanon. Although Tehran is reported to have financed *Hizb Allah* with between $16 and $60 million annually,[46] it refused to lend unconditional support to Fadlallah as the embodiment of Shi'i ideology in Lebanon. Fadlallah, who believes in popularizing *Hizb Allah* and its theories, contested *Amal*'s dominance among Lebanon's Shi'a by winning over some if its supporters in Beirut's suburbs and in South Lebanon. He seemed too independent to Tehran, however, and Iran sought to cultivate direct relations with Tufayli and Musawi as well as witha Sunni cleric (of Shi'i origin) from Tripoli, Sa'id Sha'ban, leader of the "Islamic unification movement" *(Harakat al-Tawhid al-Islamiyya)*.

---

[45]Wright, op. cit., 84–87.
[46]See, for instance, *Middle East International*, July 25, 1987; *U.S. News and World Report*, May 2, 1988.

Fearing injury to its alliance with Syria, Iran has also refused to denounce Nabih Birri and *Amal*. Birri played the role of a mediator who diligently guarded the hijackers' interests during the TWA hijacking in June 1985, but otherwise he has systematically sought to eradicate *Hizb Allah*'s position in both Beirut and South Lebanon. Fearing *Hizb Allah*'s commitment to establishing an Islamic republic in Lebanon and its willingness to continue fighting Israel across the frontier, both *Amal* and Syria tried to rein in *Hizb Allah*. Fadlallah indirectly criticized Syria's role and Birri's activities,[47] but Iran's president, 'Ali Khameneh'i, avoided a denunciation of Birri by insisting that a "Muslim should not fight a Muslim under any circumstances."[48]

Iran's hesitation over Shi'i representation and its lack of sufficient control over *Hizb Allah* had an impact on Tehran's relations with Syria. Damascus's relations with *Hizb Allah* were tense. *Hizb Allah* kidnapped a group of Syrian soldiers in November 1986 and again in February 1987. The Syrians, in turn, leaked the facts of the U.S.-Iranian arms deal to the Beirut paper, *al-Shira'*, where it was first published in November 1986. And, in April 1987, the Syrians had to swallow the kidnapping of an American journalist, Charles Glass, and the son of the Lebanese Defense Minister, 'Ali Usighan, just a stone's throw from a Syrian outpost in Beirut.

Relations between Iran and Syria were further strained in late 1987 and 1988 when *Hizb Allah* attempted to expand at the expense of *Amal* in South Lebanon and among Shi'i communities in southwest Beirut.

Following the showdown that ensued in south Beirut in May 1988, Fadlallah complained of a plot "to crush and annihilate" *Hizb Allah* and vowed as a last resort to

---

[47]Fadlallah's interview with *Al-Hawadith*, March 27, 1987.
[48]*Christian Science Monitor*, July 1, 1985.

fight back.[49] The Syrians, on the other hand, made it clear that they would stop the fighting, which challenged their dominance.[50] Iran acted as a mediator meeting with representatives of Syria, *Amal* and *Hizballah*. The influence of Iran's deputy foreign minister, Husayn Shaykh al-Islam, delayed Syrian interference in the fighting for some days. But sources from Iran's embassy in Damascus indicated that *Hizb Allah* was "blackening Tehran's face" with its behavior and that Iran did not enjoy full control over *Hizb Allah*.[51] The *Hizb Allah* triumph in Beirut only produced a death toll of several hundred Shi'a on both sides and led to a Syrian military takeover of the hitherto autonomous Shi'i quarters. Iran did little more than oversee the destruction of its own revolutionary effort in Lebanon.

Iraq's Strategy: Anti-Iranian Terrorism

Iraq's participation in the Arab radical camp after the conclusion of the Camp David accords did not result in a new campaign to promote left-wing revolution. In fact, Iraq's support for insurgency, which had already begun to moderate in the late 1970s, was virtually abandoned as Baghdad developed a new regional strategy in the 1980s. The changes in Iraq's policy reflected the spirit of the new Arab National Charter stating that "disputes among Arab states should be resolved by peaceful means" and that "the recourse of armed force [should] be prohibited."[52]

A more compelling cause for Iraq's moderation can be traced to the outbreak of the war with Iran and to Iraq's

---

[49]*Washington Post*, May 14, 1988.
[50]*Washington Post*, May 10, 1988.
[51]*Washington Post*, May 10, 14 and 25, 1988.
[52]Based on Mohammed Tawabila, *Al-Qadiyya al-Qawmiyya bayn al-Manhaj al-Kihafi wal-Tadhlil al-Maqsud*, (Baghdad, 1980), 101–105; quoted by Adeed Dawisha, *The Arab Radicals* (New York, 1986), 53.

growing dependence upon its Arab neighbors. Led by the ambitious Saddam Husayn, Iraq sought to achieve a leading role in the Arab world through a more responsible policy toward Baghdad's neighbors. As the decade progressed, Iraq's need for warmer relations with its Arab neighbors increased. Iraq received more than $10 billion annually from the Gulf states and depended crucially upon transportation services and political support provided by these states and Jordan. Later, in the mid-1980s, Iraq received men and some arms from Egypt and North Yemen. Iraq had little choice but to maintain friendly relations with these states. As Baghdad came to view the surrounding Arab states as an indispensable support system, its enthusiasm for revolution waned.[53]

In the years that followed, as Iraq's position in the war grew weaker and its dependence on Arab states grew proportionately larger, Iraq's outlook moderated still more. Thus, Baghdad minimized its activity in the "radical" camp (or "bloc of steadfastness") pitted against not only Israel but also the pro-Western Arab states. Iraq also toned down the radical rhetoric of its spokesmen; Iraqi media no longer described the Gulf states as "reactionary" and handmaidens of "imperialism." The new criterion by which Iraq evaluated its relations with Arab states was the measure of assistance they provided to its war effort. Baghdad cloaked this calculation in terms of Arab solidarity, rating the contributions of most states to the Arab cause by their support for Iraq.[54]

Iraq also changed its attitude toward the Arab-Israeli peace process when Jordan began to search for a suitable framework by which to enter the process initiated when Egypt made peace with Israel. Iraq's attitude toward the Camp David accords began to soften appreciably. Indeed,

---

[53]See the analysis in Dawisha, op. cit., 53–54.
[54]Ofra Bengio, "Iran" in *Middle East Contemporary Survey*, vol. 7 (1982–83), 604.

as it became more preoccupied with its own war, Iraq became less interested in escalating the Arab-Israeli conflict. Instead it tended to disengage, offering passive support to the states involved in settlement efforts. Hence, during 1983, Saddam Husayn and his foreign minister, Tariq 'Aziz, pointed out that Israel was entitled to "conditions of security" and declared that Iraq had "no objection" to a peace settlement which other Arab states would support.[55] Since then, Iraq has reiterated this position on various occasions.

Iraq's support for leftist revolutionary terrorism was curtailed accordingly. It has been suggested that Iraq instigated the assassination attempt by Abu-Nidal's group against Israel's ambassador to Britain, Shlomo Argov, on June 5, 1982, which precipitated Israel's invasion of Lebanon. On this view, Iraq deliberately sought to precipitate a war between Israel and Syria in Lebanon in order to embarrass its bitter rival.[56] Syria, after all, had become Iran's main ally in the Arab world, had supported Iraq's Kurdish opposition, and had closed the pipeline that transported Iraqi oil exports to the Mediterranean. However, at the time of the attempted assassination, Abu Nidal had already moved from his shelter in Baghdad and had begun to cooperate with Libya and, indeed, with Syria. Still, it is possible that Nidal acted at the behest of his erstwhile protector in Baghdad, a step not unthinkable to this Palestinian renegade.

Iraq is also said to have sheltered Abu al-'Abbas who devised the hijacking of the Italian ship *Achille Lauro* in October 1985 and who was wanted by both Italy and the United States. Although Baghdad never openly admitted granting haven to Abu al-'Abbas, an unnamed Iraqi official said that he "would be welcome" in Iraw and that he

---

[55]Ibid., 583–585.
[56]Thomas Friedman, *New York Times*, April 23, 1986.

carried an Iraqi passport. Sheltering him complemented Baghdad's attempts at the time to host the PLO head-quarters and assist in building up new PLO units. By pro-tecting 'Abbas, Baghdad sought to boost its pro-Pales-tinian image and underscore its loyalty to the Arab nationalist cause. Baghdad's support for the PLO was also an aimed at discrediting Damascus as a power that op-posed the Arab cause by aligning with Iran and splitting the PLO. The support the Iraqi-based ALF gave to Arafat's negotiations with King Hussein a year earlier indicates that Baghdad was not seeking to undermine its new Arab allies, however controversial, through radicalism and in-surgency. Supporting anti-Western, or anti-Israeli, PLO activity was attractive to Iraq, but gave way in importance to maintaining Arab unity.

Iraqi Support for Anti-Iranian Insurgency

In order to support its war efforts, Iraq attempted to foment insurgency in Iran. These attempts hardly reflected the burning ideological zeal of the early 1970s. Rather, Baghdad meddled with Iranian minorities—the Arabs of Ahwaz and the Kurds—principally to weaken the new Iranian regime. Iraq's increased support for in-surgency in the 1980s reflected the interests of a state en-gaged in a war of survival.

Iraq directed the bulk of its insurgency support to Kurdish guerrillas operating in Iran. Kurds live both in northeastern Iraq (constituting about one-fifth of the population in Sulaymaniyya, Irbilo, Dohuk, and Kirkuk) and in adjacent northwestern Iran (where they repre-sent one-tenth of the population in West Ayzarbayjan, Kurdestan, Jamjan and elsewhere). Historically, the Kurds had rebelled against both states in order to achieve autonomy. In Iraq, a Kurdish revolt of long duration was suppressed in 1975, following the Iran-Iraq Algiers

agreement which led the Shah of Iran to cut off his assistance to the Kurds.

The Iranian revolution generated new opportunities
for the Kurds. Iranian Kurds formed a tactical alliance
with leftist elements (notably the *Mujahidin Khalq*) in the
Iranian revolutionary coalition and asked for national autonomy from the new regime. Negotiations between the
Kurds and the government took place in 1979 but led no-
where. The outbreak of the war and the consolidation
of theocracy in Iran brought an end to Kurdish hopes.
Tehran soon set out to subjugate the Kurdish areas.

At this point, Iraq began to make contact with different Kurdish groups in the hope of establishing a cooper-
ative relationship with them.[57] In 1981, Baghdad started
to work with the Patriotic Union of Kurdistan (PUK), led
by Jallal Talabani. The PUK's main rival, the Kurdish
Democratic Party (KDP), led by Masud Barzani, tended to
cooperate with Syria and Iran in opposition to Baghdad.
Thus the alliance of the PUK and the Iraqi government
was in part a natural one strengthened by the leftward
inclination of both parties. Iran's July 1983 "Hajj 'Umran"
offensive into Iraqi sections of Kurdistan served to inspire
pro-Iraqi and anti-Iranian emotions among most segments
of Kurdish society and helped to isolate the KDP.[58]

The growing cooperation with the PUK led to a more
far-reaching connection with the Kurdistan Democratic
Party of Iran (KDPI). The KDPI, led by 'Abd al-Rahman
Qasimlu, was regarded as the largest Kurdish nationalist
body in Iran, commanding 12,000 "warriors" *(Peshmerga)*
and 60,000 armed peasants. Threatened by the Iranian

---

[57]Martin van Bruinessen, "The Kurds Between Iran and Iraq," *Middle East Report*, July–August 1986, 14–27.
[58]Charles D. MacDonald, "The Impact of the Gulf War on the Iraqi and Iranian Kurds" in *Middle East Contemporary Survey*, vol. 7, (1982–83), 261–272; Ofra Bengio, "Iraq" in *Middle East Contemporary Survey*, vol. 8, (1983–84), 480–82.

regime, the KDPI became receptive to Baghdad's assistance. Iraq gained even more as cooperation increased between KDPI and the Leftist *Mujahidin*, led by Mas'ud Rajavi. In early 1982, the KDPI joined the National Resistance Council, founded by Rajavi and Bani Sadr in Paris, following their escape from Tehran. Negotiations, and a *rapprochement* between the Iraqi government and PUK leader Talabani, led to the formation of a coalition which included Iraq, the PUK, the KDPI, and the *Mujahidin*.[59]

Iraq thereby succeeded in establishing partial tranquility in its own Kurdish areas—only partial, since the KDP was still fighting against the regime—while fomenting a Kurdish separatist insurgency against Iran. The alliance with the KDPI had been a continuous irritant for Iran since 1983; and *Mujahidin* operations gradually stepped up. In 1986 Qasimlu's warriors reportedly tied down 200,000 Iranian soldiers in the Sardasht area and weakened Iranian forces through assassination and sabotage.[60] The *Mujahidin* have made exaggerated claims of success against the regime in Tehran but did carry out terrorist attacks even in the Iranian capital itself.

In 1985 a group called "The Arab Front for the Liberation of Ahwaz," led by 'Abd al-Husayn 'Abd al-Razzak, expressed its disappointment over Khomeini's discrimination against the Arabs of Ahwaz and claimed to be receiving Iraqi assistance. 'Abd al-Razzak asserted that his front's violence inside Iran was "at a high level," but the front attracted little world attention and its activities were scarcely known.[61] No major Iraqi initiatives to instigate a full-scale revolution among Ahwazis were reported.

The inaccessibility of Kurdish areas made it difficult for Iraq to uphold the coalition against Tehran. Thus while

[59]Ibid.; *Al-Hawadith*, September 30, 1983.
[60]*Boston Globe*, December 27, 1986.
[61]*Al-Yarmuk*, August 25, 1985; Joint Publication Research Service, February 18, 1986.

Iraq was reported to have offered supplies to the KDPI, their safe arrival was known to depend on the attitude of Talabani who controlled the adjacent area. Iraq's influence was therefore not always a factor behind Kurdish anti-Iranian operations. To a large extent, the KDPI's own will to fight the Iranian regime sustained operations. Their motivation was summarized by one activist in these words: "The price of everything in Iran has gone up except the price of human beings."

Moreover, the Kurds retained the option of playing the two governments against each other. Thus, amidst the fighting, the KDPI conducted another fruitless round of negotiations with Tehran in late 1984–85. The ambivalent loyalties of the insurgents tested both parties, but seemed to wear more on Baghdad. In 1981–82, the Iraqi government was still willing to woo Kurds with a general amnesty for every previously armed rebel, but the old suspicions were rekindled by Iraq's brutality and the Kurds' own vacillating loyalty in the following years. Negotiations with the PUK over Kurdish autonomy broke off in the middle of 1984 with no results.

An agreement between Iraq and Turkey signed on October 15, 1984, was aimed at reinforcing Iraq's grip over the Kurds with Turkey's assistance along the frontier between the states.[62] The agreement was counterproductive for Iraq. In November 1986, after increasing disappointment over Baghdad's policies, Talabani's people attacked a group of *Mujahidin* and turned towards a new collaboration with Iran.[63] During the next several months, the pattern of the 1960s recurred: Kurds once again attacked Iraqi armed forces, triggering brutal Iraqi reprisals. Iraq still has guerrilla allies who terrorize Iran's

---

[62]Bengio, "Iraq" in *Middle Eastern Contemporary Survey*, vol. 8 (1983–84), 480–82; vol. 9 (1984–85), 470–72.
[63]*Al-Dustur*, November 24, 1986.

cities and countryside. But these allies have been unable to bring about the level of subversion Iraq desired, much less a full-fledged revolutionary process.

Conclusions

The outbreak of the Iran-Iraq war and the burden it brought to both antagonists made survival and victory the paramount concerns in the decisionmaking process of both Baghdad and Tehran. In the case of Iraq, the war accelerated a preexistent trend toward moderating its support for leftist revolutionary and pro-terrorist activities in the Middle East. Eventually, Baghdad even revised its perception of the Arab monarchies and withdrew its objections to the Arab-Israeli peace process.

In the case of Iran, the necessities of war did not cause Tehran to abandon its support for Islamic revolution, but did force Tehran to modify its tactics. The result was that both Iran and Iraq sought to promote terrorism, sabotage, assassination and hijacking and insurgency as means of reinforcing their war efforts. Both sides enjoyed moderate success. Iran developed a network which spread over the entire Arab world and proved capable of damaging Western states as well. Iraq focused its sponsorship of such acts on the Kurdish-*Mujahidin* nexus inside Iran.

But Iran's revolutionary campaign was compromised by strategic priorities and contained by the GCC states' effective use of counterinsurgency techniques. Consequently, instead of seeking to generate a substantial change in the socio-political structure of the area, Iranian-inspired terrorist activity became far more narrow in aim, limited in scope, and sporadic in frequency. Iran's efforts failed to produce either a bold local leadership or a mass constituency. The extensive Iranian propaganda coverage among Gulf societies could not compensate for these deficiencies. As Adeed Dawisha has argued, it is the ability to draw the masses over to the revolution that renders the sponsor of that process truly effective.[64] Tehran failed to achieve this in the Gulf.

In Lebanon, Iran's activities were compromised by a different process. Iranian-inspired efforts did result in mass recruitment and terrorism. However, the Shi'a eventually factionalized and developed conflicting pro-Syrian and pro-Iranian orientations. Wavering between its revolutionary protégé in Lebanon, *Hizb Allah*, and its ally, Syria, Iran had only limited influence and effectiveness in the Lebanese area.

Iraq's revolutionary aspirations may be over, but Iran still upholds its gospel. The war efforts diluted Iran's revolutionary efforts though Tehran still spreads terrorism relentlessly. As peace negotiations proceed, the impact of an eventual termination of the war is unclear. Would an end to the fighting discourage Iran's support for terrorism or would Tehran still find this technique a useful adjunct to its diplomacy? The temptation to continue such methods to intimidate opponents will be a powerful one for Iran.

---

[64]Dawisha, op. cit., 43–44.

5

TERRORISM AS A REVOLUTIONARY STRATEGY: PERU'S *SENDERO LUMINOSO*

David Scott Palmer

Peru is a country with a long and distinguished past as center of the Inca Empire and capital of Spain's largest Vice Royalty. Rich and diverse in human and material resources, it is also a country which has had a very tentative political and economic system for most of its independent existence, limited to a small portion of the population included within its national boundaries.

Within that system, Spanish to the core, governments have ranged from personalist dictatorships to institutionalized military rule, with occasional forays into limited formal democracy, and economic policies have ranged from mercantilism to *laissez faire* to state capitalism. Outside the system, a different reality has prevailed, sometimes individualistic and entrepreneurial, often communitarian and collective, frequently Indian. The country's key development challenge in the modern period has been to meld these distinctive patterns and components in ways that enhance stability and predictability, improve access to economic and political resources, and protect core national characteristics and values in the process.

Commentary by Cynthia McClintock, Barry Rubin, Simon Serfaty, and Carlos Pareja on an earlier draft of this essay is gratefully acknowledged, as is the crucial data on elections and terrorist incidents which Sandra Woy-Hazelton and Cynthia McClintock kindly provided.

Evidence abounds that, in spite of strenuous efforts by groups and by individuals to meet this key challenge at national and local levels, inside or outside the system, the process has produced results that are often quite different. The return to formal democracy in 1980 coincided not only with virtually universal adult access to national politics, but also with increasing instability in individual lives and continued erosion in economic well-being. The modernization challenge also strained, over a long period, more traditional ways of viewing and dealing with citizen-system relationships and put increasing pressure on both Spanish and Indian core values.

From this context and into this dynamic emerged the radical alternative of development by revolution and, in due course, of revolution by terrorism.

In an effort to understand better the spiral of violence which has affected much of Peru since the early 1980s, it may be useful to distinguish between terrorist organizations and revolutionary organizations. The former see force or threats primarily as a means to demoralize and intimidate. Terrorism is by definition a terrifying act which breaks the rules of civil society and which may well accomplish its purpose by its very perpetration. Revolutionary organizations, on the other hand, carry out their activities as part of a larger effort to overthrow a government or undermine a social system. To them force or threats are generally seen as a means to accomplish a larger, longer-term goal. Such distinctions can blur in practice, of course, and considerable confusion can arise over the perpetrators' own definition of their activities. Nevertheless, the situation in Peru might most usefully be analyzed in terms of viewing the leading violent actor, *Sendero Luminoso* (SL or Shining Path), as an organization with revolutionary goals which often uses terrorist means in its quest to achieve them.

However defined and analyzed, the human and material cost to Peru of the spiral of violence over the past eight years has been staggering: from 11,000 to 15,000 deaths and an estimated $5 billion in damages.[1] This has occurred at a time of considerable economic difficulty due to high foreign debt, natural disasters, and lack of business confidence. For the ten years, 1976–1985, economic growth trailed population growth, except for a brief period in 1981–82, and real wages declined by some 35 percent to 50 percent.[2] But the violence has also developed in a political context of return to formal democratic practices, the inclusion in the system of the largest range of political actors in Peruvian history, and the coming to power of a long-standing, mass-based political party after a sixty-year struggle. Violence against the system has increased, in other words, even as that system has become more representative of the Peruvian population, more legitimate to more Peruvians, and more expressive of a reformist, middle-ground alternative.

The challenge for the analyst is to explain why this has happened. Examining the leading instigator of the violence, *Sendero Luminoso*, should give us much of the answer. One can note, for example, that the set of circumstances which gave rise to *Sendero* over a number of years was very unusual, if not unique, and contributed to a militancy, a fervor, and a conviction among both leaders and followers rarely seen in modern Latin America, much

---

[1] Foreign Broadcast Information Service (FBIS), *Latin America Daily Report*, FBIS-LAT-88-030, February, 1988, 47.

[2] Cynthia McClintock, "Democracies and Guerrillas: The Peruvian Experience," *International Policy Report*, Washington, D.C.: Center for International Policy, September 1983, 3. Washington Office on Latin America (WOLA), *Peru in Peril: The Economy and Human Rights, 1985–1987*, Washington, D.C.: WOLA, Special Report, November 1987, 7.

less in Peru.[3] Furthermore, just when this militancy threatened to turn the organization inward and narrow its base of support to core Indian areas, the *Sendero* leadership substantially altered its strategy, thereby widening the range of its activities and, conceivably, both its appeal and chances for eventual success.

The historical tension in Peru between center and periphery—between central governmental authority and local populations as well as between Indians and non-Indians—may also contribute to the persistence of violence, including that sponsored by the government itself. Much of the explanation for the spiral of violence in Peru in the 1980s may well be found in the long-standing indifference of the center to the periphery's needs (Metropolitan Lima now contains about one-third of the population, but well over two-thirds of the country's industry, electrical consumption, and government services) and in inappropriate actions by central governments reflecting ignorance and bureaucratic politics. The origins of these errors in perception and action are to be found at least in part in the long-standing cultural gulf between Spanish and Indian (approximately 35 percent of Peru's 20 million people are Quechua speaking).

Sendero Luminoso is distinctive in a number of ways. The organization developed in a small provincial university which was isolated from the concerns and perspectives of the center. It originated in a region of Peru in which the Quechua-speaking Indians comprise the vast majority of the population. It developed in a university which originally saw itself as the key instrument of modernization in one of Peru's most traditional and isolated areas. *Sendero's* leaders and members worked to bring

---

[3]David Scott Palmer, "Rebellion in Rural Peru: The Origins and Evolution of Sendero Luminoso," *Comparative Politics*, vol. 18, no. 2 (January 1986), 127–46, but especially 138.

their ideology to the Ayacucho peasantry, but often through various forms of basic assistance—from literacy to new agricultural techniques—which, unlike most radical movements, they themselves delivered. They were a good deal more patient than their Peruvian guerrilla cousins in 1965, working for some fifteen years in the Indian communities of Ayacucho to build support, rather than venturing forth impetuously and disastrously into *foco*-based armed struggle.[4] They had the luxury of being able to develop their theory of revolution in a university which they controlled for most of the period prior to launching the armed struggle in 1980, and to use the vehicle of teacher training as a major instrument for placing their cadres back into the Indian communities in key positions as literate and bilingual school teachers. Finally, they had an extremely intelligent and charismatic leader in the person of Abimael Guzmán Reynoso, with the capacity both to provide theory and strategy and to legitimate his role as the preeminent leader whom *Sendero* members would follow without question.[5]

The context within which *Sendero* evolved was also distinctive in a number of ways. The University of San Cristóbal de Huamanga in Ayacucho, which nurtured this radical group, was largely autonomous during most of the 1965–1980 period, which permitted *Sendero* to develop quite unimpeded. The Department of Ayacucho is isolated (connected to the rest of the country by a one-lane dirt road until the late 1960s), heavily rural (90 percent in 1961), and largely Indian (73 percent illiteracy in 1961). The university itself, of colonial origin, was refounded in 1959 and given the special mission of reaching out to

---

[4] Héctor Béjar, *Perú 1965: Una Experienca Guerrillera* (Lima, 1969).
[5] The author taught at the University of Huamanga in 1962 and 1963, and he shared an office with him in 1963, Guzmán's first at the university. See "Rebellion in Rural Peru," 143, for additional information on the author's personal experience in Ayacucho.

assist the largely impoverished population to become more integrated into the social, economic, and political life of the nation.[6] A plethora of modest development projects of diverse national and international sponsorships operated in the region in the 1960s, both reinforcing and moderating those undertaken by the university.[7]

For a variety of reasons, these development programs were supplanted in the 1970s by a reformist military government's agrarian reform initiatives, which employed hundreds of university graduates for a time, but which affected only a small percentage of the rural population in Ayacucho (11 percent) and inadvertently and unintentionally left most of the presumed peasant beneficiaries worse off by the end of the decade.[8] Government budget expenditures in most areas of Ayacucho actually declined from the 1960s to the 1970s, except for education.[9] The military government (1968–1980) also facilitated the development of leftist forces by introducing reformist rhetoric and initiatives, by encouraging the left through legalization of Marxist unions, and by adopting a tolerant approach to radicals in universities and elsewhere.[10] These various elements provided an environment that was

---

[6]Fernando Romero Pintado, "New Design for an Old University: San Cristóbal de Huamanga," *Américas,* December 1961, n.p.

[7]Palmer, "Rebellion in Rural Peru," 133–135.

[8]David Scott Palmer, *"Revolution from Above": Military Government and Popular Participation in Peru, 1968–1972,* Ithaca, New York, Latin American Studies Program, Cornell University, 203–227. Also Cynthia McClintock, "Peru's Sendero Luminoso Rebellion: Origins and Trajectory," in Susan Eckstein, ed., *Power and Popular Protest,* Berkeley, forthcoming—see especially p. 124 of MS and Table 2.3, "The Impact of the Agrarian Reform in Highlands Peru."

[9]Instituto Nacional de Estadística, *Censos Nacionales: VIII de Poblacion, III de Vivienda, 12 de junio de 1981,* Vol. 1, Lima, 1983, vii–xii.

[10]Among the various retrospective analyses of the reformist military government, perhaps the most comprehensive is Cythia McClintock and Abraham F. Lowenthal, eds., *The Peruvian Experiment Reconsidered,* (Princeton, New Jersey, 1983). Also David Scott Palmer, "The Changing Political Economy of Peru under Military and Civilian Rule," *Inter-American Economic Affairs,* 37 (Spring 1984): 37–62.

quite favorable for *Sendero*'s development into a full-bodied revolutionary movement.

Sendero was originally one more splinter group of a rapidly dividing left in the 1960s, whose precursors included *APRA Rebelde*, the *Movimiento Social Progresista* (MSP or Social Progressive Movement), the Trotskyite *Partido Obrero Revolucionario*, (POR-T or Revolutionary Workers' Party) and the pro-Castro *Ejército de Liberación Nacional* (ELN or National Liberation Army). After the Moscow-Peking rift of 1959–61, the *Partido Comunista del Perú* (PCP or Communist Party of Peru) also split. *Sendero* was part of the Maoist faction *Bandera Roja* (PCP-BR or Red Flag), but formally broke with the national organization in 1970 to become the *Partido Comunista del Perú en el Sendero Luminoso de Mariátegui* (PCP-SL or Communist Party of Peru in Mariátegui's Shining Path), after José Carlos Mariátegui, a leading Marxist intellectual of the 1920s and founder of the Peruvian Communist party.

By the end of the 1970s several other groups on the Marxist left had formed or had broken away, including *Vanguardia Revolucionaria* (VR or Revolutionary Vanguard), *Movimiento Institucional Revolucionario* (MIR or Institutional Revolutionary Movement), *Vanguardia Revolucionaria-Proletaria Comunista* (VC-PC or Revolutionary Vanguard-Communist Proletariat), and, among the Maoists, *Partido Comunista del Perú–Patria Roja* (PCP-PR or Communist Party of Peru–Red Flag) and *Partido Comunista del Perú–Puca Llacta* (PCP-PL or Communist Party of Peru–Red Town). To complicate matters even further, elements of each group aligned with *Sendero* between 1978 and 1982 as it moved into the armed insurrection phase.[11]

---

[11]Lewis Taylor, "Maoism in the Andes: Sendero Luminoso and the Contemporary Guerrilla Movement in Peru," Working Paper 2, Liverpool: Centre for Latin American Studies, University of Liverpool, 1983, 7.

With the return to electoral processes in 1980, much of the left coalesced into a tenuous coalition known as *Izquierda Unida* (IU or United Left), though in some cases with new names or as new factions. *Sendero* stayed away, however. Adamantly opposed to "bourgeoise electoral procedures," *Sendero* formally initiated the armed struggle with the burning of ballot boxes in the Indian community market town and district capital of Chuschi, Ayacucho, during the May 1980 presidential elections, the first since 1963.[12]

Sendero's ideology derives fundamentally from Maoist principles, as does its strategy for waging revolution and taking power.[13] It views Peru as a semi-feudal, neo-colonial society, with a bureaucratic bourgeoisie government tied to feudal landlords and the "consumption bourgeoisie" nationally, and Yankee imperialism internationally. Members see the peasantry as "the principal force of the revolution," and assert that "the popular army will be forged in the countryside." The organization is to build a Maoist four-class alliance, with peasants, workers, and parts of the petite bourgeoisie and medium-scale bourgeoisie. In addition, there is to be a protracted revolutionary war, "which could last 50 years," conducted along classical Maoist lines, in which liberated areas will be established in the countryside and gradually expanded to encircle the cities and bring about their eventual collapse. *Sendero*'s revolutionary objectives build sequentially: first, the organization seeks to convert backward areas into solid bases of revolutionary support; second, to attack symbols of the bourgeoisie state; third, to generalize violence and

---

[12]For background on this important community, see Billy Jean Isbell, *To Defend Ourselves: Economy and Ritual in an Andean Village*, Austin: Institute of Latin American Studies, University of Texas, 1978.
[13]The following discussion of ideology is derived in large part from Taylor, "Maoism in the Andes," 16–25. Also see Henry Dietz, "Sendero Luminoso: Its Generalizabilities and Ideosyncrasies," paper presented at the Sixth Annual Defense Academic Research Support Program on "Revolutionary Changes in the Third World, held in Washington, D.C., June 28–29, 1988, 8–11.

develop guerrilla war; fourth, to expand the revolutionary support bases; and finally, to lay siege to the cities and bring about the collapse of the state.[14]

The new order that *Sendero* seeks to establish in Peru is to be agrarian, based on communitarian and collectivist principles of pure communism, self-sufficient and characterized by the absence of private property, along the lines envisioned by Mao and pursued by the Gang of Four in China's Cultural Revolution of the 1960s, eventually betrayed by "revisionist elements." In *Sendero's* view, only Albania succeeded for a time in maintaining the purity of Maoist principles in practice, so that country, not China, came the closest to developing a true Maoist revolution.

A combination of factors—substantial Marxist party support in the 1978 constituent assembly elections (over 31 percent of the vote, compared to 6 percent in the 1962 presidential elections); growing control by the left of organized labor; and a surge of strike activity in the late 1970s in the face of growing economic difficulties—led *Sendero* to conclude, along with several other radical groups, that a pre-revolutionary situation existed in Peru during the 1977–1980 period. While the other Marxist groups opted for electoral politics, however, *Sendero* persisted with its preparations for beginning the revolution. These included withdrawing its cadres from the universities, where they had been concentrated. It also included moving from a strong focus on radical analysis and revolutionary theorizing to building practical field experience among adherents. Other adjustments included restructuring the party into a cell network and deepening relationships with peasant communities, particularly in the Ayacucho area. All of these were designed to prepare *Sendero* for the initiation of the armed struggle.[15]

---

[14]*Caretas* (Lima), September 20, 1982, 20–23ff.
[15]Palmer, "Rebellion in Rural Peru," 128.

Organizationally, *Sendero* divided Peru into five strategic zones, South, Central, Lima, South-West, and North, with primary emphasis in the Central zone, which includes Ayacucho, Huancayo, and Huancavelica. The central committee of *Sendero* was made up of leaders from each zone, with Abimael Guzmán Reynoso, "Comrade Gonzalo," as general secretary. Following the Chinese model of the civil war period, the membership was organized into five- to nine-person cells, each with a leader. Normally there was no contact across cells, and leaders had direct contact with no more than eight other *Sendero* members. A number of the leaders were believed to have been trained in China and North Korea, and all members received instruction in the use of firearms. As of 1981 there were an estimated 200 functioning cells, with considerable expansion since.[16]

The initial debate in *Sendero's* central committee over strategy did not question the appropriateness of pursuing armed struggle; rather it revolved around whether to follow the Chinese approach of prolonged rural guerrilla war or the Albanian strategy of armed actions in both city and countryside. The rural strategy eventually prevailed and was the dominant approach pursued by *Sendero* for the first years of the armed struggle.[17] When the central government finally responded with massive military force in the Ayacucho area at the very end of 1982, *Sendero's* strategy shifted, in part out of necessity, toward increased operations in the cities, particularly the sprawling capital of Peru. Whereas more of the reported terrorist incidents between 1980 and 1984 took place in Ayacucho than any other department (about one-third), since 1985 Lima has had the highest number (more than 30 percent of the total).[18]

---

[16]Taylor, "Maoism in the Andes," 13–16.
[17]Ibid., 12–13.
[18]McClintock, "Peru's Sendero Luminoso Rebellion," MS, 109.

The *Sendero* leadership also adapted by decentralizing its organizational structure, giving more autonomy to the regional zone committee to conduct operations.[19]

Metropolitan Lima has an estimated population approaching seven million, about one-third of the country's total. Upwards of two and one-half million have migrated there within the past ten years. Many came from poorer rural highland areas, particularly the predominantly Indian regions of the south-central and southern Andes. A large proportion of *Sendero's* recruits since 1984 have come from these "urban villager" elements.

The emergence in 1984–85 of a rival guerrilla organization, *Movimiento Revolucionario Tupac Amaru* (MRTA or Tupac Amaru Revolutionary Movement), in a new zone of conflict in the coca–growing and cocaine paste–producing Upper Huallaga River basin, gave *Sendero* another opportunity to expand. *Sendero's* leaders could justify their activities on several grounds: protecting the coca leaf grower for traditional, Indian use; challenging both the government and a rival guerrilla organization; and contributing, by helping to maintain drug supply routes, to the long-term undermining of the United States.[20]

The zonal organizational structure of *Sendero* permitted a more flexible response to the new guerrilla groups and the new zone of conflict in the Upper Huallaga valley. The North Zone Committee assumed greater importance, becoming closely involved with the coca producers in this area in competition with the MRTA, but apparently without enmeshing the rest of the *Sendero* organization

---

[19]Gabriela Tarazona-Sevillano, "The Personality of Shining Path and Narcoterrorism," Center for Strategic and International Studies (CSIS), Terrorism Seminar Paper, Washington, D.C., February 29, 1988.

[20]"Crack Secret Policy Outfit to Combat the Shining Path's New Offensive," *The Andean Report* (Lima), March 1987, 38–39.

in the drug business.[21] The government's response to the growing Upper Huallaga problem in 1984–85 was a series of military actions aimed exclusively against *Sendero*; in 1987–88 expanded efforts to displace the narco-traffickers were much more violent, difficult, and inconclusive. As one observer said, ". . . [A]nti-narcotics activity adds fuel to the insurgency. Trying to gain the support for the local inhabitants against Sendero means wooing a population that is almost entirely dependent on cocaine for a livelihood."[22]

Recent adjustments in *Sendero* strategy also include active recruitment in Lima universities previously considered "hopelessly bourgeoise," some public pronouncements, infiltration of "reactionary organizations," support for strikes, and the organization of unions and student front groups. Among the more dramatic developments are *Sendero's* first plenary session in September 1987 and the publicity given to its results; the decision to hold its first national party congress in 1988; and its May Day 1988 march down some of Lima's main avenues.[23] At least part of *Sendero's* continuing capacity to operate and even expand is the result of a good deal more flexibility in strategy and a greater ability to decentralize operations than most analysts predicted.[24]

The use of terrorism as an instrument in the strategy of revolutionary warfare to intimidate, immobilize, or neutralize is widespread. *Sendero* has adapted this instrument to its own purposes with great effect in at least three areas.

---

[21] Tarazona-Sevillano, "The Personality of Shining Path," and Tarazona-Sevillano's seminar presentation for CSIS at the International Club of Washington, February 29, 1988.

[22] "Counterinsurgency and Anti-narcotics Measures Become Intertwined in the U.S.-Financed Upper Huallaga," *The Andean Report,* June 1987, 107.

[23] Sandra Woy-Hazelton, "Peru," in *Yearbook of International Communist Affairs (YICA) 1988,* (Stanford, California, 1988) 23–24, and *Seminario SI,* May 9, 1988, 26–27.

[24] The author included. See, for example, Palmer, "Rebellion in Rural Peru," 146.

One major arena of *Sendero* terrorist activities has been within the Indian communities themselves. Of the estimated 5,600 Indian communities in Peru (2,337 recognized by the central government as of 1971), with a population probably in excess of four million, in no more than 600 does community or collective property actually predominate.[25] For the rest, private ownership, although usually limited to community members, is the norm. This means that in most communities there exists considerable economic differentation based on private property holdings. Since part of *Sendero's* objective is to restore "true" Indian communism to Peru, the leadership believes that the wealthier peasants and local petite bourgeoisie must be eliminated or reformed and their property distributed, either to other members of the community or to the community as a whole on a collective basis. Thus many of the Indian fatalities at the hands of *Sendero* have been the result of a conscious strategy to achieve their ultimate objective.

A second area has been the official sector where selective terrorist actions by *Sendero* have been directed against elected public officials with national party identification. Initially these were local officials, but more recently national figures have been targeted. During the Fernando Belaúnde Terry administration (1980–85) the targets of political assassination were mostly local district governors or municipal council members of the president's party, Acción Popular (AP or Popular Action). During the Alan García administration (1985–90), the targets have been party officials and mayors of the Alianza Popular Revolucionaria Americana (APRA) party of the president and

---

[25]CENCIRA, "Reestructuración de las Comunidades Campesinas: Las Communidades Campesinas Contemporáneas," Lima, 1970, 8; Instituto Nacional de Planificación, *Primer Censo Nacional Agropecuario,* República del Perú, July 2, 1961, Lima, 1966, 8, 13–24; and Palmer, "Revolution from Above," 143–144.

have included top local elected officials in Arequipa, Pisco, and Huanta, among others.

Another focal point of selective terrorist actions is the murder of government technicians, such as engineers and agronomists, sent to Ayacucho since 1985 to help rebuild sabotaged infrastructure and to assist in the micro-development projects to which the central government belatedly committed itself. The basic objective in both cases seems to be to demonstrate that the state cannot protect elected officials or public servants at the periphery and that a high cost may accompany any decision to run for election on a national party label or to serve the government in the contested countryside.

Sendero terrorism has also been active against state security, with the selective assassination of policemen—invariably for weapons, but also to intimidate and show *Sendero's* capacity to strike with impunity even those entrusted with the keeping of public order. The results of this terrorist strategy seem to have exceeded *Sendero's* fondest hopes. There are reports that more than 4,000 police have resigned to protest the failure of their employer, the central government, to protect them from mortal danger or provide adequate compensation.[26] This exacerbates the already acute shortage of trained police and adds to the ranks of thousands of potentially disgruntled former policemen fired or removed from their posts for alleged corruption or incompetence who could be persuaded to turn against the government they once served.[27]

By and large these various uses of terror appear to be quite consciously designed and applied to accomplish specific objectives as part of *Sendero's* revolutionary strategy. The number of deaths attributed to guerilla actions over

---

[26]FBIS, *Latin America Daily Report,* FBIS-LAT-88-105, June 1, 1988, 43–44.
[27]For background on difficult condition, underpay, and under-staffing of national police see Taylor, "Maoism in the Andes," 35–36.

several years, however unconscionable, is relatively small, suggesting considerable selectivity. For the seven years between the onset of armed violence in 1980 and 1986, some 133 civilian authorities were killed, along with 340 members of the armed forces and police. During this same period, 4,144 alleged *Senderistas* perished, as did 3,225 civilians.[28] During 1987, at least 11 important figures of the ruling APRA party were assassinated, including 8 mayors.[29]

Furthermore, although the total number of deaths attributed to subversive and countersubversive activities declined sharply in 1985–1987 from the 1984 peak before rising again in 1988 (see Table 1), the number of police and military killings actually increased from 81 in

Table 1. Deaths in Peru Attributed to Terrorist Activity

Year	Total	Military	Police	Peasants	Terrorists
1980	12				
1981	82				
1982	93				
1983	1,977				
1984	3,587				
1985	1,476	31	45	770	630
1986	1,451	28	91	448	884
1987	1,115	53	137	584	341
1988	1,490	138	137	817	398

(Source: DESCO [Centro de Estudios y Promoción de Desarrollo], *Resumen Semanal*, compiled by Sandra Woy-Hazelton)

---

[28]Thomas G. Sanders, "Peru: Alan García's First Two Years," *UFSI Reports,* 1987 #12 Latin America (Indianapolis: University Field Staff International, 1987), 7. Other figures are higher. For example, Cynthia McClintock, "Peru's Sendero Luminoso Rebellion," MS, 109, quotes various *Caretas* reports of 283 civilian authorities and 568 security personnel killed.

[29]Sandra Woy-Hazelton, "Peru," *YICA 1987* (Stanford, 1988), 25.

1984 to 190 in 1987, and 275 in 1988.[30] This indicates both the growing involvement of the police and armed forces in the anti-terrorist campaign and the conscious strategy of *Sendero* to target such officials for their weapons and to avenge their own losses.

Even though *Sendero* terrorist activities do not appear, on the whole, to be random, wanton, or indiscriminate, excesses by *Sendero* have occurred, primarily in rural areas. Reported incidents include revenge on specific communities for insufficient support, for participating in government-organized militias, or against alleged government informers. These excesses can reasonably be expected to reduce local support for *Sendero*; most occurred after the military's stepped-up presence in 1983 in the Ayacucho-Huancavelica-Apurímac Emergency Zone, which affected considerably *Sendero*'s original strategy of gradual expansion of its support bases in the area. This combination of massive military presence (perhaps as many as 7,000 troops and police) and *Sendero* misdeeds may well have changed active local support to passive acquiesence in a substantial number of communities.[31]

Electoral data for Ayacucho strongly suggest retention of a popular base open to *Sendero* influence, although it is unclear whether this reflects active support or acquiescence by fear. In the 1983 municipal elections, for example, more than 75 percent of those eligible in Ayacucho's Huamanga province did not vote or spoiled their ballots, as *Sendero* directed. (The victor was a small, left, independent party, known by its acronym, PADIN.) While this

---

[30]Sanders, "Peru," p. 7 for 1984 figure. DESCO *Resumen Semanal*, compiled by Sandra Woy-Hazelton, for 1987 and 1988 figures. Due to different sources for different figures totals may not add exactly. For example, DESCO figures on military and police deaths are higher than those presented in Sanders "Peru," but lower than those from official sources.

[31]"Spread of Guerrilla Activity Makes Police Reform a Priority," *The Andean Report*, June 1985, 94.

figure declined to 47 percent for the whole department of Ayacucho in the 1985 presidential elections, it increased to 64 percent in municipal elections held in 1986. The 1985 decline may be explained largely by new electoral procedures, of which the most important was a new electoral register. By replacing the register in effect for more than 20 years, since the presidential elections of 1962 and 1963, inaccuracies stemming from death or nonvoting due to change of residence far from the location of the original registration were sharply reduced.[32] Nonvoting or ballot spoiling in 1985, then, may well have been more purposeful even though lower. It probably cannot be attributed to a decline in support for *Sendero* among the Ayacucho population.

In comparative terms, the Ayacucho abstention or spoiled ballot totals for both the 1985 presidential election and the 1986 municipal elections were the highest of any department in Peru, with neighboring Huancavelica and Apurímac, also in the Emergency Zone and part of *Sendero's* core area of operations, very close behind. Looked at another way, just 25 percent of registered voters in Ayacucho supported Alan García and victorious APRA in 1985, and only 20 percent went for APRA in Ayacucho in the 1986 municipal elections.[33] This suggests the weakness of the center and the frail legitimacy of the electoral process in the Ayacucho heartland of *Sendero*, and may also indicate the considerable influence which *Sendero* retains there in spite of its penchant for violence.

---

[32]"The APRA Received More Votes Than All Other Candidates Together," *The Andean Report,* May 1985, 73.

[33]The 1983 electoral data is reported in FBIS, *Latin America,* November 14, 1983, J4–J5. The 1985 and 1986 data is reported in Fernando Tuesta Soldevilla, *Perú político en cifras,* Lima: Fundación Federico Ebert 1987, Tables 5.2 and 6.2, 192 and 200. Totals for all three elections include abstentions, blank ballots cast, and spoiled ballots cast.

Military or official terrorism also helps to win support for *Sendero*. Such actions appear to have been substantial in the Ayacucho area since 1981, but especially during the first eighteen months after the region was declared an Emergency Zone at the end of 1982. According to newspaper accounts, the number of deaths attributed to the violence increased almost forty-fold between 1982 and 1984 (see Table 1 on page 143). Almost two-thirds of the killings that resulted from *Sendero* and counter-guerrilla activity in 1983 occurred in the provinces of the Emergency Zone (4 in Ayacucho, 2 in Apurímac, and 3 in Huancavelica; expanded to 6, 2, and 5 respectively in 1984) many of them apparently the result of a massive and indiscriminate military response.[34]

Over 1,000 documented cases of disappearances after detention by government forces in the Emergency Zone were reported from January 1983 through September 1984, along with the discovery of scores of bodies in at least 15 unmarked graves and dumping grounds.[35] In spite of official military denials, the suspicion was that most of these grisly findings were individuals executed by the armed forces themselves. Evidence was later presented which provided conclusive proof of military or police complicity in some cases. In only one case, however, were measures initiated, in 1984, after extensive journalistic scrutiny, to submit the individuals involved to judicial proceedings.[36]

Since the number of deaths and disappearances during this period far exceeded official estimates of *Sendero* militants, one can only conclude that the military and police were quite brutal in their efforts to restore order and central government authority to the region. This may have

---

[34]*Caretas,* July 9, 1984, 11.
[35]Amnesty International, *Peru Briefing,* London, 1985, 1.
[36]Ibid., 2–9.

been due in part to poor intelligence, as well as to overlapping and conflicting jurisdictions between the different armed services and the police. It is also likely that many of the excesses were exacerbated by the historic tensions between the capital and the countryside and by the cultural and ethnic gulf between the mostly Indian periphery and the armed enforcers of the Spanish center.

However brutal the means employed, one result desired by authorities was accomplished: *Sendero*'s capacity to operate in its original heartland was sharply curtailed. Another consequence of those actions, both unintended and undesirable, was *Sendero*'s shift in operations to other areas of Peru. This resulted in a sharp increase in activity in such places as Lima, Puno, San Martín (the Upper Huallaga), Huánuco, and Cerro de Pasco. Attacks in Lima, for example, increased from 38 in 1980 to 834 in 1986.[37] Far from being defeated, *Sendero* was merely displaced.

Sendero's continuing ability to carry out operations and sow selective terror in defiance of the massive military and police response seemed to encourage other groups inclined to violence. In 1984 the *Movimiento Revolucionario Tupac Amaru*, identified with the goals and strategies of the Cuban revolution, began organized actions directed against the government, the U.S. embassy, and selected foreign businesses. At first MRTA operated almost exclusively in Lima. Subsequently, they carried out a number of quite dramatic operations in the cocaproducing Upper Huallaga valley, including the temporary occupations of such important towns as Tocache. *Sendero*, not to be outdone, also expanded its activities in the region. The direct competition between *Sendero* and MRTA produced a number of violent confrontations in the valley from 1986 onward, with *Sendero* establishing dominance by the end of 1988. Like *Sendero*, MRTA gained

---

[37]Sanders, "Peru," *UFSI Reports,* 7.

notoriety through its bombings and armed confrontations with military and police authorities; unlike *Sendero*, MRTA eschewed assassinations and worked to evoke a sympathetic response among some of the elements of the *Izquierda Unida* coalition in spite of IU's continuing commitment to electoral politics.[38]

The steady annual increase in terrorist incidents reflects the capacity of first *Sendero* and then MRTA to continue to harass the government in spite of large efforts to contain them (see Table 2). This rise in terrorist incidents suggests that *Sendero*'s activities have gradually given a perverse legitimacy to radical violence; the growth of the MRTA since 1984 is one clear indication of this, as are the growing signs in Peru of connections between guerrilla groups and drug producers and traffickers.[39] *Sendero*'s "contagion" very likely also influenced any number of nonpolitical criminal elements to adopt some of the same tactics, contributing further to the marked increases in violence and illegal activities recorded during the period. Official figures indicate that 574,393 individuals were arrested in Peru from 1985 through early 1988 for various crimes, almost 3 percent of the country's total population.[40]

The García administration took office in July 1985 committed to new initiatives to try to stem the terrorist-guerrilla problem in Peru. These included the establishment of a peace commission to make contact with *Sendero*, establish a dialogue, and work toward mutually satisfactory approaches towards reducing armed confrontations. It was hoped that, by taking *Sendero* seriously, some kind of ceasefire and amnesty, along the lines of the Venezuelan government success with the 1960s guerrilla movement there might eventually be worked out. But

---

[38]Woy-Hazelton, "Peru," *YICA 1987,* 27.
[39]Tarazona-Sevillano, "The Personality of Shining Path," *passim.*
[40]*Caretas,* May 9, 1988, 33.

Table 2. Terrorist Incidents in Peru, 1980–1987

Year	Incidents
1980	219
1981	715
1982	891
1983	1,123
1984	1,760
1985	2,050
1986	3,731
1987	4,039
1988	4,446

(Sources: 1980–1985, Ministry of the Interior, cited in Gordon H. McCormick, "The Shining Path and Peruvian Terrorism," RAND/P-7297, January 1987. 1986–1988, DESCO, *Resumen Semanal*, compiled by Sandra Woy-Hazelton and adjusted by the author. Media-reported incidents in 1985 were about one-third of ministry figures—695 DESCO, 2,050 Ministry—so 1986–1988 DESCO figures are multiplied by three in the absence of official ministry data for these years.

Sendero consistently rejected the peace commission's overtures and steadfastly refused to negotiate.[41]

Commission members resigned (and the commission itself was eventually disbanded) after the *Sendero* prison riots of June 1986 provoked a massive military reaction sanctioned by the president and the cabinet in which 279 prisoners were killed, including every *Sendero* prisoner in Lurigancho Prison, 100 of them after surrendering.[42] Although President García himself promised to investigate the incident and punish severely those responsible, no action was taken beyond accepting a number of resignations. More than a year later, the hard-hitting recommendations of the investigative commission headed by IU Senator Rolando Ames were shelved and an APRA

---

[41]Sanders, "Peru," *UFSI Report*, 7–8.
[42]Ibid. He reports 234 deaths. The 279 figure is Sandra Woy-Hazelton's compilation, from DESCO, *Resumen Semanal*.

summary report absolving the government passed the Congress in a late night session.[43] Meanwhile, *Sendero* proceeded to follow through on its promise to kill 10 APRA officials for every martyred *Senderista*.

The García administration also attempted to address problems of corruption, human rights violations, and terrorist intelligence-gathering weaknesses in the police and military by firing a large number of police officials, reorganizing the military commands, consolidating the three services into a single ministry of defense, and forging one centralized intelligence agency from the eight which had previously existed. Police resentment spilled over into a police strike in May 1987 which lasted four days and resulted in trials for 383 and the sacking of 39 officers, including the heads of the Republican and Civil Guards.[44]

Streamlined intelligence operations did appear to produce some results, including the breaking up of several *Sendero* cells in Lima, more precise military actions against guerrillas in Ayacucho and the Upper Huallaga, and, in June 1988, the dramatic capture of *Sendero*'s elusive second-in-command, Osmán Morote.[45] This operation also produced the first conclusive evidence that *Sendero*'s top leader, Abimael Guzmán, was still alive and actively directing the organization.[46] President García's efforts to address official abuses of authority also produced some positive results according to human rights reports, with a substantial decline in offenses recorded through 1987.[47] "In comparison with the Belaúnde years,"

[43]Woy-Hazelton, "Peru," *YICA 1987*, 19.
[44]Ibid., 15.
[45]*Washington Times*, June 14, 1988, 2.
[46]FBIS, *Latin America Daily Report* LAT-88-123, June 27, 1988, 39–40. In July 1988, Guzmán gave an extensive clandestine interview to the director of *El Diario*, Luis Arce Borja, published July 24, 1988.
[47]Department of State, "Peru," *Country Reports on Human Rights Practices for 1985*, submitted to the Committee on Foreign Affairs, House of Representatives and the Committee on Foreign Relations, U.S. Senate, February 1986, 664 and *passim*. Also 1986 Report, submitted February 1987, 614.

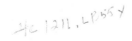

it was noted, "there has been a decline in the number of of reported disappearances and extrajudicial executions in the emergency zones, though such abuses do continue. When Belaúnde left office, an average of 600 cases of disappearances a year were being reported; over the last two years that has declined to between 100 and 150."[48] In addition, the APRA government has placed more emphasis on economic assistance to the impoverished regions of the Emergency Zone, has helped achieve an increase in national agricultural production, and followed economic policies, however controversial internationally, which contributed to national growth rates of 8.5 percent in 1986 and 7 percent in 1987, the best since the early 1970s. Developments in 1988 were not heartening, however. Inflation increased to over 1,700 percent, highest in Peruvian history, and the economy declined by at least 10 percent overall. In addition, the number of incidents and deaths attributed to terrorist activity increased substantially, as did reports of government human rights abuses. This combination of trends further undermined President Garcia's government (a year-end poll showed that a bare 4 percent of the population supported the president); not surprisingly, rumors of a *golpe* (coup) were again rampant in early 1989.

In principle, a reformist government such as that now in Peru should be the best antidote to a terrorist or guerrilla threat. A political context which gives openings to the Marxist left should also help defuse an active insurgency situation. The paradox of contemporary Peru is that while the political system was opened and economic conditions were temporarily improved, *Sendero* still managed to expand, other movements inaugurated guerrilla activities, and popular confidence in the government's

---

[48]WOLA, *Peru in Peril*, 26.

capacity to control the situation has eroded.[49] Peru is far from being on the verge of a guerrilla takeover, but it seems just as far from being able to provide the dynamic equilibrium and security sought so avidly by central authorities and the general population alike.

---

[49]President Garcia's approval ratio fell from 70 percent early in his term to 34 percent by June 1987. Woy-Hazelton, "Peru," *YICA 1987*, 9. A survey conducted in April–May 1988 found 15 percent who thought "the subversives" might win, compared with 4 percent who held this opinion a year earlier. FBIS, *Latin American Daily Report* LAT-88-105, June 1, 1988, 43.

6

GOVERNMENT AND OPPOSITION TERRORISM IN SOUTH AFRICA

Herbert M. Howe

In 1987 and 1988 South Africa had a partial and temporary respite from the violence and terror of 1984–86. Yet South Africa may soon face a significant upswing in violence that could further polarize black and white forces and enlarge terrorist groupings. If the violence is not contained, it could plague the majority-rule negotiations that eventually will take place or cripple any new government that results from such negotiations.

"Terrorism" is the deliberate use of physical violence against noncombatants for political ends. It is not easy to characterize the nature of terrorist groups or organizations. Both states and sub-national groups can practice terrorism. Nor is it a simple matter to define the targets of terrorism. Who, in a given situation, are the combatants? And, who are the noncombatants? Also, how can we be sure that the victims of any act or series of acts are the *intended* targets? Yet, the basic distinction is clear: terrorism is distinguished from other forms of political violence by having noncombatants as its specific targets.

Both the South African government and—to a much smaller degree—such opposition groups as the African National Congress (ANC) have committed acts of terrorism. The perpetrators cannot be neatly divided along clear racial lines because there are white terrorists who fight for the ANC and black terrorists who fight for the South African government. Yet, the underlying causes of much of the terrorism can be traced to South Africa's fundamental racial conflict. It will be impossible to contain the growth of terrorism in South Africa without first addressing that country's institutionalized racism.

Terrorism is used by specific forces on both sides of the conflict: the South African security establishment, black vigilantes sometimes allied with the government, and reactionary white paramilitary groups one side and the ANC's *Umkhonto We Sizwe* (Spear of the Nation) and the urban "comrades" on the other.

The South African Defence Force (SADF) has used substantial violence and terrorist tactics when entering the neighboring frontline states in search of purported ANC terrorists. And the South African government has aided insurgencies, notably in Angola and Mozambique, both of which have often resorted to terrorism.

Police and army officials in black townships have shot and tortured numerous people. Like the losing forces in colonial Mozambique and Rhodesia who employed inadequate white manpower against rising black protest, the South African government has exploited splits among blacks by increasingly supporting "black on black" terrorism and violence. Through devolution of responsibility to township and homeland governments, the South African government has reduced its own administrative presence and made black officials the target of black rage.

The South African government must also contend with non-sanctioned terrorism committed by conservative whites opposed to the "sellout" policies of the Nationalist party. Through such paramilitary groups as the *Afrikaner Weerstand Bewiging* (AWB), whites have carried the struggle into black areas, against liberal whites, and even against government officials.

The ANC has benefited from its resolve to use only limited violence and to de-emphasize terrorism over the last twenty-five years. Yet, the ANC faces increased internal pressure from black youth in the townships to be more aggressive. Frustrated by continued repression and slow government change, they want the ANC to expand its military operations from attacking physical installations or security personnel to "soft" civilian targets. Beginning in early 1988, suspected ANC bombings in South Africa killed larger numbers of innocent civilians. The unemployed and sometimes nihilistic township youth often beyond the control of the ANC or the United Democratic Front (UDF), have displayed a terrifying and arbitrary brutality.[1]

Despite the present lull in violence, South Africa's various political groupings could create a mutually reinforcing escalation and force South Africa to enter a terroristic "Peoples War" or an "African Lebanization" process fought by white civilians and the military against a similar black combination. The West has a limited but important role in lessening South African terrorism.

The South African Government

Violence by the South African government, some of which can be considered terrorism, stretches beyond its own borders. Since the late 1970s, the South African government of P.W. Botha has mounted its "total strategy" against a perceived "total onslaught" from internal and foreign foes. Regional military destabilization is a major component of the total strategy and aims, at least partially, to avert any external military threat to South Africa.

---

[1] Founded in August 1983, the United Democratic Front is an umbrella organization of some 700 organizations comprising two million members. Much of its leadership, philosophy, and methods are similar to those of the ANC.

The SADF has entered Mozambique, Botswana, Zambia, and Zimbabwe at least eight times and killed 150 people. Yet over a period of almost ten years, South Africa's direct military involvement in these countries has remained sporadic.

The SADF's actions in Angola, where South African forces have been engaged almost continuously during the 1980s, have, however, inflicted numerous civilian casualties. The SADF is ostensibly in Angola to combat the Namibian Southwest Africa People's Organization (SWAPO) whose rebels use Angola for sanctuary. The SADF's level of professionalism usually precludes it from singling out civilian targets, although individual South African units, notably the Thirty-Second Battalion in Angola and the *Koevoet* ("Crowbar") unit in Namibia, have often been accused of terrorism. The South African government justifies its regional intervention as necessary to prevent future domestic terrorism—invoking a sovereign nation's right to self-defense against a terrorism-prone foe. However, by defining terrorism broadly as any activity likely "to endanger the maintenance of law and order"[2] in South Africa, the government unilaterally enlarges the scope of justifiable targets. Since the government can thus consider as supporters of terrorism the noncombatants actively aiding SWAPO or the ANC, it would argue that actions against these noncombatants do not constitute terrorism.

The South African government has aided insurgent groups in the region, notably UNITA (the National Union for the Total Independence of Angola) in Angola and RENAMO (Mozambican National Resistance Movement) in Mozambique. These groups are partially responsible for the deaths of more than 200,000 civilians. Angola has the world's largest percentage of civilian amputees, caused

---

[2]*South Africa: A Country Study* (Washington, D.C., 1981), 243.

largely by mines planted by UNITA. In Mozambique, RENAMO has acquired a reputation for widespread terrorism. In August 1988 the U.S. Department of State reported that "the level of violence reported to be conducted by RENAMO against the civilian population of rural Mozambique is extraordinarily high. . . . It is conservatively estimated that 100,000 civilians may have been murdered by RENAMO."[3] South Africa is partially responsible for these actions because it apparently still supports RENAMO, despite a 1984 nonaggression pact between South Africa and Mozambique. Although the Angolan and Mozambican government troops have occasionally employed terrorism, most observers believe that UNITA and especially RENAMO are more culpable.

Internationally, alleged "hit squads" have attacked exiled ANC activists, most notably the Paris representative Dulcie September in March 1988 and lawyer Albie Sachs in April 1988. The South African government attributes these assassinations or attempts to divisions within the ANC. Government critics contend that an organization known as Z-Squads International carries out these operations for South Africa's National Intelligence Service. INTERPOL has issued an arrest warrant for a former South African diplomat and policeman for the murder of Dulcie September.

Internally, the difficulty that the government experienced in quelling the protests that began in September 1984 persuaded it to beef up supporting manpower, to take measures to reduce white fatalities, and to weaken black forces by assisting groups engaged in black-on-black violence.

---

[3]Robert Gersony, "Summary of Mozambican Refugee Accounts of Principally Conflict-Related Experience in Mozambique," Bureau for Refugee programs, Department of State, April 1988, 41.

The government's involvement in direct terrorism includes unjustified, often unreported, shootings and torture on a scale greater than that of its black opposition. Since August 1984, 3,000 blacks have been killed, and the government is directly responsible for perhaps 40 percent of these deaths. While some physical force may be justified, notably for self-defense, the security forces have repeatedly crossed the line from force to terrorism. For example, live ammunition is too frequently used against protesters.

On March 23, 1985, at Langa in the Eastern Cape, police killed twenty blacks. The government later paid $650,000 to resolve civil claims in what legal experts said was equivalent to an admission of liability. The *New York Times* characterized such out-of-court settlements as almost routine, serving to minimize "courtroom exposures of police interrogation, torture and negligence." A commission of inquiry found "that the stone attacks as described by [officer] Fouche and his men were a falsification in order to justify the killing."[4]

Since 1985, the government has arrested 25,000 citizens. Section 29 of the Internal Security Act allows minors to be detained and held incommunicado indefinitely with little recourse to the courts. The state has reportedly tortured many of the detainees.[5]

The government has increased its police and army forces in the townships, as is strongly reflected in budgetary increases. A recent addition to its forces has been the *kitskonstabels*, or "quick policemen." The *kitskonstabels* are blacks, many of them being "turned" (former) comrades. Their lack of formal education and training has

---

[4]"Pretoria Will Pay $650,000 to 51 For Shootings By Police in 1985," *New York Times*, August 19, 1987.
[5]See, for example, "South Africa 1986: A Permanent State of Emergency," Southern Africa Project of the Lawyers' Committee for Civil Rights Under Law, Washington, D.C., 1986.

induced many of them to engage in terrorist acts against township residents. Six hundred seven disciplinary actions were filed against the 6,137 *kitskonstables* in Transvaal, within the unit's first year.

The introduction or growth of what several observers call "death squads" is a possible new development. Evidence is lacking to support some accusations, but state security men in mufti have been linked to physical beatings of civic activists. In one,case, an apparent hit squad, code named Group 16 and comprised of army personnel, abducted and assaulted a Duduza Civic Association member.[6]

The best-known case of black-on-black violence has arisen in Natal province, where the predominantly Zulu *Inkatha* organization and its paramilitary *impis*, or warrior regiments, have been fighting the UDF. By late March 1988, blacks had killed 600 other blacks in Natal, most in Pietermaritzburg. The Natal-based *Inkatha*, while proclaiming its support for a black-led South Africa, differs from the ANC and the UDF. *Inkatha* promotes a single ethnic-geographic unit and a pro-capitalist South Africa. In part, the struggle of *Inkatha* versus the UDF and other competitors is one where the rural past meets the proletarian future—a traditionalist peasant-based reaction against modern industrial South Africa. The struggle is also one of entrenched black commercial and government elites against sometimes well-educated but politically disadvantaged people. Advertised as a moderate black organization, *Inkatha* has often resorted to violence against totally innocent civilians. In return, according to South African sociologist Fatima Meer, UDF violence is "as personalized and brutal as that of *Inkatha*. The dictate 'two eyes for one' prevails."[7]

---

[6]"A Diary Lost At Kidnap Site Leads Trail to . . . Army HQ," *Weekly Mail*, February 17, 1988.
[7]Fatima Meer, "Violence in South Africa—Some Forms and Some Causes," unpublished manuscript, 17.

Substantial violence between *Inkatha* and the UDF began in 1985. At the memorial service for UDF activist Victoria Mxenge, herself a victim of black terrorism, *Inkatha* apparently killed nineteen mourners. In retribution, *Umkhonto* placed a limpet mine at an *Inkatha*-frequented Durban hotel and injured thirty children. The UDF's growing popularity, especially among educated and urbanized Zulus, sparked a coercive *Inkatha* membership drive to which UDF partisans responded in kind. In January 1987 *Inkatha* killed (with automatic weapons) twelve UDF members. In October 1987 UDF followers trapped thirteen *Inkatha* members in a Kwashange house and set it ablaze. Those who fled certain death inside were slain outside.

Some observers worry that the Natal, specifically the Pietermaritzburg, violence appears relatively independent of the top *Inkatha* command and that it could take on a life of its own. Meer claims that the "Central *Inkatha* Committee appeared to have lost all control. . . . The organization [of violence] is highly localized and each local 'war lord' appears to operate according to his own dictates. . . . [Violence has] become a sort of sport."[8] UDF-related bands have also shown themselves to be resistant to central control. And there is growing fear that the South African government may grant *Inkatha* chief Buthelezi's Kwazulu homeland more police power by offering de jure or, more likely, de facto incorporation of Pietermaritzburg.

Although Buthelezi cautioned against violence in December 1987, *Inkatha* and the UDF have failed in several truce attempts. By mid-1988, terrorism had declined somewhat in Pietermaritzburg, and one hopes that the visions of men like Thomas Shabalala, an *impis* commander, will never be realized. "I long for the day," Shabalala once remarked, "when there will be open war

---

[8]Ibid., 16.

vs the UDF and *Inkatha*. I will leave hundreds of UDF supporters dead on the battlefield."[9]

The conflict between vigilantes (known as "fathers") and the comrades (or *maqabane*) forms a second nexus of often terroristic violence. Backed by the town councilors in the cities and the homeland leaders in the rural areas, the vigilantes enjoy varying degrees of popular support. In 1985, township terrorism by the youths angered many innocent residents—some of whom began to fight back. The vigilantes tend to be older, have stronger rural ties, and are more conservative than the younger, urbanized comrades.

During May 1986, in Crossroads, outside of Capetown, the vigilantes left 30,000 homeless and, in June 1986, razed 70 percent of a squatter settlement and left 70,000 homeless. In rural areas, they have served government objectives by attacking opponents of homeland "independence." In 1986 the forced incorporation of largely non-Ndebele Moutse into the KwaNdebele homeland triggered Moutse anger. In response, vigilantes in the presence of senior KwaNdebele officials "viciously thrashed" 400 presumed opponents of incorporation and shortly thereafter killed 19 KwaNdebele opponents of independence.[10]

The vigilantes are sometimes financed by homeland leaders who have encouraged terrorism against civilians whom they perceive to be opponents to their rule. In August 1983 the Ciskeian government unilaterally raised bus fares. Ciskeians protested by boycotting buses. The government responded with terrorism, and in one incident, the Ciskeian Defence Force fired on train commuters. Shortly thereafter, many bus boycotters and other

---

[9]Quoted in Steven Davis, *Apartheid's Rebels* (New Haven, 1987), 109.
[10]Nicholas Haysom, *Apartheid's Private Army: The Rise of Right-Wing Vigilantes In South Africa,* Occasional Paper No. 10, Center For Applied Legal Studies, University of the Witwatersrand, 1986, 71.

perceived troublemakers were taken to a football stadium where many were brutally tortured. Former life-president of Ciskei Lennox Sebe stated that "potential insurgents should expect to be tortured."[11]

The conflicts of the Zulu-based *Inkatha* or the conservative vigilantes against the UDF and the comrades have some indigenous causes. These conflicts are not solely instigated by the South African government. Nicholas Haysom, author of *Apartheid's Private Army*, points to the "intense hostilities between groups and political factions which have competing aspirations"[12] and observes that the terrorism of township youth in 1985 and 1986 angered many older residents. In addition, some of the violence is the result of preliminary jockeying for power in the new South Africa, whether between *Inkatha* and the UDF or between the UDF and black-consciousness organizations.

Yet the South African government has exacerbated the terrorism by aiding both *Inkatha* and the vigilantes. The two states of emergency, which severely restricted the activities of the UDF and other groups, were not applied to them. According to Haysom, this special treatment apparently convinced many vigilantes that the government approved of their activities. If they needed more evidence, the government sometimes supplied transportation, intelligence, access to troubled areas, limited weaponry and perhaps, on occasion, police uniforms. In court testimony about the destruction of the squatter camp, a doctor testified that "it was clear the role of any peacekeeping force would be to try and stop the aggressors. However I didn't once see the police try to stop them [the vigilantes]. On the contrary it seemed they were assisting them."[13] Just

---

[11]*London Sunday Times*, November 24, 1985, quoted in Haysom, 57.
[12]Haysom, 100.
[13]"I Watched A Man Burn In Tent While Police Stood By," *Weekly Mail*, November 6–12, 1987.

before the trial was to have begun on August 8, 1987, the minister of law and order stated that he no longer wished to contest the case and that the state would pay costs.

Empowered by the South African government, the township and the homeland governments both used force, sending either the *impis* or the vigilantes against groups that threatened their authority and sometimes their lives. South African police often stood by or actively assisted during some of these operations. The vigilantes' effectiveness was obvious. Writing about Leandra, a shanty town in the eastern Transvaal, Haysom notes, "What the might of the police and the intrigues of the development board could not achieve in five years [to reduce opposition to the government] has been accomplished in two months by vigilante violence."[14]

The South African government made black officials the targets of antiapartheid wrath by increasing their responsibility—although not their financial ability— through such legislation as the Black Local Authorities Act of 1982. One responsibility increased was financial self-sufficiency. The authorities' increasing of rents during a prolonged economic recession helped trigger the unrest that began in September 1984. Wide-scale violence between the government and protesters continued for at least two years and the most readily available official targets were the local black officials.

The advantages of such terrorism for the government are that it further divides black opposition, requires fewer white security personnel (and causes fewer white casualties), confuses the issue internationally, absolves the government from charges of terrorism, and sparks the whites' worst fears of majority government. Some observers wonder whether the government may also have encouraged such violence hoping that the UDF, which has

---

[14]Haysom, 46.

generally articulated nonviolence, may adopt violence and thus invite further government repression.

Support for the *impis*, the vigilantes, and local govern-ment officials is one expression of the government's farm-ing out of security responsibility. Such contractors and their families thereby face possible reprisal. Another pos-sible target for reactive violence could be the business community, which the government would like to recruit for security purposes. The National Key Points Act re-quires owners of strategic facilities to provide security for the installations. The legislation also grants police power—including the use of arms—to employees at these key points. Recently, the Joint Management Centers, in which businessmen work with the disliked township coun-cils and security forces, have publicly aligned more civilians with perceived government repression. The government, facing a rent shortfall of one billion rand (half a billion dollars) from rent-boycotting urban dwellers has also considered ordering businesses to de-duct from workers' wages any rent that they owe in ar-rears. Should business increasingly aid the government, activist blacks would picture it as an agent of South African repression and could take action against the businesses.

The Joint Management Centers illustrate a relative-ly peaceful means of fighting terrorism and violence. The centers discover and mediate local grievances through substantial communication and spending on social ser-vices. Special attention is paid to such potential hot spots as the Mamelodi and Alexandra townships. The govern-ment hopes that timely economic assistance will forestall black political violence.

Not all white terrorism comes from the state. Reac-tionary whites fearing a Botha sellout have increasingly enlarged their vigilante potential. The AWB, until recently a fringe group, doubled its membership in 1986. Members or sympathizers of AWB have so far limited themselves to random violence against blacks or the disruption of major Nationalist party rallies. The AWB is consistently rumored to have substantial support within the security forces, notably the police, and the potential for terrorism is apparent. Chief Buthelezi worries about the liberation forces provoking the AWB to engage "in sabotage and killing which would make the ANC's best look like amateurish bungling."[15] An AWB paramilitary trainer stated recently that the AWB's combat training will be needed "during the chaos of the coming revolution."[16] Just as white government violence in the early 1960s forced a black violent response, terrorism from private whites could step up the level of terrorism by prompting a black response.

The African National Congress

The ANC has a largely undeserved reputation for terrorism. Prime Minister Margaret Thatcher, at the 1987 Vancouver Commonwealth meeting, termed it a "typically terrorist organization."[17] More predictably, General Magnus Malan, South Africa's minister of defense told the South African parliament, "The ANC, as you know full well, is a Marxist-controlled terrorist organization. It acts across international borders—against all our inhabitants indiscriminately, blindly, and regardless of age, sex, or color...."[18] Many students of the ANC believe, however, that the group was forced to use violence, that it has renounced terrorism, and that the purpose of its violence

---

[15]"Buthelezi Slams Tambo's Insults," *Windhoek Advertiser*, March 24, 1988, reproduced in *Facts and Reports*, April 22, 1988, 6.
[16]"Far Right Afrikaners Won English Recruits," *London Sunday Times*, October 25, 1987.
[17]Thatcher, quoted in "Britain Boycotts Opening of ANC's Conference," *Independent*, December 2, 1987.
[18]Malan, quoted in Barry Streek, "Preparing For War," *Africa Report*, March–April, 1986, 23.

is not to overthrow the state but to force it to negotiate with the black majority.

Historically, the ANC has proved a most reluctant dragon. From its creation in 1912, the ANC has largely been a nontribal organization of blacks promoting black rights. Its tactics of constitutionalism and peaceful petition reflected the ANC's Christian middle-class origin and membership and an assumption that black groups could persuade the white government to make changes. For forty-eight years, until the Sharpeville killings in 1960, it persevered in nonviolent strategies.

In 1944, Nelson Mandela and others formed the Youth League within the ANC. In 1949, the year after the Nationalist party gained control of South Africa, Youth League members gained control of the ANC. Despite the Youth League's anger, compounded by the implementation of apartheid in the early 1950s, the ANC increased only its militancy while forswearing violence. The Defiance Campaign against the pass laws greatly expanded the ANC's following and membership but did not lessen the tide of apartheid legislation, and the government cracked down on the ANC. Between 1956 and 1961, the government tried 156 activists for "treason." Although the courts eventually acquitted all of the activists, the government's legal system successfully neutralized much of the black leadership during that period.

Events at Sharpeville, outside Johannesburg, on March 23, 1960, changed South Africa's political topography. South African policemen panicked when confronted by a noisy but peaceful protest and killed 69 blacks and wounded 270 others. On April 8, 1960, the government banned both the ANC and its offshoot, the Pan-Africanist Congress (PAC). Fourteen months later, in June 1961, the ANC formed its military wing, *Umkhonto We Sizwe*. In February 1962, *Umkhonto*, led by Nelson Mandela, initiated its first attack.

Four points about *Umkhonto's* early history are crucial: (1) the ANC was reluctant to create a violent organization; (2) it determined that whatever violence it employed should be nonterroristic; (3) it took the view that violence must be a secondary means to supplement a basically political struggle; and (4) the ANC hoped that its limited violence could serve a peaceful purpose by persuading the government to accept changes lest greater violence ensue. The ANC chose limited violence as one of its means of achieving a political—not military—settlement. Prolonged terrorism would prove difficult for the ANC and the government to control, not only before but also after the introduction of black majority rule. It would escalate casualties and, by embittering all parties, could complicate negotiations. Terrorism would cause both a flight of skilled whites and widespread destruction to South Africa's physical assets. Finally, terrorism runs counter to the ANC's conciliatory and nonracist concepts, as expressed in the 1955 Freedom Charter, which states that South Africa belongs to all of its citizens.

During his trial in April 1964, Mandela noted that "we shrank from any action which might drive the races further apart than they already were. But the hard facts were that fifty years of nonviolence had brought the African people nothing but more and more repressive legislation and fewer and fewer rights."[19] Faced with four possible methods of violence—sabotage, guerrilla warfare, terrorism, and open revolution—Mandela continued, the ANC selected sabotage and determined "to exhaust it before taking any other decision. . . . On no account were they [ANC soldiers] to injure or kill people."[20]

---

[19]Mandela, "I Am Prepared To Die," in David Mermelstein, *The Anti-Apartheid Reader* (New York, 1987), 222.
[20]Ibid.

Between June 1961 and July 1963, 194 "scattershot" operations took place at communication-transport facilities, fuel dumps, and government buildings. On July 11, 1963, South African police arrested most of *Umkhonto's* high command and put them on trial at Rivonia. Although little financial damage or loss of life occurred, the court gave life sentences to Mandela, Walter Sisulu, and Govan Mbeki. Following Sharpeville, other violent opposition groups had emerged, notably the PAC-affiliated *Poqo* ("we alone") and the radical white African Resistance Movement. The ANC's *Umkhonto*, however, was and has remained the largest and most effective source of military opposition.

Following the Rivonia trial, an exiled *Umkhonto* struggled to survive. A 1967 military operation that originated in Zambia and was annihilated by Rhodesian military forces was the only ANC military operation against South Africa in the 1960s. Based in London and then Zambia, the ANC continued to rely on peaceful protest and politicization.

The Soweto uprisings of 1976 and the 1984–86 disturbances swelled the exiled membership of the ANC but threatened its staunch opposition to terrorism. The government's killing of over 1,000 blacks, convinced many of the fleeing students to undertake counterviolence. Before 1975, the ANC's external cadres numbered about 1,000. By 1980, they numbered 9,000. Three-quarters of the 12,000 refugees from Soweto joined the ANC. *Umkhonto's* average age fell sharply from thirty-five to twenty-eight. Present ANC exile strength is about 17,000. *Umkhonto* has an estimated 10,000 members, about 800 of whom are within South Africa.

The ANC is being radicalized not by external forces, such as the Soviet Union, but by forces within South Africa—government policies and the emergence of activist youth in the townships. Baptized in violence and frustrated by slow political change, the ANC's youth over the past twelve years have pressed the National Executive Council (NEC) for a broader definition of acceptable methods and targets. In *Apartheid's Rebels*, Steve Davis notes that "the most frequent point of friction between the generations is the question of how intense and how central a role armed resistance should play in overall ANC strategy."[21] Youth comprise about two-thirds of the exiles but have only a few representatives on the NEC.

The ANC's leadership worries about a more violent future: "It is only a matter of time before the younger men take over," cautions a high-ranking ANC official in Tanzania. "This is our fear: the wholesale burning of the country. We want to avoid that. We are not mad. It's easy to destroy, much harder to rebuild."[22]

The ANC leadership, which Davis describes as "remain[ing] dominated by Christian-educated men and women of the Rivonia generation"[23] have reluctantly acceded to compromises concerning the youth's desire for a broader acceptance of violence. In 1985, against the backdrop of rebelling townships, the ANC held its third Consultative Congress in Kabwe, Zambia. Rank-and-file caucus members forced agreement on a landmark resolution to abandon the traditional avoidance of human casualties in *Umkhonto* missions. As reported in *Sechaba*, the ANC's official journal, it was agreed that "The distinction between 'hard' and 'soft' targets should disappear."[24] Soon the ANC's Radio Freedom urged that the war be expanded into white, especially farming, areas. Late in 1985, landmines near the Zimbabwean border exploded, and similar, sporadic attacks have continued.

---

[21] Davis, op.cit., 60.
[22] Ibid.
[23] Ibid., 59.
[24] Ibid., 60.

Soft targets are government security personnel and innocent white civilians. *Umkhonto* has also singled out black agents of the state, notably police informants and officers as soft targets. ANC officials sometimes argue that the infamous "necklacing" is not terrorism but a response against security forces. Yet, innocent people have been necklaced, and ANC officials have appeared to be divided on the tactic. Winnie Mandela once justified necklacing as a means of liberation. The ANC later renounced necklacing and disassociated itself from her remarks.[25]

ANC attacks have killed a small number of innocent civilians and thus could be considered terroristic. Urban bombings by the ANC have claimed some civilian casualties. Landmines and occasional AK-47 and rocket-propelled grenade attacks have killed farmers. The ANC justifies the bomb attacks by noting that the targets are usually security installations and not the citizens passing by. It has criticized rogue *Umkhonto* actions aimed only at civilians, notably the 1985 bombing of a Durban shopping center. Farmers along the border, the ANC argues, consciously serve a security function as an intelligence and "first alert" capability for the government.

These actions point up the difficulty of clearly defining "terrorism." A farmer and his family basically are noncombatants but may assist the government and its security operations. ANC external officials, like Dulcie September and Albie Sachs, are noncombatants but assist an opposition force that sometimes employs violence. Does any form of support to a political-military organization

---

[25]"ANC Chief Urges Blacks To Carry Armed Fight...," *London Times*, January 9, 1987, and "ANC Rebuke For Wife of Mandela," *London Times*, October 1, 1987. Ms. Mandela's statement was "Together, hand in hand, with our sticks of matches, with our necklaces, we shall liberate this country." Quoted in "Blacks Take Tougher Stand," *Christian Science Monitor*, April 15, 1986. The ANC criticism of necklacing appears largely stimulated by international outcry against the method.

sanction violent reprisals? The ANC has usually aimed its bombs and limpet mines at strategic targets. Yet the ANC knows that innocent passers-by may, however regrettably, be killed in the blast. When judging the terrorism of an act, should one distinguish between the intended target and the affected individuals?

Much of the horrific South African township terrorism came from non-ANC sources. Quasi-nihilistic youth, most notably in Port Elizabeth and the Vaal triangle, utilized terror during 1985 and 1986, holding impromptu "peoples courts" to investigate and then physically punish alleged traitors. The government claims that between 1984 and 1988, 706 blacks were burned alive, 390 of them by the gas-filled tires known as "necklaces."[26] These youth did have a certain connection to the ANC—they furthered the ANC's desire to "make the townships ungovernable" and thus were conducive for *Umkhonto* sanctuary and basing. Some of them did have sympathies, however ill-defined, for the ANC. But they were not part of *Umkhonto*, did not receive *Umkhonto* training, and were not carrying out direct *Umkhonto* commands. Ironically, some terrorist victims in the townships may have been genuine activists killed on the basis of sellout rumors initiated by South African security.

The ANC officially continues to reject the terrorism of indiscriminate killing, which its legions of supporters within South Africa—from domestics to bus drivers—have the ability to perform. In 1978, the ANC signed a protocol of the Geneva Convention that bound it to "humanitarian conduct of the war" and to foregoing civilian targets. The ANC has also rejected assassinations and the kidnapping and torture used by terrorist groups elsewhere (and probably by the South African government).

---

[26]"Black Activist Hanged in Pretoria For Killing During a 1986 Protest," *International Herald-Tribune*, March 27, 1988.

The ANC worries about these possible terrorist trends. Through education and politicization, it has defused and sidetracked insistence on terrorist methods. The ANC's Soloman Mahlangu Freedom College (SOMAFCO) in Tanzania provides a nonviolent channel for anger and training for a postapartheid South Africa. Political commissars work with SOMAFCO students to inculcate and enforce ANC views on nonracialism and nonterrorist violence.

The ANC's nonracialism limits racial terrorism. One ANC defendant stated that "in South Africa I was so hardened that I decided that all whites should be killed." After joining the ANC, "I was taught that the whites and the blacks in South Africa have got to live together. That was the greatest thing I received in the ANC teachings."[27] Most SOMAFCO graduates enter *Umkhonto* or the ANC's administration.

Despite its efforts, the older leadership may see its antiterrorist position erode further. First, an absence of substantive government changes accompanied by continued physical repression will intensify a belief that only terrorism, that is, white civilian deaths, can prompt governmental change. "More MK [*Umkhonto*] soldiers," writes Davis, "were attributing the persistence of white confidence in governmental power to the paucity of white casualties."[28]

South Africa's regional destabilization activities and its increased border patrolling have forced insurgents further into South Africa's townships and have allowed *Umkhonto* units greater de facto autonomy. *Umkhonto* cells, comprised of young recruits cut off from the moderating influences of older ANC leaders, may expand the area of violence. While the 700 local organizations affiliated

---

[27]Quoted in Joseph Lelyveld's *Move Your Shadow* (New York, 1985), 334.
[28]Davis, op. cit., 124.

with the UDF exercised some authority, the February 24, 1988, bannings restrict the influence (and status) of these groups. *Umkhonto* cadres now enter South Africa largely as trainers and recruiters rather than as liberating guerrillas. Of the 132 guerrillas arrested between January and September 1987, 77 were locally trained.

The ANC's limited violence has served several purposes well. As "armed propaganda," it has bolstered nonwhite morale and increased support for the ANC, while the lack of terrorism suggests to some whites that the ANC is a pragmatic and possible negotiating partner. Sensitive to the inevitability of change and impressed by the ANC's disavowal of terrorism, influential whites have met with ANC leaders outside of South Africa. After meeting with a group of white businessmen, Oliver Tambo concluded, "It is the armed component which has made them want to come."[29]

The ANC leadership has good reason not to cross the borders of violence into terrorism. As the NEC stated at Kabwe, "If we seriously consider ourselves as the alternative government of our country then we need to act and operate both as an insurrectionary force and a credible representative of a liberated South Africa."[30] Fearing destruction, the white population might shelve internal differences to unite against "barbarism." An ANC nod toward terrorism would not only trigger a powerful white government and vigilante reaction, but would possibly also spur new and less manageable violent black groups similar to the township youth. The often violent excesses of these youth could, as occurred in 1985 and 1986, provoke counterviolence from older township residents and further divide the black struggle. As in Rhodesia, a white government facing a more dangerous threat might

---

[29]Quoted in ibid.
[30]Ibid., 30.

seek a political accommodation with moderate black leaders. In Rhodesia it was Bishop Abel Muzorewa; in South
Africa it probably would be Zulu Chief Gatsha Buthelezi.
Davis mentions that in the mid-1980s, "The more anti-
apartheid violence *Umkhonto* caused, the more whites
sought cooperation with Buthelezi as the black leader
most willing to leave minority power intact in a postapartheid South Africa."[31]

The South African government would also undoubtedly respond by pounding the frontline states, which, if
Rhodesia serves as an example, would then pressure their
ANC guests to leave or to limit their activities. The international community, which presently perceives a clear
moral distinction in the South African conflict, could reduce its already limited support of the ANC and slacken
the struggle for economic sanctions. The ensuing loss of
commercial, financial, and technical capability could in-
flict economic hardship on a future ANC-ruled South
Africa.

The Future

The South African government is taking a big gamble, betting that its repression of opposition groups, combined with a significant bettering of township economies,
will restrict the opposition's appeal. As more blacks enter
"the system," the argument goes, they will feel less dis-
posed to oppose it with force.[32] Indeed, like some of the
homeland leaders, they may actively oppose *Umkhonto* and
other groups.

---

[31]Ibid., 130.
[32]Malan, "I think that for the masses in South Africa, democracy is not a
relevant factor. They are just concerned with meeting their own material
needs." Quoted in "Key Townships Targetted For Upgrading," *Southscan*,
January 13, 1988.

The question of whether terrorism will increase or change form in South Africa has several possible answers. First, it is possible that the government's gamble will pay off and that black cooptation will stifle revolutionary and terroristic tendencies. While a growing black middle class vigorously campaigns to resolve the gap between economic and political rights, its struggle would prove more militant than military.

Critics argue that the government is seeking only to manage rather than to resolve South Africa's problems and that as long as the state denies political equality it will continue to face an opposition dedicated to its overthrow. The history of apartheid's abuses is too long, continuing physical repression of even nonviolent groups and civilians has been too strong, and the economic reforms will never reach or convince the required audience. Each outbreak of violence—Sharpeville in 1960, Soweto in 1976, and the Vaal triangle-East London from 1984–86—introduced still more terrorism and violence and took longer to subdue.

The present troubles, which began in September 1984, were sparked by formal exclusion of blacks from parliament, increased rental and transport charges during an extended economic downturn, and continuing inferior education. Until the government satisfies at least some of these grievances, it can only expect continuing terrorism in return. Thus, at least in the medium term, military force and acts of terrorism by both sides will continue.

Terrorism against and by the state is highly unpredictable, but several disturbing trends are evident. The ANC's longstanding opposition to terrorism faces challenges from within, and the state's continuing crackdown on black leadership may be fostering a more independent and violent generation of youth.

ANC youth have been pressing for increased terrorism, and *Umkhonto* is hitting more innocent civilians, notably farmers on the northern borders, with its increasing bomb blasts. By mid-1988, a new faction within *Umkhonto* was challenging the relatively gentle Rivonia generation. In June, Chris Hani, *Umkhonto*'s chief of staff, stated that he considered Nationalist party military police, "reactionary judges," and other enforcers of apartheid as legitimate targets of violence. Oliver Tambo publicly rebuked Hani's remark and its implication of wider attacks on civilians. Yet, two weeks later, a limpet mine at an East London restaurant and a car bomb at a Johannesburg sports stadium killed two civilians and wounded forty.

The quasi-anarchistic township youth demonstrated a frightening ability in 1985 and 1986, according to Meer, to unleash "a terrible and terrifying energy. . . one that society cannot control."[33] Reports in late 1986 indicated "that as police action skims off the leadership of black organizations, there is less control over the angry black youths."[34] Terrorism, especially from the young, will probably increase. One terrorism expert notes that "in prolonged conflicts. . . the attitudes, vocabulary, and goals change, often to the point where terrorism is deemed not only justifiable, but natural."[35]

Conflicts between blacks, notably *Inkatha* and the UDF fighting in Natal, continue and may gain a life of their own whatever the level of government encouragement. If continuing black anger is not allowed to channel itself through nonviolent but now banned organizations, it might seek underground terrorism as the only alternative.

The government continues to employ physical repression, including terrorism. Along with longstanding police actions in the townships and interrogation rooms,

---

[33]Meer, op. cit., 22.
[34]"South Africa's Violence Shifts Pattern," *Washington Post*, June 10, 1986.
[35]Robin Wright, "The Rage of the Children," in *TVI Report*, vol. 7, no. 3, 1.

several new groups have emerged, notably the *kitskon-stabels* and possibly unsanctioned hit squads. Also, paramilitary groups conjure up fears of a "last stand" by embittered whites.

The worst-case scenario is that of black South Africa becoming an African Lebanon with a growing fractionalization of political power and widespread terrorism, a land where violence-prone groups owe primary allegiance to individual warlords and where the government sanctions or cannot control growing terrorist organizations. Violence and terrorism would feed on themselves, with black gangs entering white areas for guns and whites responding violently, possibly with security force cooperation.

Nongovernment firepower has grown at a worrisome rate in recent years. Over 1 million whites have gun licenses. A U.S. official has stated that "very significant amounts" of small arms exist in the townships.[36] In May 1988, police arrested *Umkhonto* insurgents carrying at least one SAM-7 missile system. A rise in political terrorism would encourage what Haysom calls "a criminal subgroup taking advantage of a situation of deteriorating law and order."[37] Such rampant violence would reduce the prospects of any serious negotiations leading to a peaceful transition to majority rule. Even following a transfer of power, the ready availability of arms would pose continuing security problems.

Yet this scenario may not be the most likely to develop. First, the ANC may have concluded that the military struggle must remain secondary given the government's proven ability to respond in kind. Moreover, a turn toward terrorism would damage the ANC's increased international legitimacy. As one of his major reasons for

---

[36]State Department interview, spring 1988.
[37]Haysom, op. cit., 127.

condemning necklacing and other forms of terrorism, Oliver Tambo cited international criticism of the practice. In addition, the ANC has a centralized target—the Vaal triangle—that is the nation's economic jugular. The ANC and other organizations may have embarked on a concentrated program of industrial sabotage. The University of South Africa's School of Business Research data indicate widespread sabotage as a major problem in South Africa's troubled economy.[38] The Soviet Union, *Umkhonto's* biggest financial backer, has apparently recommended negotiations rather than prolonged conflict. Additionally, increased *Umkhonto* recruitment and training within the townships may permit the ANC to exercise more control over the youth. Although the military struggle may increase in intensity, the ANC and the UDF affiliates may use this partial respite to intensify grass-roots activity.

Finally, South Africa's blacks still retain their hopes for a peaceful transition to majority rule. Local civic associations and trade unions have shown remarkable resilience during the past three years and are agents for peaceful transformation. The Institute for Black Research conducted a poll during the unrest in September 1985 that showed that 90 percent of blacks favored change "through genuine negotiations" and 73 percent favored disinvestment. Only 36 percent favored armed struggle as a possible option, while 28 percent approved of terrorism against suspected government collaborators.[39] Given an alternative, most blacks reject terrorism.

Although the United States and other Western governments face limitations—notably the intensity of animosities within South Africa and the suspicion or

---

[38]"Sabotage By Blacks 'Hitting Economy,' " *Guardian*, June 8, 1986.
[39]See Fatima Meer, "Political and Economic Choices of Disenfranchised South Africans," Institute of Black Studies, Durban, 1986.

dislike of many Western nations by the major actors—
the West has an obligation to act even despite its limited
influence. The West can either deal indirectly with the
causes of much of the terrorism—apartheid and white
rule—by applying economic sanctions or it can take a
more direct course by aiding the opponents of apartheid.

Numerous critics of the South African government
urge increased sanctions to help destroy apartheid and
its violence. William Gray, a leader in the U.S. Congress,
and Bishop Desmond Tutu and Reverend Alan Boesak
in South Africa see sanctions as the last instrument for
peaceful change. If black terrorism exists partly because
of the lack of hope, they argue, comprehensive Western
action would strengthen proponents of the nonterrorist
alternatives. And sanctions would demonstrate a powerful but peaceful international resolve against apartheid
and press the South African government to end such
causes of violence as the legislative pillars of apartheid,
to lift the ban on ANC and other groups, and to release
political prisoners for eventual negotiations. Officially
designating South Africa as an international terrorist state
is one means of placing sanctions against South Africa.[40]

Critics of sanctions reply that such measures would
increase black unemployment, anger, and willingness to
adopt terrorism while driving whites into the armed
laager, isolated from Western influence. The Heritage
Foundation suggests stimulating the South African economy as a means of black empowerment leading to black
majority rule.

The West hopes for a peaceful transfer of power to
a new and democratic government. It has several options

---

[40]Section 15 of HR 1580 requires the secretary of state to report to Congress whether South Africa is involved in, or supports, international terrorism. If the U.S. decides that South Africa is an international terrorist,
it would be obligated to apply sanctions found within the International Emergency Economic Powers Act and the Export Administration Act.

that are less dramatic and intrusive than sanctions. In order to encourage a relatively peaceful transition, the West must encourage the growth of such nonterrorist groups as the UDF and its 700 affiliates. Equally, it must press the ANC not to increase terrorism and the South African government to reduce state terrorism.

The Reagan administration delivered mixed messages to South Africa. While criticizing apartheid, President Reagan partially justified the police shooting of twenty blacks at Langa in 1985 when he claimed it was the result of black provocation. The first American ambassadorial contact with the ANC's headquarters in Lusaka was in July 1986 (although lower-level contacts had occurred earlier). Yet, during the same month, President Reagan spoke of "elements of the ANC" urging "calculated terror."[41]

The United States and other Western nations could more forcefully signal their hopes for peaceful change. High-level Western contacts with the ANC, such as Secretary of State Shultz's meeting with Oliver Tambo in January 1987, and possibly even the granting of medical and educational supplies to the Lusaka headquarters and SOMAFCO could strengthen the NEC's rejection of most terrorism, signal American displeasure of state terrorism, and promote the United States as an honest broker in eventual negotiations. Extending military support or diplomatic recognition to the ANC would prove unwise for numerous reasons, not the least of which is that the ANC is only one of several opposition political groupings.

Increased official and press attention to terrorism—whether by the ANC or the government—could also help to reduce excesses. The United States could publicly

---

[41]Reagan, quoted in "U.S. Envoy Holds Talks With 3 Key ANC Officials," *Baltimore Sun*, July 31, 1986. Although accurate in itself, the statement reflects President Reagan's strong dislike of the ANC.

criticize the indefinite detention and torture of prisoners and expose Pretoria's support of extra-legal terrorist organizations. The U.S. Department of State, which currently channels several million dollars a year to legal and human rights centers in South Africa, could increase its outlays. Material or verbal opposition can lessen terrorism. The Carter administration's stress on human rights may have helped cause the drop in deaths by blacks in detention. The Ciskei government disbanded its vigilantes after press coverage and a U.S. warning to American citizens not to enter Ciskei in 1983 attracted international attention.

Another option is increased economic and security assistance to the frontline states of southern Africa. Economic aid through such regional organizations as the Southern African Development Coordinating Conference as well as defensive and nonlethal military assistance to the frontline states would serve at least three purposes: to limit South Africa's regional destabilization, to signal U.S. displeasure to Pretoria about its internal policies, and to improve U.S. relations with the nations sheltering the ANC.

There is no simple or quick solution to South African terrorism. But without more forceful Western action, terrorism from the Right and Left will continue in South Africa not only up to the negotiation period—at which time it may actually intensify—but also possibly into the rule of a black majority government as remnants of the *impis*, the vigilantes, the security forces, the AWB, and disenchanted or revenge-seeking *Umkhonto* members continue to use terrorism to advance their distinctive political aims.

7

THE POLITICS OF TERRORISM: A CONTEMPORARY SURVEY

Cecilia Albin

In the 1980s terrorism has become an increasingly significant feature of interstate wars, civil strife, and insurgencies in the Middle East, Latin America, Asia and Europe.[1] Measured by the number of people killed and wounded, it remains a minor, seriously exaggerated, problem compared to more pressing world ills. In 1987 some 832 international terrorist attacks worldwide killed 633 people and injured 2,272.[2] The figure for 1988 is estimated to be about 1,200 incidents.[3] In 7,343 international terrorist attacks recorded between 1975 and 1987, 416

---

[1] I am grateful to Barry Rubin, Jim Wootten and I. William Zartman for their valuable comments on this article.

[2] "International Terrorism Statistics, 1968–87," U.S. Department of State, Office of the Ambassador at Large for Counter-Terrorism, Washington, D.C., 1988; *Patterns of Global Terrorism: 1987,* U.S. Department of State, Washington, D.C., 1988, 1. It should be noted that the figures reflect the extraordinary increase in terrorist bombings in Pakistan, which, according to these sources, killed 234 and wounded 1,200 people in 1987. Of the bombings, 127 were believed to be attributable to the Afghan secret police.

"International terrorism" is defined here as terrorism involving the citizens or territory of two or more countries, and does not include the extensive political violence used by indigenous insurgencies (as in Peru and Colombia) and nationalist-separatist groups (as in Sri Lanka and India) against *domestic* targets, or by governments and national armies against internal opposition (as in Guatemala and El Salvador).

[3] FBI source quoted in David C. Martin and John Walcott, "How to Survive the Coming Terrorism Boom," *Washington Post,* June 26, 1988, C1.

U.S. citizens were killed, most in a few especially bloody incidents, such as the 1983 bombing of the U.S. Marine headquarters in Beirut, Lebanon.[4] Looking coldly at these figures, it may be surprising that terrorism has so preoccupied the media and that it has become such a priority in U.S. foreign policy.

Terrorism represents a growing danger, however, because of three factors: it involves risks of escalation of tension between countries; it poses a threat to the stability of numerous governments; and it has become a valued tool of extremist regimes and zealots in spreading their influence and blackmailing others. Those menaced include fragile democracies and countries where the United States has important strategic interests.

Particularly worrisome is the drastic increase in state-sponsored terrorism and the use of political terrorism by narcotics smugglers. While only 56 (1.4 percent) of all terrorist attacks between 1976 and 1983 are believed to have been state-sponsored, the figure increased to 456 (15.3 percent) between 1984 and 1987.[5] The April 1986 U.S. raid on Libya at first seemed to help reduce Colonel Qadhafi's terrorist activities, but they began to reoccur in early 1988.[6] Another important development has been the sharp increase in the number of terrorist incidents targeted against people rather than property. Only about 20 percent of all terrorist attacks were directed against persons in the early 1970s. In the 1980s, the figure had increased to 50 percent.

While terrorism is one of the most closely observed phenomena of our time, it is also, as Walter Laqueur has noted, one of the least understood.[7] Much scholarly treatment of the subject has stumbled over the difficulty of

---

[4]"International Terrorism Statistics, 1968–1987."
[5]Ibid.
[6]Martin and Walcott, C1.
[7]Walter Laqueur, *The Age of Terrorism* (Boston and Toronto, 1987), 7.

defining the term in a manner that is at once meaningful, comprehensive, and consistent. Virtually all scholars and policymakers agree that terrorism involves the use or threat of force to create a state of fear among many by striking only a few. In the longer run, it aims at achieving certain political goals. It is the instrument of movements and certain states which lack, or believe they lack, sufficient traditional diplomatic, political, military, and economic power to further their interests. To be effective, terrorists depend on publicity to establish a general atmosphere of fear and to tell the world about their causes.[8]

Some experts have argued that because each terrorist actor is unique in its motives, ideology, composition, organization, choice of targets, operational environment and effectiveness, it is impossible to construct a theory of terrorism's cause.[9] Laqueur is quite representative of this view. In *The Age of Terrorism,* he notes only one common denominator among terrorist groups—the generally young age of their members—and concludes: "Generalizations [about terrorist groups] are of limited validity because so much depends on the political and social conditions in which terrorism has occurred, on the historical and cultural context, on the purpose and character of the terror, and, of course, on its targets."[10]

---

[8]Walter Laqueur, "Reflections on Terrorism," *Foreign Affairs,* Fall 1986, 88. Compare also the common elements in over 100 definitions of terrorism quoted by Alex P. Schmid in *Political Terrorism: A Research Guide to Concepts, Theories, Data Bases and Literature* (Amsterdam and New Brunswick, 1983), 119–52.

For terrorism viewed essentially as a strategy to gain world public attention through the media, see Alex P. Schmid and Janny de Graaf, *Violence as Communication* (London and Beverly Hills, 1982).

[9]For an excellent overview of various attempts at constructing a theory of terrorism, see Schmid, *Political Terrorism,* 160–243.

[10]Laqueur, *The Age of Terrorism,* 77.

Others experts have identified the actor's underlying motives as the key to distinguishing terrorism from other forms of violence. In this view, groups fighting for a "just" cause, such as freedom and liberation from foreign domination or repressive regimes, are not terroristic, whatever the means used. Hence, the United Nations General Assembly has condemned "terrorist acts by colonial, racist and alien regimes," but endorsed the legitimacy of the struggle of "national liberation movements."[11] In 1974 Yassir Arafat, chairman of the Palestinian Liberation Organization (PLO), stated before the Assembly that "[h]e who fights for a just cause—for the liberation of his country—against invasion and exploitation or single-mindedly against colonialism, can never be defined a terrorist."[12] Similarly, the Reagan administration has condemned, and taken military action against, terrorists that it says seek to destroy Western democratic systems and values, while supporting anticommunist "freedom fighters" that use similar methods and employ the very same political strategies used by the alleged "terrorists." Thus Secretary of Defense Caspar Weinberger stated in 1987: "When we can no longer distinguish between the terrorist's murder of innocents, and the freedom fighter's sacrifice for liberty, at that point, tyranny wins."[13]

A directly opposite view is that whatever the intent, certain acts such as hostage taking, kidnapping and bombing are inherently terroristic.[14] The actor's choice of

---

[11]*Everyone's United Nations,* 9th edition, Department of Public Information, United Nations, New York, 1979, 332.

[12]Yassir Arafat's speech to the United Nations General Assembly, November 13, 1974, quoted in Schmid, *Political Terrorism,* 100.

[13]"Remarks prepared for delivery by the Honorable Caspar W. Weinberger, Secretary of Defense, to the International Conference on Terrorism, Washington, D.C., Wednesday, January 21, 1987. *News Release,* No. 38–87, Office of Assistant Secretary of Defense, Washington, D.C., 1987, 1–2.

[14]See, for example, *Report on the European Convention on the Suppression of Terrorism,* Council of Europe, Strasbourg, January 27, 1977, 20–21.

targets—particularly civilian targets—has also been considered a key element distinguishing terrorism from other forms of warfare, including guerrilla wars. Today, however, civilians are certainly heavily victimized in wars and insurgencies, and military personnel and installations are deliberately targeted by many terrorist groups, including the Irish Republican Army (IRA), the Basque *Euzkadi to Azkazatuna* (ETA), and the Philippine New People's Army (NPA). Similarly, many definitions of terrorism stress the intentional victimization of "innocents" (often without defining the meaning of the term),[15] although there is little evidence that terrorists consider innocence as a key criterion in their choice of targets.

This chapter seeks to compare how some of the most important state and substate actors use various types of terrorist strategies to further their political goals. It will focus on how terrorism is used—and how successfully it has been used—as a political strategy in four, often overlapping, but nevertheless distinguishable ways:[16]

1. The use of terrorism by *internal opposition groups* against the existing government (or some of its policies), the political system, or other groups within the country. These include revolutionary movements in Latin America, Europe, and South Africa; groups opposing the North Atlantic Treaty Organization in Europe; and domestic terrorist groups in the United States.
2. The use of terrorism by *nationalist-separatist groups* which seek to gain political independence or establish their own state primarily on the basis of a national identity,

---

[15]See Hannah Arendt, *The Origins of Totalitarianism,* (New York, 1951); R.A. Friedlander, *Terrorism and the Law: What Price Safety?* (Gaithersburg, 1981); Herbert Howe, "Government and Opposition Terrorism in South Africa" in this volume.
[16]These distinctions correspond, in part, to those of R. Moss in *Urban Guerrillas: The New Face of Political Violence* (London, 1972), 32ff.

ethnicity, or religion (for example, the ETA, the IRA, the Puerto Rican Armed Forces of National Liberation, the Armenian Secret Army for the Liberation of Armenia [ASALA], and the PLO).

3. The use of terrorism by *governments* and *national armies* to subdue internal opposition (for instance, in Nicaragua, Iran, Syria and Guatemala), whether of ethnic, religious, political or other nature.

4. *The use of terrorism by states* or regimes against other states or outside groups.[17] Generally, these are non-democratic states that attempt to close the gap between their (sometimes overambitious) foreign policy goals and (insufficient) power by the use of terrorist strategies. This type of terrorism takes place at various levels of involvement ranging from directly state-directed terrorism (Syria, Libya, Iran) to less direct forms of support, including provision of money, arms, training and protection, either directly (Cuba, East Germany, Bulgaria) or through proxies (the Soviet Union).

Terrorism as a Separatist and Revolutionary Strategy: The U.S. Experience

Since 1980 the United States has become an increasingly important target of many terrorist actors. While only 8.5 percent of all international terrorist incidents worldwide between 1975 and 1979 were believed to have been directed against U.S. citizens or property, between 1983 and 1986 the figure rose to 22–35 percent. In 1984, 38

---

[17]In many cases, as Schmid argues in *Political Terrorism* (105), it would be more appropriate to speak of regime-sponsored terrorism, for a small political elite or even a single leader is often the only user and supporter of the terrorist strategies (for example, Muammar Qadhafi of Libya). Here, however, the terms "state-directed" and "state-sponsored" terrorism will be used, without suggesting that most of the country's population necessarily supports it.

Americans were killed and 157 injured in about 600 international terrorist attacks targeted against U.S. personnel or installations;[18] that is, a terrorist incident has been directed against U.S. citizens or property about once every 17 days. Although the number of American casualties still remains relatively low, as many U.S. diplomats have been killed in the past 17 years as in the previous 180 years.[19]

Only an insignificant number of these terrorist acts have taken place inside the United States: Between 1984 and 1986 the yearly average of internal incidents was 12; in that time, one person was killed and ten were injured. Actors classified as "domestic" terrorists were behind all of these attacks.[20] It may be more relevant, therefore, to seek to explain why the United States has so rarely experienced terrorist incidents internally in comparison with many other countries; why terrorists prefer to attack Americans overseas rather than at home. Networks of terrorists do exist in the United States, and although they have been responsible for only a few attacks mainly against property, they have the capability to become much more active and violent.

Domestic Terrorism in the United States. Some terrorist groups operating in the United States are supported, directed, and financed exclusively by indigenous sources, and target the U.S. government or groups within the country. By far the most active and violent domestic groups are the various Puerto Rican terrorist organizations, which a Federal Bureau of Intelligence researcher in 1987

---

[19]James P. Wootten, *Terrorist Incidents Involving U.S. Citizens or Property, 1981–87: A Chronology,* Foreign Affairs and National Defense Division, Congressional Research Service (Washington, D.C., 1987), 1.
[20]Garrett in *Defense Issues,* vol. 2, no. 3, 1.
[21]*FBI Analysis of Terrorist Incidents in the United States, 1986* (hereinafter cited as *FBI Analysis 1986*), Terrorist Research and Analytical Center, Terrorism Division, Criminal Investigative Division, FBI (Washington, D.C., 1986) i, 10.

judged to be "the most viable domestic security threat at
the beginning of the 1980s."[21] Between 1980 and 1986,
Puerto Rican terrorist groups were responsible for 74 incidents or 54.8 percent of all terrorist attacks in the
United States.[22] Although the names of these Puerto Rican
groups have frequently changed, they all reject U.S. juris-
diction over Puerto Rico, subscribe to Marxist-Leninist
ideology, and believe that armed struggle alone can
achieve Puerto Rican independence from U.S. "imperialist domination."[23]

At least nine different Puerto Rican groups have
claimed responsibility for terrorist attacks in the United
States since the mid-1970s, but the ties among them remain close and many incidents were planned and carried
out jointly. They have often bombed U.S. government and
military installations, particularly on the island; carried
out robberies; and occasionally assassinated Puerto Rican
military and police officers and U.S. military personnel.[24]

Some groups stand out for their longevity and high
level of violent activity: the Armed Forces of National
Liberation (FALN), which has close ties with the M-19
group in Colombia and has claimed responsibility for
over 150 bombings; the Organization of Volunteers for
the Puerto Rican Revolution (OVRP), closely connected
with the FALN; and the *Macheteros* (Ejército Popular
Boricua—EPB), generally considered the most violent.
The OVRP and the *Macheteros* were long based in Puerto
Rico only, but have recently established cells on the U.S.
mainland; the FALN traditionally has operated from the

---

[21]Johns W. Harris, "Domestic Terrorism in the 1980s," 7, in *FBI Law Enforcement Bulletin,* October 1987.
[22]*FBI Analysis 1986,* 14, 56.
[23]James Stinson, "Domestic Terrorism in the United States," *The Police Chief,*
September 1987, 63–4.
[24]Oliver B. Revell, *Terrorism: A Law Enforcement Perspective,* U.S. Department
of State, Federal Bureau of Investigation (Washington, D.C., 1988), 48–50.

U.S. mainland. Typical activities have included the October 1979 bombings and attempted bombings of U.S. government installations, for which the OVRP, FALN, and FARP (Armed Forces of Popular Resistance) claimed joint responsibility; the May 1982 killing of a U.S. marine in Puerto Rico and the September 1983 multimillion dollar robbery of the Wells Fargo Depot in Connecticut, both incidents claimed by the *Macheteros*; and the April 1986 assassination of a former Puerto Rican police officer for which the OVRP claimed responsibility.[25]

Left-wing revolutionary and black nationalist terrorist groups in the United States gained momentum during the unrest of the mid-1960s and early 1970s. By far the most important group today is the May 19 Communist Organization (M19CO), named for Ho Chi Minh's and Malcolm X's birthdays and the date of the death of Cuban nationalist José Martí, which springs from the Weather Underground Organization. M19CO has developed close ties with the FALN and with black nationalist organizations such as the New Afrikan Freedom Fighters (NAFF), the New African People's Organization (NAPO) and the Republic of New Africa (RNA), which seek the establishment of a black socialist state within the United States through revolution. Externally, the M19CO has associated itself with Third World causes and has established contacts with Palestinian, South African, and Latin American movements.[26] Although the M19CO has mainly relied on legal instruments such as demonstrations and rallies to advocate political change and revolution, a few terrorist attacks in the 1980s were attributed to the organization or to front or allied groups (such as the Red Guerrilla

---

[25]*FBI Analysis 1986*, 16; Revell, op. cit., 56–7.
[26]Harris, 10.

Resistance, the Armed Resistance Unit, and the Revolutionary Fighting Group).[27]

The United Freedom Front (UFF) has used terrorist strategies more extensively to further the same goals and has claimed responsibility for eleven terrorist incidents between December 1982 and September 1984.[28] In all, left-wing and black nationalist groups committed twenty-nine terrorist attacks between 1980 and 1984, but only one in 1985 and none in 1986.[29] Virtually all these incidents were actual or attempted bombings of symbolically significant targets such as U.S., Israeli, and South African installations. Since the 1960s, black terrorists have focused almost exclusively on attacking policy-related targets. An example is the 1984 NAFF plan to bomb police cars and kill several police officers in New York City, which was averted by law enforcement personnel.[30]

Different in motives and choice of targets, the Jewish Defense League (JDL) and its spin-offs—the United Jewish Underground, the Jewish Defenders, and Jewish Direct Action—have been most active in the United States in recent years. Between 1981 and 1986, these groups claimed or were assigned responsibility for twenty-four terrorist acts.[31]

The JDL operates on the premise that only through armed struggle against anti-Semitism can another Holocaust be avoided and adequate international attention be directed to the fate of Soviet Jews. Terrorist attacks, ranging from arson and bombings to vandalism and threats, have been made against alleged Nazi war criminals and Soviet, Arab, and Arab-American individuals, organizations, and property. In September 1986, for example, the

---

[27]Revell, op. cit., 34, 41–2.
[28]Harris, op. cit., 7.
[29]*FBI Analysis 1986*, 14.
[30]*FBI Analysis 1986*, 4; *FBI Analysis 1984*, 4; Harris, op. cit., 10.
[31]*FBI Analysis 1986*, 4, 14.

JDL released a tear gas grenade during a Soviet dance performance at the Metropolitan Opera House in New York City, injuring seventeen people.[32] In April and July 1982, the same organization set off bombs in the Iraqi and Lebanese missions to the United Nations, and in the offices of Lufthansa Airlines in New York.[33]

Right-wing terrorist groups in the United States, particularly the Ku Klux Klan, were active in the decades preceding the 1960s. Anti-black, anticommunist, anti-Semitic and often neo-Nazi, these groups are closely intertwined and advocate the overthrow of the U.S. government and the creation of a racially "pure" (all-white, Christian or Protestant) America. Much of this racism is religiously rooted in the Christian Identity Movement and the teachings of the Reverend Richard Butler, which hold that whites are God's chosen race and the descendants of Israel, while Jews are the children of Satan. Most right-wing groups engage in paramilitary training in preparation for a racial war to precede the Second Coming of Christ or in expectation of a Communist takeover.[34]

Other elements of right-wing terrorism include vehement tax-protest groups which are also anti-black and anti-Semitic, such as the Sheriff's Posse Comitatus and the Arizona Patriots. However, the Aryan Nations led by Butler and its affiliates, including the Order, are by far the most active and violent. These were behind virtually all of the seven right-wing attacks initiated between 1980 and 1986. They have assaulted and killed law enforcement personnel, but typically their attacks have involved bombings of state and federal buildings in Butler's home state of Idaho.[35]

---

[32]Ibid., 21.
[33]Ibid., 21–22.
[34]Harris, 10–11.
[35]See, for example, *FBI Analysis 1986*, 22–23.

The failure of terrorism as a revolutionary and sep-aratist strategy in the United States so far essentially reflects lack of public support for the terrorists' goals. For example, the FALN has about 200 hard-core members and 2,000 supporters,[36] and electoral results suggest that the overwhelming majority of Puerto Ricans favor either the current commonwealth or change by peaceful means. Most domestic terrorist groups have even fewer adher-ents: the Aryan Nations has an estimated 150 hard-core members and 1,500 supporters,[37] and the UFF has only seven members. In addition, law enforcement agencies have managed to prosecute many of the most commit-ted leaders and adherents of these groups (all in the case of the UFF), which has taken a heavy toll on their vigor and activities. Finally, lacking support from any substan-tial segment of the U.S. population or from outside states or groups, domestic terrorists have had to rely on rela-tively limited means to finance their activities.

International terrorism in the United States. International ter-rorists in the United States, defined as those who are directed from abroad and/or who principally target for-eign groups or governments, have been far less active than domestic terrorists. Between 1980 and 1983, 54 interna-tional terrorist acts were committed in the United States, killing three and injuring eighteen—far fewer than the 99 domestic attacks which killed twelve and injured thirty-five in the same period. Since 1984 no successful inter-national terrorist operations have been recorded in the United States. It should be added, however, that 12 inci-dents were prevented, and that in April 1988 a suspected member of the terrorist Japanese Red Army (JRA), Yu

---

[36]Stinson, 64.
[37]Ibid., 62–3.

Kikumura, was arrested in New Jersey with a fraudulent passport and visa and homemade bombs in his car.[38]

Yet international terrorism in the United States can be regarded as a greater potential threat to U.S. national security than this low level of activity suggests. First, international terrorist groups operating in the United States have been able to garner considerable support—ranging from donations of money and weapons to refusals to provide information on the terrorists' activities to law enforcement authorities—among corresponding ethnic populations, including Armenians, Sikhs, Palestinians and Cubans. Such groups use the United States primarily as a base for training, collection of intelligence, and procurement of weapons and financial support to overthrow the government in their home countries. Second, an infrastructure is in place to escalate terrorist activities by exploiting the presence of Libyan, Iranian and Syrian offices; of international terrorist groups using the United States as a base of operations; and of students from countries which support terrorism. While thus far states sponsoring terrorism are known to have used these networks only to track and punish their own dissidents in the United States and to fight groups and governments outside of this country, these networks could be utilized to direct attacks against the American government and population, particularly in retaliation for U.S. actions against the sponsors.[39]

An important example of groups enjoying support among corresponding ethnic populations are Armenian terrorist groups, notably the Armenian Secret Army for the Liberation of Armenia (ASALA), the Armenian Revolutionary Army, and the Justice Commandos of the

---

[38] *Washington Post,* April 15, 1988, A3.
[39] Oliver B. Revell, "Terrorism Today," *FBI Law Enforcement Bulletin,* October 1987, 2.

Armenian Genocide (JCAG). Thirteen attacks in the United States were attributed to these groups between 1980 and 1983. Both the ASALA and the JCAG seek revenge for Turkey's massacre of Armenians in 1915, and favor the establishment of an independent state in historical Armenia (the ASALA through Marxist-Leninist revolutionary means). Attacks have been made against Turkish personnel and installations and against governments which hold Armenian terrorists. In 1982 members of the JCAG shot and killed the Turkish consuls general in Los Angeles, California, and Somerville, Massachusetts. Typically, however, Armenian terrorist incidents have involved bombings or attempted bombings and few if any casualties. In May 1982, for example, ASALA attempted to place a bomb in the Air Canada cargo facility at Los Angeles International Airport.[40] In November 1981, the JCAG placed an explosive device at the Turkish consulate in Los Angeles, which caused some damage but no casualties.[41]

The anti-Castro Omega 7 group was by far the most active international terrorist group in the United States in the mid-1980s: twenty-one attacks were committed between 1980 and 1983.[42] Through the substantial financial support and loyalty it enjoyed among Cuban exiles in the United States, Omega 7 succeeded in establishing a solid base of operation for trying to overthrow Castro's Communist regime. Selected targets ranged from Cuban government representatives and installations to people and businesses dealing with or suspected of being sympathetic to Castro's regime. The group carried out two assassinations in the late 1970s, but in the early 1980s its operations were for the most part limited to bombings

---

[40]*FBI Analysis 1982*, 13–14.
[41]*FBI Analysis 1981*, 11.
[42]*FBI Analysis 1986*, 14.

that resulted in very few casualties.[43] The 1983 arrest of Omega 7's founder and leader—Eduardo Arocena—and of many of its members ended the groups' organized activities, but bomb attacks by anti-Castro individuals continued.[44]

Other international groups that operate in the United States with ethnic support and that, prior to 1983, were believed responsible for terrorist attacks include Sikh, Croatian, Palestinian, Irish, anti-Khomeini, and anti-Qadhafi organizations.

State-run and state-supported terrorism in the United States is perhaps the most difficult kind to assess, for, while the necessary networks are clearly in place, they have so far been little utilized. These networks consist essentially of Libyan and Iranian representatives (including their missions to the United Nations and the Iranian interests section at the Algerian embassy) who organize and direct pro-Khomeini and pro-Qadhafi groups and student organizations in the United States. Only a few incidents have been initiated by them and these were predominantly assaults upon opponents of the leaders in Tripoli and Teheran. In July 1980, for example, a pro-Iranian group of American Shiite Moslems called Islamic Guerrillas of America assassinated the Freedom Foundation's anti-Khomeini leader, Ali Akbar Tabatabai.

While the Nicaraguan and Cuban governments are also known to be capable of launching terrorist operations in the United States, the networks linked to the Libyan and Iranian regimes have the greatest potential for becoming a threat to U.S. security. In March 1985, a Libyan student at Georgetown University was caught planning, with other members of the Libyan Revolutionary

---

[43]For examples of these terrorist incidents, see *FBI Analysis 1982*, 18–19; *FBI Analysis 1983*, 16–17.
[44]Revell, op. cit., 86–88.

Committee, a series of terrorist attacks in the United States.[45] Eight men, seven of whom were believed to be Libyan agents, were charged in July 1988 with using a Washington, D.C., travel agency and a McLean-based Libyan student group to gather intelligence and to violate the U.S. trade embargo against Tripoli. According to the federal prosecutor, they had collected the names of U.S. officials involved in the 1986 raids against Libya and specifically planned to assassinate former White House aide Oliver North.[46]

Groups such as Omega 7 and the Provisional Irish Republican Army (PIRA) have occasionally been involved in joint criminal activities with narcotics traffickers and accepted money from the drug trade, but there is at present no narco-terrorism in the United States of the nature or extent found in Latin America and the Middle East.[47] In the final analysis, although there is a potential particularly for international terrorist groups to become more active, political violence inside the United States has to date been an amazingly small problem in view of the experience of many other countries and the fact that the United States has been a primary target of many terrorist groups.

Terrorist Strategies in Western Europe: The Cases of Spain and Ireland

In contrast to the pattern in the Middle East, Asia and Latin America, international terrorism in Western Europe declined between 1986 and 1987 as a result of improved security measures and the expulsion of some

---

[45]Revell, op. cit., 63, 67.
[46]*Washington Post*, July 21, 1988, A1, A6; July 29, 1988, A12.
[47]Daniel Boyce, "Narco-Terrorism," in *FBI Law Enforcement Bulletin*, October 1987, 25–27.

100 Libyan "diplomats" from European capitals. Between 1981 and 1985, there was an annual average of 220 international terrorist attacks in Western Europe, but in 1986 it fell to 156 and in 1986 to 150 attacks. Even Middle East "spillover" terrorism in Europe declined from 1985 by about 40 percent to 43 attacks in 1987. Still, Western Europe ranked second only to Latin America for the number of terrorist acts involving U.S. citizens and property.[48] Particularly in operations against NATO and U.S. personnel and installations in Europe, extreme left-wing groups such as the German Red Army Faction, the French *Action Directe*, and the Italian Red Brigades cooperated closely. Terrorism in Europe remained concentrated in countries historically most plagued with political violence: Spain, Italy, Ireland, France, and West Germany.

While the specific causes behind the uses of terrorism vary among countries, European terrorists are generally motivated by ethnic nationalism (in the cases of Spain's ETA, Ireland's IRA, and Corsica's National Front for the Liberation of Corsica) and revolutionary ideology (the Red Brigades, the Red Army Faction, and *Action Directe*). With regard to ideology, as Richard Rubenstein has noted, terrorism has often emerged from frustrations with leftist parties not militant enough to provide a clear alternative to democratic-socialist and conservative politics.[49] Moreover, the radicals themselves are generally too few and espouse causes—or at least use tactics—too unpopular to gain mass support. This section compares how Spain's ETA and Ireland's IRA have used terrorism as a political strategy to further their nationalist, revolutionary goals.

---

[48]"International Terrorism Statistics, 1968–1987."

[49]Richard E. Rubenstein, *Alchemists of Revolution: Terrorism in the Modern World* (New York, 1987), chapter 5, especially 78–82.

ETA: surgical, partly successful, terrorist tactics. The most important terrorist group in Spain is the Basque ETA, although Catalan organizations such as *Terra Llivre*, the Red Catalan Army and the Catalonian Red Army of Liberation also use political violence in their struggle for an independent state.

Euzkadi to Azkazatuna was formed in 1959 in reaction to General Franco's suppression of Basque historical rights and privileges (particularly cultural autonomy) and the failure of the Basque National Party (PNV), in the eyes of its younger members, to resort to revolutionary means.[50] The nationalist goal of achieving a Basque country through political violence has been at the heart of ETA from the very beginning. Ideologically, however, serious splits soon emerged within the organization over how important Marxist-Leninist ideology and armed struggle should be in seeking this objective.

The predominant faction, which by 1974 had split with the more revolutionary ETA members to become "political-military" ETA (ETA–PM), sought under its leader Moreno Bergareche to reconcile primary loyalty to Basque nationalism with Marxism-Leninism in a strategy of "revolutionary nationalism." Armed struggle was necessary, Bergareche argued, but the emphasis should be placed on developing a political program to win the Basque working masses over from the PNV and to emphasize Basque national liberation within a socialist class struggle. By contrast, the faction which became "military" (ETA–M) favored the creation of a Marxist-Leninist vanguard party primarily engaged in military action to bring about revolution in all of Spain.[51]

---

[50]Laqueur, *The Age of Terrorism*, 223; Peter Janke, "Spanish Separatism: ETA's Threat to Basque Democracy," in William Gutteridge, ed., *Contemporary Terrorism* (New York and Oxford, 1986), 141.
[51]Janke, op. cit., 143–150.

While ETA-PM later participated in elections and supported the Spanish government's 1979 statute granting greater Basque autonomy, the ETA-M rejected these initiatives of the new democratic regime as "bourgeois politics" that could never lead to true Basque independence. Indeed, the ETA-M escalated its terrorist attacks as Spain developed into a constitutional monarchy. Repression of ETA militants became much milder after Franco's death, and greater local powers were granted to the Basques; yet the number and cruelty of ETA-M operations continued to increase under Spanish democracy.[52]

While the IRA and other terrorist groups have often sought to gain attention through the massive casualties and damage caused by bomb attacks in public places and other forms of random killing, ETA-PM and ETA-M have both sought to further their goals by engaging in discriminate, "surgical" terrorism that maximizes the political and symbolic impact of the acts while minimizing unnecessary killings. Typically, Basque terrorists have preferred to use guns and firearms rather than less precise bombs and explosives. They have attacked individuals and small groups rather than large crowds and have carefully chosen their targets with a view to the likely impact in the Spanish and Basque political arenas.[53] Of course, much of the difference between the IRA's and ETA's terrorist strategies and degree of success is due to their drastically different operational environments. ETA operates in an overwhelmingly Basque region against "outside" enemies (the Spanish government and non-Basque Spaniards) and can therefore target a relatively tiny group. The IRA, however, is active in an area in which the Catholic population is a minority (about 35 percent

---

[52]Laqueur, *The Age of Terrorism*, 225.
[53]Robert P. Clark, "Patterns of ETA Violence: 1968–1980," 123–24, 127–30 in Peter H. Merkl, ed., *Political Violence and Terror: Motifs and Motivations* (Berkeley, Los Angeles, and London, 1986).

of the total population) and sees two-thirds of the population as potential targets.

Of 2,812 ETA terrorist acts recorded between 1968 and 1980, most were aimed at lower-ranking *Guardia Civil* personnel (about 23 percent of all persons killed) and senior members of the national and local police in the Basque provinces (almost 50 percent of all people killed). The third most common, but politically most significant, target was the higher ranks of the Spanish armed forces: twenty senior military officers were assassinated between 1968 and 1980, including Prime Minister Admiral Luis Carrero Blanco in 1973 and the military governors of Madrid in 1979. Among civilians, the most popular ETA targets were government representatives in the Basque region and rival political leaders, particularly top members of the then-ruling Democratic Center party (UCD). In 1980 three high-ranking UCD members were assassinated.[54]

Apart from attacks on politically and symbolically important individuals, ETA has frequently blackmailed industrialists and businessmen (some were killed for refusing to give money to the organization), and undertaken kidnappings and bank robberies to finance its activities. In 1976 José Luis Arrasate was kidnapped and later ransomed for 30 million pesetas; in 1973 Felipe Huarte Beaumont, a wealthy businessman, was released in exchange for 50 million pesetas.[55] While ETA-M was responsible for most of the killings, ETA-PM carried out more than half of the kidnappings between 1968 and 1980.

How successful has ETA's terrorist strategy been? Clearly, the group's increasing use of political violence played an important role in inducing the government in

---

[54]Janke, 159; Clark, 136–39.
[55]Janke, 158–59.

Madrid to take important steps toward Basque self-government. Yet, by the early 1980s, ETA's terrorism threatened to become counterproductive. First, as the Spanish government extended greater regional powers to the Basques, ETA's terrorist acts continued to escalate. Despite Madrid's concessions, at some point this escalation is bound to undermine the government's willingness to further expand Basque autonomy. Second, by the early 1980s the increasing number and cruelty of ETA attacks began to endanger democracy, the only type of political system likely to uphold or allow for greater Basque rights. In the entire 1968–1980 period, ETA carried out 80 percent (2,352) of its terrorist actions and about 80 percent (188) of its killings after Franco's regime ended in 1975. In 1979, as Spanish democratization was being completed and the first Basque regional government was about to be elected, ETA's terrorism peaked with 1,471 incidents and 75 deaths.[56]

Third, ETA has failed to gain support among the majority of the Basque people, including the working class. Most Basques feel that their particular interests, including nationalist aspirations, are better served by the PNV. Hence, only an estimated 10–15 percent of the Basque people support ETA and its terrorist tactics.[57] The growing violence of ETA operations has also caused controversies among the relatively few active members (ranging from 50 to 200 at any one time),[58] and has led to new arrests, further weakening the group.

There is considerable evidence that ETA presently receives or has received support, including training, from countries such as Algeria, South Yemen, Cuba, and Libya. By far the most important foreign assistance, however,

---

[56]Janke, 159; Clark, 134.
[57]Laqueur, *The Age of Terrorism,* 224.
[58]Ibid., 225.

was the freedom of operation that ETA long enjoyed in France and that was severely curtailed in the early 1980s.

In the final analysis, the case of ETA illustrates how terrorist strategies can be carefully designed to maximize their political impact but also how, in the process, they can become so violent and threaten young democracies to the extent of becoming self-defeating.

The IRA: less discriminate terrorism with bleak prospects. While the struggle over Northern Ireland between, roughly speaking, Catholic Republicans and Protestant Loyalists is more than a century old, the fierce contemporary terrorism campaigns on both sides grew out of the Catholic civil rights movement of the later 1960s. Between 1969 and 1982, more than 2,200 people were killed in the longest period of political terrorism experienced by a Western European democracy since the end of World War II.[59]

The demand for an end to political and social discrimination against the large Catholic minority in Northern Ireland (over one-third of the population) at first won sympathy among many Protestants and even in the British government. British troops were deployed there in 1969, originally to protect the Catholics from the growing sectarian violence. Some Protestants in the north, however, felt their safety and privileges were threatened by the prospect of a Catholic-Protestant reconciliation. In 1966 the Ulster Volunteer Force (UVF) was formed as a Protestant-Loyalist paramilitary organization opposing the granting of greater Catholic minority rights and favoring continued British rule in Northern Ireland.[60]

---

[59]Paul Wilkinson, "The Orange and the Green: Extremism in Northern Ireland," 105, in Martha Crenshaw, ed., *Terrorism, Legitimacy, and Power: The Consequences of Political Violence* (Middletown, Connecticut, 1983).
[60]Adrian Guelke, "Loyalist and Republican Perceptions of the Northern Ireland Conflict: The UDA and Provisional IRA," 92–93 in Merkl, ed., *Political Violence and Terror.*

Three years later mounting clashes between the UVF and the Irish Republican Army provoked a split within the latter. The dissidents called for more militant terrorist action and formed the Provisional IRA (PIRA) or the "Provisionals," which soon became the better-equipped, more nationalistic and larger wing of the IRA. By 1972 the official IRA ("the Officials") had ended virtually all of its political violence.[61] The Provisionals have since been the major Republican terrorist group in Northern Ireland, and their strategies have been quite similar to those of Loyalist-Protestant forces[62] as well as other Republican groups such as the Irish National Liberation Army.

Rejecting the 1921 agreement partitioning Ireland, the PIRA seeks the withdrawal of British troops from Northern Ireland, the overthrow of the current government of the Irish Republic, and the establishment of an Irish republic uniting the predominantly Protestant north with the Catholic south. According to its program, this would be a Marxist-Socialist republic brought about by revolution throughout Ireland, with an economy based on cooperatives and extensive nationalizations.[63] Even the PIRA has admitted, however, that the deep sectarian divisions among the Irish working class have in practice precluded the possibility of proletarian unity.

While its legal arm, the Provisional Sinn Fein Party, engages in political campaigns and support work, the PIRA carries out terrorist attacks to undermine the will of the British government and people to continue London's rule in Northern Ireland. The primary targets are the British military and police as well as members of the Protestant paramilitary forces in Northern Ireland. On June 15, 1988, for example, a PIRA bomb killed six British

---

[61]Laqueur, *The Age of Terrorism*, 209.
[62]See, for example, Wilkinson, 109–116.
[63]Laqueur, *The Age of Terrorism*, 209–210.

soldiers and injured at least ten civilians in Lisburn outside Belfast. This was the bloodiest PIRA attack against
the British Army in Northern Ireland since a 1979 bomb
blast claimed by the same organization killed eighteen
soldiers. The same day the PIRA shot and killed Robert
Seymour, a leading member of a Protestant paramilitary
group.[64]

At times, however, the PIRA has also conducted terrorist attacks in England, and against British military and
diplomatic personnel abroad. In 1979 the British ambassador to the Netherlands was assassinated by the PIRA.
In May 1988 the PIRA in separate bomb and gun attacks
killed three British Royal Air Force members and injured
another three in the Netherlands.[65]

Unlike ETA, the PIRA has often bombed public sites
with large crowds, including pubs, department stores,
hotels, and even hospitals.[66] On occasion, hostages have
been taken for ransom and several prominent British
citizens have been assassinated, but the general pattern
is one of indiscriminate violence. This has resulted in extensive random killings. Only a few of the victims of PIRA
attacks have been active upholders of British rule in
Northern Ireland; most have been Protestant civilian
bystanders. When the number of casualties in Irish terrorist incidents peaked in 1972, less than 25 percent of
the 467 people killed were army personnel. Subsequently, the level of violence declined, but the percentage of
accidental victims remains high. Of the 49 people killed
by the PIRA in 1985, for example, only 2 were British
army members and 25 were British police.[67]

While many Irish Catholics support the goal of ousting the British from the north and reuniting the island,

[64]*Washington Post,* June 16, 1988, A1, A37.
[65]*Washington Post,* May 2, 1988, A1, A27.
[66]Wilkinson, 118.
[67]Laqueur, *The Age of Terrorism,* 210–12.

they bitterly resent PIRA methods. Indeed, the organization's relatively indiscriminate, brutal terrorism has undermined any remnants of sympathy among the Protestant population and even among many Catholics and Republicans who have also been the victims of PIRA attacks. Presently, the approximately 300 PIRA fighters and 2,000 active supporters have virtually no political support in the Republic of Ireland. In Northern Ireland, they have never received more than about 10–12 percent of the vote.[68]

An important event that ultimately created antipathy for the group was the 1981 PIRA hunger strikes. When these initially brought about a surge in support, publicity, and financial contributions to the organization, the PIRA leadership insisted on continuing them until all the hunger strikers died. This decision put the PIRA on a collision course with the prisoners' relatives, the Catholic Church, and a large part of the Catholic community who wanted the hunger strikes called off for humanitarian reasons.[69] Another important incident detrimental to the group's image was the PIRA bombing of November 1987, which killed 11 civilians at a Remembrance Day ceremony for war dead in Enniskillen.[70]

If the PIRA's terrorist strategy can conceivably achieve any of its goals, it is the more immediate one of British withdrawal. Polls have repeatedly shown that most British citizens favor disengagement from Northern Ireland. In contrast to ETA, however, it is very unlikely that political violence will induce the British government or the Protestant population to agree to any significant steps towards changing the status of Northern Ireland. Rather, decades of PIRA terrorism have made the prospects of a

---

[68]Ibid., 213.
[69]Conor Cruise O'Brien, "Terrorism Under Democratic Conditions: The Case of the IRA," 102–103, in Crenshaw, ed., *Terrorism, Legitimacy, and Power.*
[70]*Washington Post*, March 16, 1988, A45.

Catholic-Protestant settlement and a united Ireland even more remote by deepening sectarian hatred and strengthening the determination of Protestant paramilitary forces to resist unification.[71] This conclusion does not imply that the PIRA (or their Protestant-Loyalist counterparts) will renounce the terrorist weapon; they undoubtedly will not.

Guerilla and Terrorist Warfare in Southeast Asia: India and Sri Lanka

Of all parts of the world, Asia has experienced the greatest increase in the number of terrorist incidents, casualties, and state-sponsored terrorist attacks since 1986. From 1985 to 1986, the number of international terrorist acts in Asia increased from 42 to 77 per year; in 1987 there were 170 attacks. These statistics reflect to a large extent the rise in Afghan-sponsored terrorist bombings in Pakistan, whose government was the conduit for military supplies to the guerrillas fighting Soviet forces in Afghanistan. In 1987 the Afghan intelligence service was blamed for 127 bombings in Pakistan, which killed 234 people and wounded 1,200.[72]

Following the August 1988 airplane crash which killed Pakistani President Mohammed Zia ul-Haq, U.S. Ambassador to Pakistan Arnold L. Raphel, and 29 other passengers, speculation about possible Afghan complicity emerged, particularly as investigations into the incident ruled out technical failure as the cause.[73] These figures and events still do not account for the enormous surge in domestic terrorist operations and victims in the region, particularly in Sri Lanka and India.

---

[71]O'Brien, 100–102.
[72]"International Terrorism Statistics, 1968–1987."
[73]*Washington Post*, October 21, 1988, A25; October 17, 1988, A1, A23; August 23, 1988, A10.

Asia has experienced all four types of revolutionary and state terrorism previously mentioned. In 1987–88 the United States added North Korea to its official list of states directly engaging in or supporting international terrorism on the basis of two key incidents: the October 1983 bombing in Burma, which was meant to assassinate South Korean President Chun but instead killed four South Korean cabinet members; and the November 1987 bombing of a South Korean airliner (Korean Air flight 858) off the coast of Burma that killed all 115 people on board.[74] Among the terrorist groups supported by North Korea is the recently reemergent Japanese Red Army, believed to be responsible for the April 1988 car bombing at a United Service Organization (USO) club in Naples that killed one U.S. servicewoman and four Italians.[75]

In some cases, pro-government forces use terrorist tactics against opposition groups. The *Alsa Masa* organization, which is the umbrella group for the antiguerrilla vigilante squads in the Philippines, has killed people suspected of supporting the Communist insurgency of the New People's Army (NPA). In July 1988 the fifth human rights lawyer in twelve months was assassinated in what was labeled a right-wing campaign of violence.[76] In India, police death squads have reportedly killed civilians or alleged supporters of Sikh terrorist groups.

Insurgencies in Sri Lanka and the Philippines are rather typical cases of guerrilla groups which use terrorism as part of (not a substitute for) a wider national-separatist and/or revolutionary strategy. Although much has been written on the differences between guerrilla and terrorist tactics, theoretical distinctions became blurred

---

[74]James P. Wootten, *Terrorism: U.S. Policy Options,* Foreign Affairs and National Defense Division, Congressional Research Service, Washington, D.C., April 1988, 5, 8.
[75]*Washington Post,* April 16, 1988, A1, A20.
[76]*Washington Post,* May 3, 1988, A20; July 3, 1988, A31.

when guerrillas come to rely on terrorist means, as in Southeast Asia and Latin America.

Guerrilla warfare is mainly rural based and fought according to a strategy which the Chinese guerrilla theorist Lin Piao termed "encirclement of the city by the countryside." Guerrilla leaders seek not only to build up military units and eventually an army to defeat government troops, but also to establish "liberated zones" and win popular support as a viable alternative to the ruling regime. This strategy does not preclude the use of terrorist tactics. Indeed, one of the most important guerrilla theorists, Mao Zedong, stressed the need to create terror for a limited period of time.[77] But terrorism, which cannot be used to build mass support, remains only one element of a larger political strategy. In contrast to guerrillas who seek to win area control, terrorists usually operate clandestinely in small units, in predominantly urban centers. Their strategy is to create a state of terror. The primary tactic is not—and cannot be—to build political support or to engage in political organization, which helps to explain why so few terrorists have attained their long-term objectives.[78]

A primary example of an insurgent group engaging in terrorism is the NPA—the military wing of the Communist party in the Philippines—whose growing strength is partly due to its successful combination of guerrilla and terrorist tactics. Indeed, since 1986, the NPA has apparently moved about 100 guerrillas into the Manila area to function as assassination squads (known as "sparrows" for the speed

---

[77]Mao Tse-tung, *Selected Works of Mao Tse-tung*, Vol. 1 (Peking, 1967), 29, quoted in Grand Wardlaw, *Political Terrorism: Theory, Tactics and Counter-Measures*, (Cambridge, 1982), 47.
[78]Laqueur, *The Age of Terrorism*, 5, 147–48. For a representative range of views on the distinctions to be made between guerrilla warfare and terrorism, see Schmid, *Political Terrorism*, 39–49.

with which they carry out their deeds).[79] In the country-side, the NPA has created a network of organizations that build political support in guerrilla-held areas, notably by providing community services to the poor neglected by the central government. At the same time, primarily in the urban centers, the NPA is escalating selective terrorist attacks against government officials, police and military officers, members of the antiguerrilla vigilante squads, and occasionally U.S. servicemen.[80] In March 1988, for example, a mayor of a Manila suburb was injured and seven of his bodyguards were killed in the bloodiest terrorist attack ever attributed to the NPA in the capital.[81] In October 1987 three U.S. servicemen were murdered near Clark Air Force Base in successive attacks later claimed by the NPA.[82]

Sikh terrorism in India. There are numerous ethnic and religious groups in India whose resentment against the central government or other communal groups has turned violent. So far, none has matched the Sikh Khalistan Commando force. In 1987, the world's most sanguine terrorist war claimed an estimated 1,238 lives; in the first five months of 1988, the number of terrorist victims was almost as large.[83]

What has triggered this phenomenal bloodshed? The demand for an independent state in the Punjab region, which is 60 percent Sikh, is rooted in the religious-political ideology of Sikhism, which holds that its followers should have their own homeland, called Khalistan ("Land of the

---

[79]*Washington Post,* March 29, 1988, A10.
[80]Steve Lohr, "Inside the Philippine Insurgency," *New York Times Magazine,* November 3, 1985, 45, 48, 52, 54.
[81]*Washington Post,* March 29, 1988, A10.
[82]*Significant Incidents of Political Violence Against Americans: 1987,* U.S. Department of State, Bureau of Diplomatic Security, Washington, D.C., 1988, 33–38.
[83]*The Economist,* May 28, 1988, 35.

Pure"). The last few years of escalating violence, however, are the result of a series of severe confrontations between the Indian government and the Hindu majority on one hand, and the Sikh minority on the other. In June 1984 Prime Minister Indira Gandhi sent the army and tanks into the Golden Temple in Amritsar, Punjab, to end an occupation by armed Sikh separatists. About 1,000 people were killed, including hundreds of innocent Sikh worshippers, and some of the most precious parts of this holiest of Sikh shrines were destroyed. The Sikh response—the killing of Mrs. Gandhi by two of her Sikh bodyguards in October 1984—in turn drove Hindu rioters to kill indiscriminately 4,000 Sikhs in New Delhi and elsewhere with little police interference. Although most Sikhs do not support the use of terrorism or even the goal of secession from India, this incident further fueled Sikh hatred of the central government.[84]

Sikh terrorist tactics typically involve massive, random killing of Hindus in gun and bomb attacks, often in response to particularly serious crises in Hindu-Sikh relations. One such crisis that helped to expand the terrorists' ranks and heighten the level of violence was triggered by Prime Minister Rajiv Gandhi's decision to suspend the Punjab state government and extend central government control to that region in the spring of 1987.[85] While the Sikhs' larger goal is to force the Indian government to give up Punjab, many attacks have been concentrated on Hindus living there to drive them out of the state, and especially against Hindu villagers along the Pakistani border to facilitate the incoming flow of weapons.

Yet another Sikh occupation of the Golden Temple was defeated by the Indian government in May 1988. Indian paramilitary units surrounded the temple, cut off all

---

[84]Paul Glastris, "Inside the Temple," *The New Republic*, July 4, 1988, 13.
[85]*The Economist*, May 7, 1988, 27.

supplies, and forced the Sikh militants to surrender. In comparison with the 1984 army assault on the temple, this operation more successfully limited the number of casualties, physical damage to the shrines, and political harm to Gandhi's government. Yet the resulting victory for the Gandhi regime only enraged Sikh militants further and provoked massive retaliatory killings. During the five days after the surrender, more than 245 people, mostly Hindus, were killed randomly by Sikh terrorists in Punjab.[86] On June 21, for example, two bomb blasts attributed to Sikh separatists killed at least 32 and wounded 75 people near the Golden Temple.[87]

To a lesser extent, Sikh terrorists also target Indian government officials and police, particularly in Punjab; Sikhs suspected of collaborating with the central authorities or of being insufficiently militant; and, most recently, Hindu migrant workers in Punjab, on which the state's agricultural economy and India's food supplies so critically depend. An example of such targeting is the assassination of the moderate Sikh leader Sant Harchand Singh by Sikh militants following his July 1985 Punjab accord with Prime Minister Gandhi.

Sikh extremism in India is perhaps the foremost illustration of how terrorism can destroy the very fabric of a society without bringing closer the goal for which the violence supposedly is used. The ever-growing force of hard-core terrorists, now estimated to include more than 2,000 people, has certainly succeeded in driving many Hindus out of Punjab, in gaining increasingly sophisticated weaponry from Pakistan, and in escalating terrorist campaigns. Above all, the militants are gaining greater support among normally law-abiding Sikhs who have become alienated by the central government's own.

---

[86]*The Economist,* May 28, 1988, 35; May 21, 1988, 34–35.
[87]*Washington Post,* June 22, 1988, A19.

often indiscriminate, abuse of the Sikh population.[88] But even so, the goal of an independent Sikh state in Punjab has not come closer. The government in New Delhi has proved forcefully that no matter how great the pressure of Sikh violence becomes, it will not concede to this demand which would entail an unacceptable economic and strategic loss to India.

The Tamil Tigers in Sri Lanka. The complex warfare in Sri Lanka between, on one hand, the central government and the Indian "peacekeeping" force and, on the other, an array of Singhalese and Tamil terrorist groups demonstrates the potential of terrorism to escalate into full-scale civil war.

The demand of Sri Lanka's Tamil minority for an independent state (Tamil Eelam) in the northern and eastern provinces, where most Tamils live, is rooted in a strong sense of ethnic identity and a long history of Singhalese-Tamil antagonisms. The predominantly Hindu Tamils, who comprise 18 percent of the country's population, have suffered considerable discrimination under the mostly Buddhist Singhalese majority that makes up 74 percent of the population and controls Sri Lanka's government and military institutions. The most important Tamil guerrilla organization using terrorist tactics— the Tamil Tigers (the Liberation Tigers of Tamil Eelam [LTTE]), led by Velupillai Prabakaran—emerged in the 1970s and has about 2,000 fighters and thousands of sympathizers.[89] Their principal source of support is the 45–50 million Tamils living in India's southern state, Tamil Nadu, and, until recently, the Indian government.

---

[88]Glastris, 13–15.
[89]Steven R. Weisman, "Sri Lanka: A Nation Disintegrates," *New York Times Magazine,* December 13, 1987, 80, 81, 85.

After years of more or less allowing Sri Lankan Tamils to be trained and armed in southern India, New Delhi declared in 1985 its opposition to a Tamil homeland on the island. In July 1987 Rajiv Gandhi entered a compromise agreement with Sri Lanka's President Junius Richard Jayewardene to extend greater political autonomy to the Tamils in the northern and eastern provinces. Although the Tamil guerrillas at first complied with the "peace accord" under Indian pressure and surrendered their arms, they finally rejected the arrangement for failing to grant full Tamil independence. The Indian peacekeeping troops sent to help implement the accord joined the Sri Lankan Army in the war against the guerrillas. Instead of ending the civil war, the 1987 Indian–Sri Lankan agreement served to escalate, at least temporarily, the terrorist violence on all sides: from Singhalese terrorist groups, mainly the revolutionary People's Liberation Front (the *Janatha Vinukthi Peramuna*) opposing Tamil autonomy; from and among rival Tamil guerrilla organizations; and from the Sri Lankan government and army launching counterattacks against both Singhalese and Tamil guerrillas.

Until the intervention by Indian troops, LTTE terrorism often involved gun and bomb attacks against Sri Lankan government officials, army, and police officers; moderate Tamil officials and rival Tamil guerrillas; and Sinhalese extremists. In a 1983 ambush, for example, the Tamil Tigers killed 13 Sri Lankan soldiers, which provoked Singhalese mobs to murder hundreds of innocent Tamils. In October 1987, a moderate Tamil civil servant, Marianpillai Anthonimuthu, was killed by a Tamil-planted car bomb. During August and September 1987 alone, the Tamil Tigers killed an estimated 150 members of the rival People's Liberation Organization of Tamil Eelam (PLOTE) and Eelam People's Revolutionary Liberation Front (EPRLF)[90]

---

[90]*FBIS*, September 15, 1987, 38.

Terrorist acts by the LTTE and other Tamil guerrillas also entailed extensive random killing of large groups of Singhalese civilians. In April 1987 the Tamil Tigers massacred 127 bus passengers; in October 1987 127 Singhalese villagers were killed in a sixteen-hour period by the same group in eastern Sri Lanka.[91] And on April 30 and May 1, 1988, 32 Singhalese and Muslim bus passengers were killed and 32 were injured in two separate mine and gun attacks attributed to the LTTE.[92] These types of events have occurred almost daily on the island.

With the Indian–Sri Lankan accord and the Indian intervention into the war, Tamil terrorism was stepped up and extended to include other targets. The new victims were particularly Indian soldiers and (potential) participants or candidates in the elections for the provincial councils that were part of the accord's plan for Tamil autonomy.[93]

Like the Punjab region in India, Sri Lanka is a primary example of a country threatened with disintegration by separatist ethnic minorities resorting to terrorist means and by an unending cycle of violence and revenge. After five years of guerrilla and terrorist warfare, which has killed more than 7,000 Sri Lankans,[94] the Tamil dream of a homeland has not come closer. Rather, it has become more distant. As in the case of ETA, the Tamils launched terrorist attacks that eventually forced the central government into making considerable concessions, but they were unwilling to compromise and stop the campaigns of violence. At this point, the Tamils' warfare has become a major obstacle to their own aspirations, for which the proposed political autonomy and provincial councils eventually could have paved the way.

---

[91]Weisman, 93. *FBIS,* October 7, 1987, 46.
[92]*Washington Post,* May 2, 1988, A29.
[93]*The Economist,* May 7, 1988, 28–29.
[94]Weisman, 37.

Latin America: Narco-Terrorism and Insurgencies in Colombia

Latin American terrorism is still chiefly domestic, part of insurgent groups' wider guerrilla strategies, and directed against local governments rather than U.S. or other foreign targets. Nevertheless, the number of international terrorist attacks against U.S. and foreign property and personnel in Latin America has increased since 1980. For local revolutionaries, assaulting foreign targets seems to be a tactic designed to attract greater international attention to their causes, to protest foreign presence, and perhaps to win support from anti-Western states such as Libya.[95]

After the peak year of 1986, in which there were 159 recorded incidents, the number of international terrorist attacks in Latin America declined in 1987 to 108 attacks.[96] Still, of all terrorist incidents involving the United States in 1987, over half (52.8 percent) occurred in this region. Most of these attacks were against the property and personnel of U.S. oil companies, multinational banks, and other businesses.[97]

Among the types of political violence found in Latin America are the use of terrorism by governments and armies against domestic opposition (for example, the death squads in El Salvador and Guatemala) and by their indigenous enemies which in some cases enjoy foreign support (for instance, the Cuban and Nicaraguan backing of Colombia's National Liberation Army [ELN] and 19th of April Movement [M-19]). One noteworthy feature of

---

[95]*Patterns of Global Terrorism: 1986,* U.S. Department of State, Office of the Ambassador at Large for Counter-Terrorism, Washington, D.C., 1988, 25.
[96]"International Terrorism Statistics, 1968–1987."
[97]*Significant Incidents of Political Violence Against Americans: 1987,* U.S. Department of State, Bureau of Diplomatic Security, Washington, D.C., April 1988, 1, 3, 4.

Latin American terrorism, however, is the link sometimes found between guerrillas using terrorist tactics and narcotics traffickers, although the latter also carry out their own terrorist operations. Virtually every Central and South American state has been affected by either the drug trade or insurgent-terrorist groups. None, however, has suffered as profoundly from both problems simultaneously as have Colombia and Peru. This section briefly examines the nature and implications of the relationship between narco-terrorism and insurgencies in Colombia.[98]

Colombian President Virgilio Barco inherited from his predecessor a tenuous truce with the country's single largest guerrilla group, the Revolutionary Armed Forces of Colombia (FARC), the military wing of the Colombian Communist party. Since 1985, however, the three major Columbian insurgent groups that resort to terrorist tactics—the ELN, the M-19, and the People's Liberation Army (EPL)—are loosely allied in the National Guerrilla Coordinator (CNG), totaling about 2,500 guerrillas. At present, the ELN seems to have replaced the M-19 as the dominant force within the CNG.[99]

While there is some effective coordination of attacks, ideological differences continue to cause divisions within the alliance. The ELN is Castroite, while the EPL is Maoist. Yet, the ideological leanings of Colombia's insurgent groups often change or remain obscure. The M-19, for instance, emerged in 1972 on the extreme Right only to announce an alliance with the leftist ELN a few years later.[100]

These guerrilla groups use terrorism as one of many strategies to further their political and military goals. All are actively involved in legal politics, especially in the

---

[98]With regard to narco-terrorism and the *Sendero Luminoso* movement in Peru, see David Scott Palmer's contribution in this volume. Concerning terrorism in Argentina, see Mark Falcoff's chapter.
[99]*Patterns of Global Terrorism: 1986*, 25–26.
[100]Schmid, *Political Terrorism*, 307; Laqueur, *The Age of Terrorism*, 205, 257.

activities of labor unions and other organizations, to capitalize on widespread grievances and build popular support.[101] Simultaneously, the guerrillas are primarily rural based, seeking to expand their fronts from the countryside to urban centers. But terrorist operations are also carried out in the cities, where appropriate targets and international attention are concentrated.

At first, the goals of narcotics traffickers and guerrilla groups may appear quite different. For the former, the enormous profits made from the sale of illegal drugs is an end in itself, while for the latter these gains simply provide the means to finance guerrilla-terrorist warfare. Yet, the drug dealers have a stake in cooperating with guerrillas and terrorists to weaken the government and to drive law enforcement agents from their production areas. Apart from receiving funds, guerrillas also have a political interest in cooperating with drug traffickers, for the latter's intimidation and bribery of police, judges, and government officials serve to corrupt, weaken, and destabilize the country's regime and political system.

In Colombia the powerful Medellín cartel, which controls an estimated 75–80 percent of all cocaine coming into the United States, has been particularly effective in this endeavor. The fact that often drug traffickers cultivate their crops and insurgent groups establish their bases in the same remote, rural areas has also promoted cooperation. In a few parts of the country, however, guerrillas fight a fierce war against drug traffickers who have become powerful landowners opposed to the guerrillas' stated goal of agrarian reform.

There is considerable evidence that in the case of Colombia the activities of drug traffickers and insurgent-terrorist groups have in general become exceptionally intertwined. Guerrillas carry out attacks against Colombian

---

[101]*Patterns of Global Terrorism*, 25.

and U.S. law enforcement personnel and engage in virtually every aspect of the drug trade (the FARC even grows and processes coca), while narcotics dealers also engage in terrorist operations. In April 1984 drug traffickers assassinated Colombian Justice Minister Rodrigo Lara Bonilla in response to his raid on several cocaine-processing laboratories and stepped up warfare against the narcotics trade. As the Colombian government started to extradite drug traffickers to the United States, drug dealers detonated a bomb outside the U.S. embassy in Bogotá in November 1984 and threatened to kill American diplomats and business people.[102]

In exchange for substantial sums of money, guerrilla groups provide physical protection for Colombian marijuana-growing areas in the northeast (the world's largest); for cocaine-processing laboratories, where about 75 percent of all cocaine entering the United States is refined from Peruvian and Bolivian coca leaves; and for the drug traffickers' transport routes. In one region, local terrorists are reported to have earned $10 million a month for their protective services. The FARC is believed to have once received $100 million to purchase weapons and guard seven cocaine laboratories and seven airstrips run by drug traffickers.[103] In November 1985, the M–19 raided the Supreme Court in Bogotá and destroyed a large number of documents to hamper the extradition of Colombian drug traffickers to the United States. More than 50 M–19 members and 11 Supreme Court justices, including Supreme Court President Alfonso Reyes, were killed in the assault on the building. It is noteworthy that although carried out by an insurgent-terrorist group, the operation was not motivated by political goals but by the interests of narcotics traffickers. Finally, both the Medellín

---

[102]Boyce, 24–25.
[103]Laqueur, 98, 257.

cartel and the M-19, and political as well as narcotics interests, have been suspected of supporting or executing
the May 1988 kidnapping of Alvaro Gomez Hurtado, the
leader of Colombia's main opposition Conservative party who had urged tougher measures against both drug
traffickers and guerrillas.[104] These are only a few examples of how the motives and operations of insurgent terrorists and narcotics dealers in Colombia have become
almost indistinguishable.

This cooperation with local drug traffickers does not
imply that Colombian guerrilla groups have reduced their
politically motivated, international terrorist activities. Of
50 international terrorist attacks in Columbia in 1986, most
were directed against U.S.-affiliated staff and property. In
July 1986, ELN guerrillas attacked the U.S.-owned
Occidental–Shell–Ecopetrol pipeline close to the Venezuelan border and followed up with dozens more attacks
on the same pipeline throughout the year.[105] Several
grenades have damaged the U.S. embassy in Bogotá. Colombian guerrillas have also engaged extensively in kidnappings of local and foreign politicians, business people, and
diplomats stationed in the country. In 1983 a U.S. ranch-
er, Russel Martin Stendhal, was kidnapped by the EPL and
later released for an unknown ransom; in 1985 the same
group kidnapped two U.S. engineers. One of them—
Edward Sohl—was found dead in August 1986, while the
other was released unharmed. In 1988, following the abduction of three Colombian journalists, left-wing guerrillas in the country held twelve people, including two West
German consuls and a French assistant press attaché.[106]

For many of Colombia's peasants and workers involved in growing marijuana or in refining and distributing

---

[104]*Washington Post,* May 30, 1988, A24; June 7, 1988, A18; July 20, 1988, A11.
[105]*Patterns of Global Terrorism: 1986,* 25, 36–38.
[106]*Washington Post,* May 5, 1988, A38.

drugs, the narcotics trade provides the only alternative to abject poverty. In contrast to the United States, for example, where Omega 7's alleged involvement with narcotics trafficking in the early 1980s undermined much of its support among the Cuban exile population, Colombian guerrillas seem to have won some grassroot support among the poor, rural population by protecting their lucrative livelihood in the narcotics business.

Colombia provides a frightening illustration of how the emergence of narco-terrorism has strengthened both drug-trafficking cartels and insurgencies using terrorist tactics, and how it has become a genuine threat to the nascent democratic institutions, political stability, and economic integrity of many Latin American countries. Although Colombian guerrilla groups so far have not seriously threatened to overthrow the regime, terrorist violence is on the rise, and drug lords keep expanding their influence in the country's political, economic, and social life.

The Middle East: state-run and state-supported terrorism. Since 1984 the Middle East has taken over Latin America's previous position as the primary stage and source of international terrorist incidents and casualties. From 1982 to 1985 the annual number of international terrorist attacks in the Middle East jumped from 51 to 357. Taking into account Middle East spillover in Europe, international terrorism occurring or originating in the region in 1987 numbered 414 attacks, or 50 percent of all recorded incidents. However, only 14 (less than 4 percent) of the incidents taking place in the Mideast in 1987 have been judged anti-American. When Middle East terrorists have attacked the United States specifically, they have preferred to do so in the European arena.[107] In 1988 the Palestinian uprising

---

[107]"International Terrorism Statistics, 1968–1987"; *Significant Incidents of Political Violence,* 1, 2, 4.

in the Israeli-occupied territories became a potential source of increase in terrorist attacks and counterterrorist reprisals in the region.

Most terrorism in the Middle East is carried out in the name of, or in support of, several predominant political or religious causes, such as the Israeli-Arab conflict, Islamic fundamentalism, and Palestinian nationalism. Widespread involvement in these causes has also allowed certain countries to use terrorism for their own purposes as an instrument of foreign policy. Three regimes in the region—Iran, Libya, and Syria—have engaged directly and substantially in terrorism.

Terrorist tactics have been used extensively to spread the Iranian revolution and to promote other foreign policy goals of the revolutionary Islamic regime. Specifically, Iran's strategy has been to work through local Shiite communities seeking to gain a larger share in their governments or to establish an Islamic republic on the Iranian model. Inside Lebanon, Iran has been able to station a number of Revolutionary Guard units during periods of heavy internal fighting between the country's various factions. The sheer number of Shiite fundamentalist groups in Lebanon is impressive but misleading: most, including the Organization of the Oppressed on Earth, Islamic Jihad, and the Revolutionary Justice Organization, are subgroups within a single organization— the *Hizb Allah* ("Party of God"). Iran is believed to have been directly involved in several *Hizb Allah* kidnappings of Westerners and to have directed many of the organization's operations.[108]

It would be an exaggeration to say that the Khomeini regime totally controls the *Hizb Allah* or is directly responsible for all of its terrorist deeds. Iranian leverage still

---

[108]*Patterns of Global Terrorism: 1986,* U.S. Department of State, Washington, D.C., 1988, 10, 20–22.

consists predominantly of military training, weapons, and money. Nevertheless, evidence of Iran's extensive influence over the organization was provided by the release of several French hostages as a result of successful French-Iranian negotiations. Three French television crew members taken hostage by the Revolutionary Justice Organization in March 1986 were freed after France repaid one-third of a debt from the Shah era. In November 1986, when Prime Minister Jacques Chirac repaid another one-third of the debt to Teheran, two more French hostages were released.[109] In May 1988 Islamic Jihad freed the last three French hostages in Lebanon following prolonged French-Iranian talks. The only concessions to Iran admitted by France were the restoration of diplomatic relations between the two countries, broken off by Paris in July 1987, and France's repayment of the remaining $340 million of the loan made by the Shah.[110] In July 1988, after Iran accepted a ceasefire in its war with Iraq, Teheran began to seek improved relations with Western countries. Iranian leaders offered, among other things, to help arrange the freeing of American hostages in exchange for U.S. concessions to Teheran (notably the unfreezing of Iranian military supplies and funds in the United States).

About twenty foreign hostages were still held by Shiite Moslem groups in Lebanon in the first half of 1988. Of these, nine were U.S. citizens—including U.S. Marine Lt. Col. Williams R. Higgins, head of the 75-man Lebanon Group of the U.N. Truce Supervision Organization, who was kidnapped near Tyre in February 1988, and Associated Press reporter Terry Anderson, who was abducted in March 1985—and three were British subjects,

---

[109]*Washington Post,* May 5, 1988, A29.
[110]*New York Times,* May 6, 1988, 1; *Washington Post,* June 6, 1988, A31, A35; May 19, 1988, A35, A38.

including Anglican Church envoy Terry Waite, kidnapped in January 1987.

The most recent example of Iranian-inspired terrorism was the April 1988 hijacking of Kuwait Airways flight 422 by Islamic fundamentalists seeking the release of seventeen pro-Khomeini terrorists held in Kuwait. Two Kuwaiti passengers were killed before Algerian mediation brought an end to the sixteen-day crisis. According to the hostages released at the plane's first and second stops in Mashhad, Iran, and Larnaca, Cyprus, respectively, several more hijackers were allowed to board the aircraft in Iran with weaponry and explosives.[111] Apart from the September 1986 bombings in Paris attributed to the *Hizb Allah* and some assaults on anti-Khomeini Iranians in Europe, the Khomeini regime has seldom sponsored terrorism outside of the region. Middle East spillover terrorism in Europe and Asia has been primarily Arab and Palestinian, made possible to a large extent by Libyan and Syrian state sponsorship.[112]

No case better illustrates the extent to which an otherwise small and weak state can attempt to use terrorist strategies to gain international attention and further overly ambitious foreign policy goals than Libya's Colonel Qadhafi. His sponsorship has been critical for many terrorist groups, including the IRA, the ETA, the Popular Front for the Liberation of Palestine (PFLP), Abu Nidal, and insurgencies in Southeast Asia, South America, Africa and the Caribbean. In November 1987, for example, French authorities intercepted a ship bound for the IRA with 150 tons of arms, including surface-to-air missiles, from Libya.[113]

---

[111]*Washington Post,* April 21, 1988, A1, A28; April 11, 1988, A1, A18; April 9, 1988, A1, A22; April 15, 1988, A23.
[112]On Iran-sponsored terrorism and the general problem of terrorism in the Middle East, see the articles in this volume by Joseph Kostiner and Barry Rubin.
[113]*Washington Post,* June 3, 1988, A23.

The targets of Libyan-sponsored terrorism have typically included Israel, moderate Palestinian leaders, Arab regimes, Libyan opponents of Qadhafi and, more recently, U.S. and British personnel and property, particularly in Europe. Libya paid and provided asylum for some of the terrorists who killed the Israeli athletes at the 1972 Munich Olympic Games.[114] In 1984, Libyan agents fired on anti-Qadhafi demonstrators from within the Libyan embassy in London, and in February 1986 wounded the owner of a radio station in Rome hostile to the Qadhafi regime.

Through his support of Abu Nidal, Colonel Qadhafi has contributed to numerous terrorist actions in Europe. These include the September 1986 attack on an Istanbul synagogue in which 22 people were killed and 6 were wounded only a few hours after four Abu Nidal terrorists had been arrested for attempting to hijack a Pan Am flight in Karachi, Pakistan; and the December 1985 attacks on the El Al ticket counters at the Rome and Vienna airports in which 18 people (including 5 Americans) were killed and 116 (22 Americans) were wounded. Libya was apparently involved in the November 1985 hijacking of an Egyptian Air flight in which Arab gunmen shot 2 Israelis and 3 Americans and another 56 passengers were killed as the Egyptian commandos stormed the plane in Malta. These bolder Libyan attacks on U.S. targets culminated with the April 1986 bombing of the La Belle discotheque in West Berlin that killed 3 people (2 Americans) and wounded more than 200 (70 Americans).

European diplomatic and economic sanctions against Libya, increased security measures, and the April 1986 U.S. air raids on Tripoli and Benghaze helped bring about a significant lull in Middle East state sponsorship of international terrorism, particulary in the attacks carried

---

[114]Laqueur, *The Age of Terrorism*, 283; Wootten, *Terrorism: U.S. Policy Options*, 6.

out in Europe. Specifically, the expulsion of more than 100 Libyan "diplomats" from European capitals made it much more difficult for Qadhafi to use Libyan People's Bureaus (the Libyan equivalent of embassies) there for terrorist missions. Overall, Libyan-sponsored terrorism dropped from 26 recorded attacks in 1984 to 19 in 1986; Iranian-sponsored terrorism declined from 64 to 13 incidents; and Syrian-supported terrorist operations fell from 26 to 6 acts in the same period.[115] In early 1988, however, Iran and Libya seemed to reemerge as major sponsors of international terrorism.

After being expelled from Syria in the summer of 1987, Abu Nidal relocated his headquarters to Tripoli and carried out numerous terrorist actions with alleged Libyan support. These include the March 1988 attack on an Alitalia Airlines crew in Bombay; the May 1988 assaults on Westerners in Khartoum that killed 6 people; and the July 1988 attack on the Greek cruise ferry *City of Poros*.[116]

Colonel Qadhafi also began supporting the Japanese Red Army (JRA). This terrorist organization gained notoriety by hijacking a Japan Airlines flight in 1970 and another in 1977, and by attacking the Lod Airport in Israel in 1972, killing 28 people. When JRA member Kozo Okamoto, jailed in Israel since his participation in the Lod Airport incident, was released in 1985 as part of a deal freeing three PFLP-held Israeli soldiers, he immediately traveled to Libya. In August 1986, Colonel Qadhafi allegedly met Hasaka Shigenobou, a woman leader of the JRA living in Damascus, to plan the organization's comeback. The following year, the U.S. embassy in Rome was attacked with gunfire and bomb devices planted in a car

---

[115]"International Terrorism Statistics, 1985–1987."

[116]*Washington Post,* July 12, 1988, A1, A19; July 13, 1988, A14. A spokesman for the Abu Nidal group later maintained that the member mainly accused for the attack—Khadar Samir Mohamad—died three years ago (*Sydsvenska Dagbladet,* July 22, 1988, 32).

rented by JRA member Junzo Okudaira. The same man is believed to have arranged the car bomb attack on the Naples USO club on April 14, 1988.[117] Yi Kikumura, most likely belonging to the JRA, was arrested in New Jersey on April 12, 1988, with homemade bombs and is suspected of planning the group's first attack on U.S. territory. Shortly thereafter, Yasuhiro Shibata, a JRA member who took part in the 1970 hijacking, was arrested in Tokyo; in May 1988, a bomb believed to have been planted by the JRA exploded at a Citibank office in New Delhi.[118] These and other incidents related to the JRA coincided with the second anniversary of the U.S. retaliatory raids on Libya, and seemed to indicate that Qadhafi's support and instructions are important forces behind the organization's growing activism.[119]

Syrian sponsorship of international terrorism appears in many aspects similar to that of Colonel Qadhafi and Ayatollah Khomeini. The Assad regime provides weapons, economic aid, training, safe haven, and operational bases in the country or in Syrian-controlled Lebanon to the Syrian Social Nationalist Party (SSNP), Kurdish, and Armenian terrorist groups; and to numerous anti-Arafat Palestinian groups including Abu Musa, the PFLP, the PFLP-General Command, the Democratic Front for the Liberation of Palestine, *al-Saiqa* and, until recently, Abu Nidal. As with Libya and Iran, Syria's involvement in terrorism ranges from direct participation by its agents in terrorist operations and near total control of certain terrorist groups, such as *al-Saiqa*, to tolerance of terrorist activities in Syrian or Syrian-held territories. In Lebanon, numerous assassinations of anti-Syrian leaders have been attributed to Damascus, including the 1982 killing of

---

[117]*Washington Post*, April 16, 1988, A1, A20.
[118]*Washington Post*, May 11, 1988, A28.
[119]See further *Washington Post,* June 3, 1988, A1, A23; June 26, 1988, C1, C4.

President-elect Bashir Gemayel. The Assad regime is also suspected of having played a role in the many attacks on U.S. targets there.[120]

Before evidence of Syrian involvement in several terrorist incidents brought about Western sanctions in the fall of 1986 and sufficient pressure to force a reduction, Syria contributed to numerous Palestinian operations in Europe. Specifically, Syrian agents were reported to have been directly involved with Palestinian terrorists in three incidents in Western Europe in 1986: the March bombing of a German-Arab Friendship Union building in West Berlin, the April attempt to bomb an El Al flight from London to Tel Aviv, and the June effort by Abu Musa's Fatah rebels to bomb an El Al flight in Madrid.[121] In October 1987, three alleged members of the Lebanon-based Syrian Social Nationalist Party entered Vermont from Canada and were arrested on charges of illegal immigration and import of explosives. They apparently planned an assassination with a car bomb in the United States as part of a factional dispute within the SSNP and no direct Syrian involvement was proven.[122] Still, like the Kikumura incident, this event points to the possibility of escalated terrorist activities on U.S. territory.

Syria's use of terrorism has been more effective than that of Iran and Libya because it has been more selective and discreet, and has been carefully combined with conventional diplomacy and military means. Iran's and Libya's open, extensive reliance on terrorism to achieve far too ambitious goals, such as worldwide revolution and control of the Arab world or the Persian Gulf, has, at most, managed to direct international attention to their causes. By contrast, Syrian President Hafez al-Assad's more

---

[120]Wootten, *Terrorism: U.S. Policy Options,* 7; *Patterns of Global Terrorism: 1986,* 9.
[121]*Patterns of Global Terrorism: 1986,* 9, 13.
[122]*New York Times,* May 18, 1988, A6.

discriminate use of terror has greatly favored his relatively limited aims, serving to increase Syrian influence in Lebanon and to discourage Israeli-Arab negotiations. The fact that Damascus has rarely admitted (let alone boasted about) its use of terrorism, or engaged in the open attacks on Israeli and U.S. targets characteristic of Libyan-sponsored violence, has helped to preserve some of Syria's standing in the West and spared the country from retaliation. Hence, while promoting many essential foreign policy goals, Assad's terrorist strategies have not entailed heavy costs and have permitted him to use conventional diplomatic and political channels simultaneously.[123]

Conclusion: Terrorism as a Political Strategy

Terrorists have been amazingly successful in gaining publicity through the media; in creating fear among the masses and in confusing political leaders; and even in bringing about concessions from major powers such as the United States and France. Still, few terrorist groups have achieved any of their stated ultimate goals. The failure of terrorism as a revolutionary strategy is particularly evident. Whenever terrorism has come to predominate over political work and organization, the terrorist group has failed to develop into a mass revolutionary movement. In such cases, the selection of terrorism as a political technique often proved to be a symptom as well as a cause of the group's inability—given the lack of support for its goals, its own nature, or prevailing political conditions—to operate effectively. Hence, terrorist and guerrilla groups in Latin America have certainly contributed to the destabilization of governments there, but have fallen short of bringing about revolution.

---

[123]See Barry Rubin, "The Political Uses of Terrorism in the Middle East," in this volume.

The use of terrorism as a nationalist or separatist strategy has been somewhat more fruitful because nationalist-separatist groups have often been able to obtain greater popular support, more committed members, and a higher degree of internal cohesion on the basis of their ethnic or national identity, surpassing ideological and class differences.[124] As part of the decolonization movement in Palestine, Algeria, Tunisia and Morocco, nationalist terror was certainly effective in the struggle against European colonial rule. As noted earlier, ETA terror helped to induce the extension of greater regional powers to the Basques, and the IRA's terrorist operations continue to raise the costs of British military presence in Northern Ireland. By the same token, however, the main victims of terror have often been the corresponding ethnic or national populations themselves. Primary examples are the Tamil and Sikh terrorists in Sri Lanka and India, whose extensive reliance on terrorism has contributed to destroying the very fabric of their societies without bringing the goal of national liberation any closer.

The most successful terrorist strategies have been those used by states or regimes against other states and internal or external groups, evidently because a state's means are much more effective and extensive than those of substate actors. The state as terrorist has at its disposal a national army, a large budget, diplomatic channels, and superior intelligence. Surrogate, or client, terrorist organizations ultimately depend on the economic aid, military assistance, and protection provided by standing governments. States such as Libya, Syria, and Iran that gain sufficient influence in a low-risk, cheap way by supporting terrorists will find it convenient to continue supporting

---

[124]Laqueur, *The Age of Terrorism,* 206–207. Rubenstein, *Alchemists of Revolution: Terrorism in the Modern World,* 91, 111, 197–198, 202–205.

them. As illustrated by the Syrian example, state-directed and state-supported terrorism has brought the greatest benefits at the lowest cost when kept low-key and discriminate, and when subordinated to a larger political strategy combining conventional diplomatic, political, and military methods.

Although terrorists will not seriously threaten Western governments or values as long as most people believe in change through the political process, state sponsorship of terrorism and narco-terrorism has undoubtedly aggravated the challenge posed by political violence. State-supported terrorism, like cooperation with drug dealers, has greatly enhanced the power and potential of several terrorist groups; has complicated efforts to combat them; and has increased the risk that retaliation against terrorism may escalate to open warfare.

By contrast, the risk of nuclear terrorism seems extremely small, though it should not be completely ignored.[125] Most terrorists and their sponsors pick strategies on the basis of political calculations, and instruments safer and more precise than nuclear weapons are readily available. There is still the small possibility that fanatics who believe they have nothing to lose will attempt to use nuclear weapons to gain political leverage, but they are also among those least likely to gain access to this type of weaponry. Since 1970, about 70 nuclear-related terrorist incidents have occurred, most of them unsuccessful. Almost half were Basque assaults on a Spanish utility company, and the rest were directed mainly against nuclear power plants.[126]

---

[125]For a full-fledged discussion of the potential for nuclear terrorism, see Paul Leventhal and Yonah Alexander, eds., *Preventing Nuclear Terrorism: The Report and Papers of the International Task Force on Prevention of Nuclear Terrorism* (Lexington, Massachusetts, 1987).

[126]Konrad Kellen, "The Potential for Nuclear Terrorism: A Discussion and Appendix," in Leventhal and Alexander, 110–111, 123–33.

The major challenge for the West is to determine how to confront those states which conduct and support terrorist operations. State involvement in specific terrorist incidents is often difficult to prove. Even when sufficient evidence exists, democratic governments are frequently handicapped in their ability to undertake military retaliation or covert action. When a major power such as the United States opts for military reprisals, the danger of escalation into international conflict is especially great, as is the risk that a large number of innocent people will be killed. Diplomatic and economic sanctions might be effective if sustained over sufficiently long periods of time by all major Western countries. Experience has proved, however, that such coordination among states is extremely difficult to achieve. Many European countries, for example, quickly relaxed their 1986 sanctions against Libya.

Addressing the "root causes" of terrorism will not eliminate this kind of political violence, for the aims of most terrorists are either unrealistic or even more unacceptable to the West than current terrorist activities. In general, satisfying the terrorists' demands would only encourage further use of terrorist strategies. In some cases, however, resolution of national and ethnic issues would reduce the popular base of terror, as the achievement of colonial independence showed.

It has become increasingly evident that if it is to be discouraged, terrorism must be treated strictly for what it is—a criminal activity threatening law and order, not a threat to vital national security interests necessitating or requiring negotiations and concessions. The record proves the significance of defensive and preventive measures. For example, the eight Middle Eastern attacks directed at airlines and airports in Western Europe in

---

[126]Konrad Kellen, "The Potential for Nuclear Terrorism: A Discussion and Appendix," in Leventhal and Alexander, 110–111, 123–33.

1986 alone, if successful, could have killed 800 people, but the actual death toll was 4.[127] Measured reprisals based on accurate intelligence, which raise the costs of engaging in terrorism, is another cornerstone of an effective counterterrorist policy. In the final analysis, however, it is important to keep in mind that even the most well-conceived strategy can only reduce—not obliterate—terrorism.

---

[127]*Patterns of Global Terrorism: 1986,* 13.

ABOUT THE AUTHORS

Barry Rubin is a fellow of the Johns Hopkins Foreign Policy Institute (FPI) and director of the FPI's program for the study of international terrorism. He is also a senior research fellow at the Washington Institute for Near East Policy. His most recent works include *Istanbul Intrigues* (New York, 1989); *Modern Dictators: Third World Coupmakers, Strongmen, and Populist Tyrants* (New York, 1987); and *Secrets of State: The State Department and the Struggle over U.S. Foreign Policy* (New York, 1985).

Cecilia Albin, a doctoral candidate at the Johns Hopkins School of Advanced International Studies, is assistant for the Foreign Policy Institute's program for the study of international terrorism. She is coauthor of *Sinai II: The Politics of International Mediation* (Washington, D.C., forthcoming).

Ami Ayalon is senior research fellow at the Dayan Center and senior lecturer at the department of Middle Eastern and African history, Tel Aviv University. He is the author of *Language and Change in the Arab Middle East* (Oxford, 1987), editor of *Regime and Opposition in Egypt under Sadat* (Tel Aviv, 1984, Hebrew), and associate editor, *Middle East Contemporary Survey*.

Mark Falcoff is a research fellow specializing in Latin American issues at the American Enterprise Institute for Public Policy Research, Inc., Washington, D.C. Dr. Falcoff is the author of *Modern Chile: A Critical History* (1989), among other works; his articles and reviews have appeared in the *Washington Post, The New Republic, The American Spectator, Orbis,* and elsewhere.

Herbert M. Howe is research professor of African politics and served as acting chairman for African studies (1987–88), School of Foreign Service, Georgetown University. Dr. Howe is a specialist in political-military relations; his articles have appeared in various books and magazines.

Joseph Kostiner was a visiting scholar at the Harvard University Center for Middle Eastern Studies at the time of this writing. His most recent book is *The Struggle for South Yemen* (London, 1984).

David Scott Palmer is professor of political science and international relations at Boston University. He has written extensively on Peruvian politics.